P9-DMI-341

BLINDED BY THE SUNLIGHT

ALSO BY MATTHEW MCALLESTER

Beyond the Mountains of the Damned: The War Inside Kosovo

BLINDED BY THE SUNLIGHT

Emerging from the Prison of Saddam's Iraq

MATTHEW MCALLESTER

HarperCollins*Publishers*

BLINDED BY THE SUNLIGHT. Copyright © 2004 by Matthew McAllester. All rights reserved. Printed in the United States of America. No part of this book may be used or reproduced in any manner whatsoever without written permission except in the case of brief quotations embodied in critical articles and reviews. For information, address HarperCollins Publishers Inc., 10 East 53rd Street, New York, NY 10022.

HarperCollins books may be purchased for educational, business, or sales promotional use. For information, please write: Special Markets Department, HarperCollins Publishers Inc., 10 East 53rd Street, New York, NY 10022.

FIRST EDITION

Designed by Elliott Beard

Printed on acid-free paper

Library of Congress Cataloging-in-Publication Data is available upon request.

ISBN 0-06-058819-5

04 05 06 07 08 ❖/RRD   10 9 8 7 6 5 4 3

For Jane and Moises, my brother

ACKNOWLEDGMENTS

I've said it before and I'll say it again: No words can express my thanks to those who worked so hard to secure our release. The list, if I had the space to compile it here, would be hundreds and perhaps thousands of names long. Many of those names I will probably never know. So perhaps if I just offered my gratitude to my colleagues, my family, and my friends, well, that might begin to cover it. They all know who they are. I would only add that my sister was astonishing in all respects; my newspaper, *Newsday*, showed that it is peopled by men and women of truly humbling strength, resourcefulness, and kindness; and my friends and colleagues, none more so than Larry Kaplow, showed true bravery and selflessness while working for our release as they continued to cover the war from Baghdad.

Once I was released, certain people helped make this book happen: Flip Brophy, Sharon Balmer, David Hirshey, Mukhaled Baban, Nick Trautwein, Catherine Philp, and, again, my always generous editors at *Newsday*.

CONTENTS

INTRODUCTION

"Moises?" I called out, into the room on the sixth floor of the Hyatt Hotel in Amman, where Moises had his own separate room.

There was no answer.

Orange light shafted through the crack in the curtains and I could not be sure where it came from or where I was. Was it the burning sky come back again, the roiling dust storm that had cast my second day in prison into a permanent sunset? The light that day had found a way in through the concrete lattice of my prison cell's window, caught in the water bottle next to where I slept on the floor. If this was the same light, that meant I was still in my cell. There would be guards at the door and beyond the window would be a high wall decorated with curls of barbed wire. Was this my cell or my hotel room? Where was Moises? I sat up in bed, wrapped in pristine white cotton sheets, and looked around for him. Perhaps he was around the corner in the room toward the bathroom, with its shower gels and deep tub. Or maybe he'd been taken away for interrogation. Maybe I wouldn't see him again.

"Moises?"

My watch said 4:32 A.M. I had slept for an hour and a half, the first sleep in two days. When I flopped onto the bed at three o'clock I had closed my eyes and immediately men in dark khaki uniforms, men without distinct faces, had started to dismember the bodies of other men. They were clean cuts, arms and legs coming off without much fuss or gore.

My feet touched the soft carpet and the breath of the air conditioner chilled my back. I stood naked in the room and waited for the guards to come in and take me to see Abu Ibrahim. Should I put on my clothes and go to the television interview so that I could explain what had happened to my friends and me for the evening viewers in the United States? But that would not be possible, because I couldn't leave the room. Nor, for that matter, could anyone else leave their rooms. Everyone in my world was locked in, except for the guards.

I did eight days in Abu Ghraib prison and then I left Iraq and took my bad dreams home to my friends, my family, and a grandfatherly psychologist in an airy, calmly decorated house next to Hampstead Heath in London. After talking to him the first time I walked across to the heath and sat on a park bench looking at the ducks and swans paddling across the surface of one of the ponds and I felt euphoric. Pretty soon the dreams went away. My newspaper picked up the tab for the shrink.

Iraq, which was its own prison for the twenty-four years of Saddam Hussein's direct rule and another eleven before that when he ruled in all but name, has no such placid refuge. Months after the collapse of the Baath Party regime, there was no reliable electricity in Baghdad, and a continuing crime wave kept women and girls off the streets and homeowners sleeping next to their Kalashnikovs. That meant that surviving—sometimes at the expense of other Iraqis—left little room for healing and reflection. And so every day the country woke up without really knowing what it was anymore. It could not quite believe that it was free. It did not know if there were regime guards at the door or if they had really gone forever. Only one thing was certain: now there were new guards, with different rules, from another country.

The entire country was in a state of trauma that goes beyond the political. In a single day—April 9—Iraq passed from being imprisoned in perhaps the most extreme fashion of any country in the world besides North Korea to being absolutely and lawlessly free. Most Iraqis thought that they and their children and grandchildren were facing life sentences—and they were just the people living lives as far away from the attention of the regime as possible. Iraq's brick-and-mortar prisons within the national prison held hundreds of thousands of inmates. Many Iraqis had long since abandoned the hope of freedom, and none had ever truly experienced it inside the borders of their own country. Their sudden introduction to a world stripped of the old barriers was barely comprehensible to many.

There was a sliver of mirror in my prison cell, glued to the wall about five feet from the ground, almost exactly above the spot where I lay my head every night for seven days. Somehow, I never noticed it. Each day I lay on the filthy blanket and ran my fingers over my increasingly stubbly face and through my knotting hair and I wondered what I looked like. There was no mirror in the cell-block bathroom. I wanted to see my face one last time. I wanted to see which of my faces my interrogators were seeing. Sometimes I would scratch myself, gnaw at my right hand with my teeth or just touch my own body to remind myself of who I was. A mirror, above all things, would have prompted that memory. And there it was when I returned after the war to the prison, stuck on the wall of the ten-by-six concrete room whose every square inch I was sure I knew with my eyes closed, a silvery cradle for light whose presence I could surely not have missed during a week of solitary confinement. But it was no new addition—it was partially spattered by the old coat of pale blue paint that covered the cinder-block walls. I can only think that somehow, for a week, I refused to see the mirror.

I've taken a fairly good look at myself since I was released, and I am, I suppose, okay. I was lucky. The Hampstead shrink told me that I had been given a great gift, and occasionally I think he is right. There was no glory in being taken to prison. In a sense, it represented a failure to me. I was in Baghdad to cover the war, to do my job, not to get locked up. But it did give me an opportunity and a responsibility to exploit my experience in the center of Saddam Hussein's machine of terror—to tilt the mirror in order to show the other, far more traumatized, inmates of Iraq's prison. An entire nation lived in prison for thirty-five years and now they are free to scream out their agony and stumble through their pain toward a new freedom.

As it did for so many Iraqis and for Iraq itself, the collapse of the regime started a quest for me, an exploration that even those prisoners who had made it out alive had never been able to enjoy before. I would walk again through the corridors and cell blocks in search of an understanding of this massive prison state that had kept me for a short while in its most isolated corner. I wanted to find out why this prison existed at all. And I became determined to find my captors, grasp their hands in some sort of perverse brotherhood, and ask them the question that they would never let me ask while I sat in front of them in Abu Ghraib. My question had many fewer ramifications than that of so many other Iraqis. But it was the same.

"I want to ask him only one question—why?" said a physician named Ahmed, whom I met after the war. He had spent ten years in Abu Ghraib's section for political prisoners. He smiled throughout a long interview until I had asked him what he would say to his interrogator and torturer if he could see him again. Tears sprung from his embarrassed eyes. "Why did you destroy me and my family? Why did you put me in prison for ten years? Why did you destroy my future? I don't know his name. But I want to find him."

BLINDED BY THE SUNLIGHT

1

Cruise Missiles
and Paper Airplanes

First came the air-raid sirens, then the pink-and-white tracer fire slicing through the sky above Baghdad like fireworks with no starburst at the end of their trajectory. I ran from my room and was on my way up the darkened concrete stairs to the roof of the Palestine Hotel when the first two bombs hit downtown Baghdad at a quarter past nine. They slammed into the Ministry of Planning, a few hundred yards upstream on the opposite bank of the Tigris. The stairwell shook under my feet. When I reached the roof, I could see black smoke pouring from the remains of the ministry building and drifting south on a gentle breeze. Flames curled outward through the remaining windows. As still as a pond on a perfect spring day, the Tigris mirrored the burning.

An emergency vehicle with a single flashing blue light on top eventually crept toward the site. Some fearless drivers, ignoring memories of how American-led forces bombed some of Baghdad's bridges in 1991, made their way across the snaking river. There were no other signs of life near the burning building.

Two hotel waiters in black and white appeared on the roof to watch. "We'll give them twenty bucks to go away if they ask us to leave," someone said. But the staff just smiled at the growing crowd of reporters and photographers and gazed across the river at their government buildings burning in the night.

We waited for more and it did not come. What did come, however, was an Iraqi voice from behind us. "Go, go, off the roof," it said. I sat between John Burns and Tyler Hicks of the *New York Times*, and like everyone else we stayed where we were, not even turning around, sure that we could sit out this threat from the hotel management to our prime viewing spots. The waiters must have told the manager, we thought. But this was not hotel management. Once we had ignored their first command to leave, they did not ask again. Tripods started crashing to the floor. A platoon of big men in suits whose patience had disappeared instantly were spreading all over the roof and pushing people away from the edge and toward the ladder that sloped down to the exit door.

"Take it easy," I heard someone say. I turned to look.

"No take it easy," said an Iraqi man in a suit, pushing the journalist hard in the chest.

A photographer tripped and fell down the ladder, smashing his knees and hands on the roofing tiles.

One of the men in suits grabbed a camera from another photographer and sent it sailing off the roof.

They had flashlights. I put my head down, scuttled down the ladder, and joined the completely silent troop of journalists. We padded quickly down the stairwell, trying not to draw attention to ourselves, not knowing who might be behind or in front of us in the darkness.

That, we all agreed as we reconvened in various rooms, had probably been the Mukhabarat, Saddam Hussein's secret police, the same guys who had been going room to room, vacuuming up unregistered satellite phones. These devices were our only way of reliably keeping in touch with the outside world, but they were strictly monitored by the Ministry of Information. If we were caught with one by the authorities we could be expelled from the country. We could not use the roof again.

That was the second bombing of the war. The first had been disconcertingly muted. At the meeting in the Azores, President Bush and Prime Ministers Blair and Aznar had set a deadline for Saddam Hussein and his sons to leave Iraq or face war. That deadline was now past, and Moises Saman and I had been up all night waiting in vain for the first missiles to crash into Baghdad. Now I couldn't sleep. So, convinced that tonight the war would not be televised, I had popped five milligrams of Valium—sold over the counter by the hundred for the cost of a Big Mac—and drifted off into an adrenaline-killing stupor.

"Dude," said Moises, his voice piercing rather forcefully through my sleep.

Moises was my frequent travel companion, a dear friend and a brilliant photographer. Although a Spaniard, Moises speaks fluent dude, the one-word language of surfers, skateboarders, and, sometimes, photographers. This time "Dude" meant: Get up, the war just started. It was moments after five thirty on the morning of March 20; the sun was still beyond the horizon but close enough for the cityscape to be softly lit in violet and mauve.

The distant boom of bombs or missiles or something—we had no idea at the time—had started it all. From our balcony we now watched red antiaircraft rounds daintily arc into the sky from several points around the city. This was the first of many nights of ineffectual gunning by Iraqi air defensemen. We had been to watch the Air Defense soccer team play a few days earlier and, given how bleak their immediate future seemed at the time, I was delighted for them when they had beaten Uday Hussein's Karkh team 2 to 0. Now I was torn between admiring their commitment and pitying their fear of disobeying orders that made them suicidally fire their blowpipe darts in the vague direction of the most sophisticated bombs and missiles and planes in history.

For days and weeks, the world had been promised "shock and awe" when the war began. By that stage, an average *Time* magazine subscriber could probably describe where the main ministries, palaces, and military bases in Baghdad were and what sort of laser-guided munitions would likely demolish them. But so far, it had been nothing but shock and bore. All we were seeing now was a silent, predawn city letting off a few pretty antiaircraft rounds into the gathering light. I thought the distant booms we were hearing were just bigger guns.

"This is a false alarm," I said. "I'm going back to bed."

"Look at that," Moises said, gazing through the spiderweb lattice balcony of our room. Far to the south we could make out smoke rising from the horizon.

"That's just a fire or something," I said, the Valium refusing to let me get excited.

"No, it's mushroom clouds. Like we saw in Afghanistan."

"That," I said, "is a fire."

And then another mushroom cloud appeared followed by another boom.

"Ah, bombs," I said. And we both ran for the roof of the hotel, which had a spectacular view of the city and most of the likely central targets. Chief among them was the enormous Republican Palace complex, the largest in Baghdad, which lay directly across the Tigris from the hotel. Its most splendorous residential building was crowned with four cast-iron busts of Saddam Hussein costumed as Saladin, the great Muslim conqueror. In the distance you could see one of his newest palaces, the Sajda, also cornered with giant Saladin Saddams, four more public projections of one of the president's favorite fantasies. Unlike most of his other homes, this one proudly—and to an American targeter, temptingly—rose above the usual cover of trees and walls that shielded most of the other palaces from street-level viewing.

At 6:40 the bombing began again. It seemed to be in the same southern corner of the city, the mushroom clouds puffing up from the same spot on the horizon. Even from there, the explosions were strong enough to set off car alarms on Abu Nawas Street, which hugs the eastern bank of the Tigris and was now deserted, apart from a stray dog who changed tack with the sound of each explosion.

"This is our day and we will fight together," Uday Hussein was telling the Iraqi people on the radio. Fight what? I wondered. These were bombs coming from out of the heavens. Baath Party militiamen stood at their positions on the deserted street corners, gazing up at the quiet sky and pressing radios to their ears in the hope of finding out what was going on. A few civilians took an early morning stroll. Just before eight, the air-raid sirens sounded the all clear and Baghdad started a new workday.

As the day progressed, we began to hear explanations of this strangely minimal start to what had been billed as the most devastating aerial bombardment in history. American officials explained that even they hadn't expected this attack, that their intelligence gathering network had provided them with a last-minute "target of opportunity" and Bush had authorized an immediate cruise missile strike from eight Navy warships in the Persian Gulf and the Red Sea. He had also sent two F-117A stealth fighters to bomb a farm area in the south of Baghdad where the CIA believed Saddam Hussein, one or both of his sons, and other members of the senior leadership were holding a meeting.

Saddam appeared on Iraqi television in the early afternoon to denounce the start of the attack on his country. It was impossible to tell whether this was the actual leader or one of his doubles, or whether this was a pretaped message of defiance or a genuine reaction to the bombing.

Our driver, Yousef Aziz, had slept in our other room at the nearby Al-Dar Hotel so that we would not be cut off from each other if the government imposed the much-rumored curfew. Anxiety had kept him awake until three, whisky had sent him to sleep, and bombs woke him up two and a half hours later. When he came round to the Palestine at nine, he seemed disappointed with the mildness of the attack but had high hopes for the evening.

"Tonight it will be with Viagra," he laughed as we drove around the almost deserted city assessing the impact of the bombing on Baghdadis. There was so little traffic that a group of boys had turned a main street into their soccer pitch.

Moises and I had agreed several days earlier that when the war began we would go to the Ministry of Information to try to convert our visas. Unable to obtain regular journalist visas, we had entered Iraq on journalists-with-human-shields visas, which only allowed us to cover the activities of the peace activists who said they were determined to bunk down at facilities such as hospitals and schools in the hope of preventing bombing attacks. Now, we decided, the time was right to apply for regular journalist visas or the pink laminated cards that the ministry issued to accredited journalists. With the war underway, we felt that it would be unwise to remain unregistered. We were already nervous about our status, and we did not want any misunderstandings about our true purpose for being in Iraq. We also picked up the feeling that the Ministry would prefer to have the few remaining nonregistered stragglers safely under its gaze.

We went to see Khadem al-Taie, director of the press center, in his glass-walled office in the ministry building. For a place of such power it always struck me as absurdly tatty: the springs in the cushions of the armchairs were loose, the paint was chipped, and the filing cabinets creaked when Khadem or one of his shifty aides pulled out the drawers. Khadem was uncovered as a Mukhabarat official after the war but he seemed pleasant enough to me at the time. He would help us out if he could, he said; but he couldn't. We knew this was a lie, as he had recently done the same conversion for friends of ours. Ask my boss, Khadem said. So we did. Uday al-Taie sat at Khadem's desk, wearing the khaki uniform that senior Iraqi officials had donned once the war began. Politely, he said that he could not help us, either. Try Khadem, he said. We tried Khadem again, who I knew happily took bribes, and again he declined, preempting my intended suggestion that giving us the pink cards would "make us all happy" by telling us that if he did break the rules and accredit us, then "someone will think you gave me money." I didn't quite understand this: the visa game revolved around bribes and Khadem was one of the biggest beneficiaries. We gave up and continued working, getting on board the Ministry buses that took us for the day's first scheduled magical propaganda tour to the Taji grain silo outside the city. Khadem saw us join the official tour but made no objection.

Outside the city we drove past about fifty soldiers forming a defensive line along one stretch of the main road north. They were picnicking under the shade of roadside trees. Their sand-colored pickups were parked about fifty yards apart, all facing the road. Some were mounted with antiaircraft guns, poking out from under dun-colored tarpaulins. Others sported heavy machine guns. They were not particularly well camouflaged and would be easy pickings if American ground forces came down that road toward their ultimate goal, Baghdad. The soldiers lay on the grass gazing through the branches at the sky and passed food around. Just outside the silo itself, little red triangular flags poked out of a wasteland of loose rocks and earth, marking three artillery guns pointed west. A single mortar launcher leaned to the north.

On the asphalt forecourt of the silo facility, two elderly human shields were ready to present the Iraqi minister of trade with a bouquet of flowers. Chanting workers at the silo promised to sacrifice their souls and their blood for Saddam.

"I think you feel the confidence from the people you are meeting with today and first of all from the speech of President Saddam Hussein," said the minister, Mohammed Mehdi Salah, wearing a military uniform like all his other high-ranking colleagues. "Our reaction has not started yet. You will see. . . . In 1991 we saw a larger-scale [American] military reaction than now. We can absorb all military threats."

That day saw the start of what became perhaps the most astounding and long-running display of public denial in television history. Minister of Information Mohammed Saeed al-Sahaf, soon to become a comedic icon in much of the world, gave his first wartime briefing.

"These villains, and in particular the villain Bush," sneered al-Sahaf from the lectern set up on the ground floor of the ornate new annex to the main ministry building, "said they had struck Iraq with forty cruise missiles to assassinate President Saddam Hussein. Not only are they disappointed, I think they are hysterical."

John Burns, the veteran *New York Times* reporter, had some inexplicable attachment to the now abandoned Al-Rashid, and so, the day after the first big attack on the Ministry of Planning, he, Jon Lee Anderson of the *New Yorker*, Paul McGeough of the *Sydney Morning Herald*, and I had a last lunch in the hotel's pastel-colored dining room. We were the only customers and the menu was limited to kebabs, bread, and grilled tomatoes. I wasn't going to stand in the way of Burns's whim—hunger and comradeship often overcome common sense, even when bombs are headed your way—but I did think there was a particularly good reason that day to avoid the Al-Rashid. All morning, the BBC World Service had been reporting that eight B-52 bombers laden with precision bombs had taken off from a military airfield in England and were making their way toward Iraq. The Al-Rashid, officials from both the American and Australian governments had indicated to us, was a likely target because of a bunker housed in its basement. It was also surrounded by other government buildings. We spent some time over lunch doing dangerously amateurish calculations about how long it would take for the B-52s to get within range. The staff, understandably, wanted to know whether the Al-Rashid might be a target. I shared their curiosity and chewed my chunks of lamb with some haste.

All the time we were eating, the B-52s were cutting through the clear spring skies over the English Channel, moving across Europe and toward Iraq. Knowing that, it was hard not to marvel at the bizarreness of Sahaf's latest press conference—"I think they are frightened," he said—where he was joined by the minister of the interior, Mohammed Diab al-Ahmed.

Al-Ahmed strutted chest first into the annex, then stood almost motionless in front of the press corps while al-Sahaf spoke. A man used to waiting for his turn to speak, I thought. He had come prepared. In his right hand he held a short-stock silver-plated Kalashnikov. He wore a khaki vest that held four ammo clips and a large knife. When it was finally his turn to address us, he skipped issues of internal security and national defense and went straight to the props.

"You ask why I am here with my machine gun," the uniformed al-Ahmed said, holding up his weapon, pointing it at the roof of the vestibule and telling us that his sons had guns too. I believed him. "The Iraqi people swear they will not give up their guns and they will sacrifice themselves."

Not even silver-plated assault rifles were going to change the course of that day, though. By eight o'clock, the sun had gone down and the BBC was reporting that the B-52s would be within range within an hour. There was the feeling that this evening would be different.

Almost exactly at nine, the Iraqi radar systems picked up something heading in their direction and the sky was suddenly full of pink, white, and yellow antiaircraft fire. From one position, two rather more substantial and purposeful ground-to-air missiles trailed white through the sky in search of a target. In my never-ending quest for the best view, I had joined Suzy Goldenberg of the *Guardian*, who had told me that she had access to a suite where some British photographers had a fine panorama of the far bank of the river. Suzy and I were in the corridor when something grabbed the entire building. The hotel shook like a cardboard box in a storm. Suzy and I had spent a fair amount of time together in uncomfortable parts of the West Bank during the Intifada. Now we suddenly found ourselves crouched on the floor, holding hands for the first time. Another unearthly force shook the hotel and we rushed toward the suite, reaching the balcony in time to see a vast fireball erupt out of a building in the Republican Palace complex. Where's the noise? I wondered. A second later, the pressurized night air rammed into my face, along with a roar that threatened to burst our ears, and Suzy and I were again squatting behind the wall of the balcony. The walls, windows, and floor shivered.

Across the river, Saddam's center of power was on fire. The Republican Palace compound, the biggest in the Great Uncle's capital, was being picked apart by American bombs. Whatever one thought of the stated motivation and justification for the war, I wonder if there would be many in the West who wouldn't want to let out a whoop of sheer exhilaration at seeing a psychopathic dictator's most symbolic base being brutally, unrelenting pounded by laser-guided bombs. I hate war. I absolutely loved this.

Downstairs in Jon Lee and Paul's room, Moises, Tyler, Burns, and my old friend Larry Kaplow of Cox Newspapers were similarly rapt. Jon Lee, on deadline, continued to write. Paul called in a radio interview to Australia on his satellite phone. The bombs kept coming and we had to remind each other to keep our excited voices down so that the Iraqi security men in the street below would not spot us. It was a bad idea to be seen as enthusiastic spectators of the bombing.

The Americans' favorite target seemed to be the huge ziggurat in the Republican Palace compound. Modeled after the ancient Sumerian temple of Ur, the birthplace of Abraham, it was where Saddam usually met his top advisers. Bomb after bomb tore into its sloping stone and steel limbs. Huge flames roared from its lower levels, and smaller fires burned brightly in the night from the upper windows. It looked like the biggest funeral pyre ever built.

At about nine-thirty, the bombing in downtown Baghdad stopped. For the next few minutes we scanned the night skyline with binoculars and noted that many obvious potential targets still remained untouched and brightly illuminated. There was the needle of the Saddam Tower, with its revolving restaurant and unparalleled views. Across the road from that was the gloriously vulnerable and boastful Sajda Palace. "What the fuck is that? A plane?" someone asked, as a screeching jet sound appeared out of nowhere and came very rapidly toward our balcony. Some dived onto the floor. Whatever it was out there in the night screamed past the hotel and across the river toward the Mansour area of Baghdad.

A fireball erupted on the horizon. The lights went out in the Sajda Palace.

The laser-guided bombs had done the general softening-up work. It was now time for the million-dollar cruise missiles to take over.

Another one ripped by us and erupted somewhere near the Al-Rashid. I guessed that, whatever was hit in that part of town, the hotel restaurant would not be open for lunch tomorrow. More cruises sliced invisibly through the night, many of them doing their best to topple the ziggurat, which burned but declined to cave in.

And then it was over. The city went quiet, the flames silently licking into the sky from the devastated palace buildings on the other side of the river. The following day, I emailed my girlfriend, who was covering the war for her newspaper in the north of Iraq: "I think this could be over soon. Maybe see you next week?"

It was the last she heard from me for a long time.

The next morning, Saturday, March 22, we joined a ministry bus trip to Baghdad's Yarmuk Hospital to see civilians injured in the night's bombing. These trips had become our nightmare because they were the distillation of Iraqi government control over our freedom to report—"bullshit" was the most common term heard before, during, and after the trips—but they also became, more or less, the only way to gain safe access to Iraqis. The alternatives were to sit in your room or to walk or drive out into a city now infested with informants and paranoia.

At the hospital there were people with some horrible injuries, but most of the 215 wounded reported by the visiting minister of health had been discharged and most of those who remained were not in critical condition.

"We were expecting a lot more," said a young doctor, Ali al-Bazzaz, dangerously off-message.

I shared the doctor's surprise. Even in our short bus trip, we had seen enormous damage. About three hundred bombs and missiles had hit the city during the night. Three civilians had died, the minister said.

The four busts of Saddam Hussein still stood untouched on the corners of the Sajda Palace, but they now gazed out from a burned hull of a building. All over town were government buildings that had precise holes bored into their side walls or roofs and their innards scooped out, leaving most of the frames intact; cruise missiles and precision bombs tend to hollow things out, not bring them crashing to the ground. The windows of the buildings next to the shattered palace engineering building were still intact.

Unlike the previous days, the bombing did not stop with the sunrise. All throughout the day we heard distant explosions, and I wondered if the Americans and British had decided to attack the rumored Iraqi ring of defenses on the outskirts of the city in preparation for the promised ground attack on Baghdad. Already, American troops were racing north toward us, but erratically, and we were spending increasing amounts of time, with increasing amounts of anxiety, debating how long it would take them to arrive. This could be a long time, American officials were now saying. There was no overt sign that the regime was crumbling as hoped.

We knew of only one restaurant open in Baghdad: Lathikia, on the otherwise deserted Arasat Street. Inside, most tables were empty. A handful of journalists and a few Iraqis quietly ate amid the potted plants and white tiled walls. Jon Lee, Paul, Burns, and I were just about to start enjoying our kebabs there at lunchtime when al-Sahaf's deputy, Uday al-Taie, walked in with some friends of his. Seeing us, he forsook the customary Iraqi pleasantries. "We have got two American pilots," he yelled angrily across the restaurant. "They are in Baghdad. They thought it was going to be a picnic with cream cakes and crates of Pepsi, but you will see—they will be slaughtered." This was no press conference. He was genuinely angry and it was alarming. Almost silently we ate our lunch and discussed whether it would be a good idea or a terribly bad idea to insist on paying for Uday's lunch.

On the sidewalk, there was a massive plume of black smoke rising over the rooftops. We wondered if we had somehow missed hearing an enormous explosion nearby.

"I think, Mister Matt, that they have set fire to the trenches of oil," Yousef said.

From our balconies at the Palestine, we could see that he was right. Within a few hours, Baghdad had become ringed by fires spewing out the blackest of smoke. Designed to confuse laser-guided bombs, these trenches filled with flaming crude oil were hopeless as a defensive tool but brilliant as apocalyptic accessories. Baghdad now seemed literally caught in a circle of fire. The smoke began to fall over the whole city, meandering through the streets, down our windpipes and into our lungs.

My phone rang. It was Larry.

"Have you blown your nose recently?" he asked.

Bombs continued to scythe their way through the patchwork eclipse.

Late that night ministry officials called us down to the lobby for another bus trip. Few of us were that keen on touring the city during prime bombing time but we went, mainly out of the ancient journalist's fear of missing something important. The buses drove through the city, deserted but for groups of armed men on street corners. The air-raid sirens started to wail just as the buses were passing the Mukhabarat headquarters, the Saddam Tower, a telecommunications hub, and the remains of the Sajda Palace—all likely targets.

It was around midnight when we arrived in the Yarmuk neighborhood, near the hospital. We disembarked in the darkness and stumbled through rubble-filled streets to a massive crater, about thirty feet deep and forty feet wide, carved into someone's backyard. Ministry men were there with a generator to power halogen lamps so that we could see the wreckage. At least five houses were heavily damaged. Pages from a magazine, cushions, and a small patch of still wet flesh and blood were strewn among the chunks of concrete and twisted iron supports.

"They are trying to deceive the world by saying they are targeting the regime, that they are targeting military positions," said al-Sahaf, who showed up at the site. "Well, you are witnessing—is this a military place?"

He said the attack had taken place at about 7:30 P.M. Several civilians had been injured, but none killed. I asked, a little gingerly, whether some senior Iraqi officials might be using private homes to hide in as they had in 1991.

"It is not only an allegation, it is a completely unbased allegation," he bellowed back, fortunately not seeing where the question had come from. "Lies and dirty lies."

The buses moved on to a second home. A songless bird in a cage was still alive inside the house, but all the other residents had left. Shoes sat neatly arranged on the staircase that led upstairs from the living room, some of them the size of a young child's foot. Twenty-four people were injured here, al-Sahaf said. At that time of night there was no way to verify the truth of his words or the scene in front of us.

Eventually it was time for bed. None of us had been getting much sleep—filing late, jumping out of bed for bombs, rising early—but this night was particularly draining. The first cruise missile had Moises and me out of bed in seconds, rushing to the balcony. And the second. By the time the third drilled its screaming way through the night—they always seemed to be bearing down on the hotel—I gave up going to the balcony and lay in bed, deeply scared but resigned. They kept coming.

On the morning of March 23, Moises and I were standing around on the sidewalk outside the Ministry of Information waiting for the latest bus tour when Khadem al-Taie approached us. "Come to my office in five minutes," he said, smiling gently. "I will give you passes. You have photographs, yes?"

Five minutes later, we had our pink passes. No explanation, no bribes, no logic. We didn't ask. We were ecstatic and relieved. We were now as legit as the next person. We assumed that we had become familiar faces to the ministry men and had been enveloped within their world, as had most other journalists on questionable or expired visas. Or perhaps, with the growing feeling that the American-led attack was not working out as planned, the Iraqi government simply felt more relaxed and confident and wanted to keep as many journalists as they could in Baghdad to chronicle their great resistance. Whatever the truth, our worries on that front seemed to be over. No one could now mistake us for spies.

As each senior official appeared before us in person at the huge press conferences sponsored by the Ministry of Information in the nearby Sheraton Hotel—that day we had the vice president and the minister of defense—the impression grew of a government that was still very much holding together.

This was also the day when Iraqi television broadcast footage of dead and captured American soldiers. In the lobby of the Palestine, a large group of Iraqi men gathered in solemn silence around a television.

"What is your name?" asked an unseen interviewer as a terrified young American soldier glanced from side to side.

"Sergeant James Riley," the prisoner said.

"Where are you from?"

"New Jersey," the man said.

The footage cut to an equally scared woman soldier. Her legs appeared to be injured.

"What is your name?" the voice said.

"Shana," the soldier said, eyes darting about as if at other people in the room around her.

"Where are you from?"

"Texas," she said.

The Iraqi men watching were silent, no one saying a word. I felt enormous sympathy for the soldiers. The possibility of being taken prisoner is something every soldier in a war has to address. But this was not just a war over territory, as the 1991 war had been. It was a war designed to topple the regime. If the Iraqi government did begin to sense that its demise was inevitable and near, it might not retain much enthusiasm for the Geneva conventions and the captured soldiers' rights. I was also not encouraged by what I had just witnessed on the west bank of the Tigris.

The news had spread in seconds throughout the city: an enemy pilot had ejected from his damaged jet and parachuted into the river, right in the center of Baghdad.

"I saw the plane go down toward the west and the pilot parachuting into the river," swore Mohammed Abdul Salah to the *Sydney Morning Herald*'s Paul McGeough as they stood on the Rashid Bridge, minutes after the pilot allegedly splashed into the current below.

Almost immediately a crowd of hundreds formed on the western bank of the river, just downstream of the bridge. Three speedboats appeared and began racing up and down the river, searching for the enemy. Soldiers set fire to the bulrushes that line that stretch of the river.

Yousef had told me that state radio had announced rewards for capturing the enemy. Shoot down a plane and you got 100 million Iraqi dinars—about $35,000. This was an enormous sum to the average Iraqi, who might hope to make $1,200 in a year. Each POW was worth half that and a captured pilot the same. A dead pilot would bring in $8,750. So perhaps there was a financial motive to the desperate frenzy that took hold of hundreds of Iraqi men. About two years earlier I had seen two Israeli soldiers lynched in Ramallah and I had a horrifying hunch that I was about to see the same thing happen again: there was the same air of vengeful celebration at the prospect of ripping apart another human being from a much stronger enemy force.

A man wearing black threw gasoline onto the six-foot-high rushes. Fires along the bank soon crackled as the river slid silently by. Men tore their shirts off and raced into the rushes with scythes, knives, and guns.

An hour after the hunt started, a cry went up from one part of the reeds and the crowd surged toward the spot, cheering at the prospect of finding the airman cowering in the shallows. The boats raced to the spot, and two frogmen—one perhaps a little over the ideal weight for the job—leaped into the cold and very polluted water.

They found nothing.

Minutes later one of the many security officers who had gathered over the past hour fired his rifle into another part of the rushes and another stampede began. Civilians hacked at the growth.

"Bring him, bring him," chanted the crowd that had formed on the walkway overlooking the river. People laughed in anticipation. Paul and I squatted among the onlookers, exchanging cigarettes and wondering if we had ever seen anything vaguely like this in our lives.

At 4:20 P.M. a man in black pants and a white shirt thought he saw something move. He pulled out his pistol, squared his shoulders with alacrity and purpose, and leveled his handgun at the greenery. The bullets ripped into the water beyond, perhaps warning shots to the discovered pilot. The mob surged forward. A teenager held up a black shoe (a roar from the crowd), and then another (roar), and then something that looked like a gun magazine or a wallet (roar). Like spectators sensing blood at a gladiator's contest, the hundreds on the riverbank called out in delighted expectation of seeing something more any minute now.

A former Iraqi airline pilot named Khaled, who was now working as a driver for another journalist, sat on the rocky slope above the river next to us.

"It is very sad," he said, not joining in the excitement. "What is this? I don't like it because I was a pilot. The thing is, they believe he's a criminal."

We went down to the rushes and talked to a soldier with wet pants who seemed in much better spirits.

"They said that there is a pilot there," he said, gesturing at the water. He seemed uncertain that there had ever been an enemy pilot in the vicinity, but he was still smiling broadly. The search was enough for him and for most people. "They are searching for him."

A very young, hormonally aggressive teenager sporting a uniform and a machine gun demanded to see my pass. He was very insistent and when I could not immediately produce it—it was not yet laminated, was not yet dangling around my neck—he became upset. I'm sure he believed it perfectly possible that I had just finished a daylight bombing raid, parachuted into the freezing cold Tigris, snuck out in front of hundreds of scythe-wielding Iraqis, and unzipped my wetsuit to reveal my ready-made journalist outfit. Bond, I wanted to say. James Bond. Instead, I found my pass in my bag and the youth went away, without the 50 million dinars he would have collected for busting me as a pilot.

"Your excellency, Mr. President, your name scares the Americans," a group of young men chanted. In Arabic, it scanned and rhymed and sounded menacing.

The heavyset frogman, wearing a blue wetsuit, took a cigarette break. A flock of white birds shaped in a V formation flew quietly overhead, oblivious to the human behavior unfolding below them and the high-tech steel birds passing over their heads, dropping bombs on the city. Throughout the search, American and British pilots continued their daily work. One plane formed an arc in one of the few remaining patches of blue left in the oil-smoke sky above Baghdad. People ran for cover. Two massive explosions hammered the city, and gray mushroom clouds rose to the west. This made the searchers even more determined to find their prey.

A deaf-mute man sat watching the tragicomedy next to Paul. After a few minutes Paul turned to me and gave me his version of what he called the first interview in his career with someone who could neither hear nor speak. In an unmistakable and universal form of sign language, the man had given Paul his theory of what was happening. He indicated with his fist that he would punch the pilot if he were found. But the man thought the pilot was smart and had dived underwater and had already swum downstream.

The man had redirected his focus to the show and now gently pushed aside a man who had stepped in front of him as if the newcomer had obscured his view of a soccer game. He and Paul began communicating again.

You would need to pull the plug out of the river to find him, the deaf man mimed. It will be one hour till darkness falls, he indicated, tapping his watch and pointing to the sun, and then the pilot will be free to swim away.

At 6:10 P.M., after several more mad, hungry dashes to various spots on the riverbank—all false alarms—the final scene of the drama played out. Someone spotted a reed floating downstream. It was vertical. Surely this was the wily pilot breathing air while remaining under the surface.

Four frogmen dove into the water and chased the fleeing reed. Soldiers and security officers fired into the water around it.

No body floated to the surface and the reed continued nonchalantly down the river.

The swimmers returned to shore. And finally, a few minutes later, nearly everyone went home. They were greeted by images on their TV screens of American soldiers who really had fallen into Iraqi hands. Someone would be claiming their multimillion dinar rewards today.

★   ★   ★

Saddam and his sons, Uday and Qusay, were feeling pretty good about things. Together with their top lieutenants, the three of them had spent months planning the defense of the country and, in particular, Baghdad. Uday was especially happy, one of his top bodyguards told me after the war. This most brutal of all Iraqis usually slept during the day and woke in the evening to begin his habitual drunken partying, which often included spotting young women on the street or even at their own weddings and taking them to one of his palaces to satisfy his sexual urges. But now that Iraq was again at war, he discovered a sense of purpose and responsibility that he had long ago lost, a slippage that had allowed his younger and more sober brother, Qusay, to assume the role of heir apparent.

"During the war he went to sleep at one-thirty or two in the morning, and he'd wake up at four to check the news and then he would sleep until six," said the bodyguard, who made me promise to call him by a pseudonym that he chose: Abu Tiba. "He slept very little. Before the war he would sleep during the day and wake up at night."

The newly responsible Uday would send orders to his fedayeen commanders in a small case carried by messengers. He did not use communications technologies, such as satellite telephones, which the Americans could track, Abu Tiba said.

Saddam's fedayeen, the militia composed of pardoned criminals, were Uday's private army. He founded it in 1992, and, rather to the surprise of the advancing American soldiers who were now pushing toward Baghdad, it proved the most deadly of Iraq's armed forces. Often wearing civilian clothes and traveling in pickup trucks, the fedayeen launched surprise attacks at the convoy of American vehicles snaking north through the desert from Kuwait. Uday's stock rose sharply in the regime's inner circles.

"When the Republican Guard morale declined, he felt like a leader because his father sent him a message congratulating the actions of the fedayeen," Abu Tiba told me in late July, two days after the death of Uday and Qusay at the hands of American soldiers. He sat on a couch in his home about an hour north of Baghdad, sporting the same black crew cut, stubble, thick eyebrows, and heavy build as his former boss. He was a calm man, apparently without the psychopathic inclinations of Uday. "He felt so happy that he was doing something for his country. . . . It was great for Uday that he was commanding a fighting force."

Even better for him and his family, the Americans had failed to kill them in that first strike of the war. They were nowhere near the targeted area, Abu Tiba said. "Because of the deadline Bush gave, they did not sleep in any of their palaces but slept in other homes. For Uday there was no meeting that night at all. But maybe there was a meeting for the other leaders."

What Uday found harder to stomach, however, was the accurate American targeting of his real estate. "Sometimes he was tense, especially when his properties or palaces were hit in the war," said Abu Tiba, who was part of a team of six bodyguards who worked in alternating shifts with another team of six. "In the 1991 war, none of his sites were hit. He felt someone inside was giving information about his palaces. Then he'd get very tense and angry. You can see that anger in his looks. You can see the agony on his face. He was most suspicious about his friends."

Nothing hurt Uday's feelings more, Abu Tiba said, than when American bombs hit Uday's palace on the banks of the Tigris where he kept his big cats.

"He loved his animals very, very much," Abu Tiba said. "His tigers and his cougars. He was affected so much."

Like his brother and his father, Uday moved every two or three days. Sometimes he stayed at one of the more modest of his many homes in regular residential neighborhoods. Sometimes he stayed with friends. Gone were his attention-drawing expensive cars. Now he drove around in Toyotas or KIAs, often with his head wrapped up in a red kaffiyeh to disguise the face so familiar to Iraqis. His bodyguards carried automatic rifles. Uday kept a machine pistol with him at all times.

Even during the war, convinced that he had a future ahead of him, Uday continued his morning physiotherapy sessions, made necessary by a failed assassination attempt in December 1996. He had a metal rod inside his right leg, Abu Tiba said, and could not fully straighten it. Every day he would lift weights to strengthen his body, which had almost been torn apart by the assassins' bullets.

The family, Abu Tiba said, was convinced that the Iraqi military would repel any American attempts to seize Baghdad. They had prepared an elaborate plan to defend the city, forming three rings of forces all around Baghdad. Not once did they consider accepting an offer from another country to flee. Nor did they consider organizing an underground resistance beforehand should they lose the war. They simply would not, could not, lose.

All chatter stopped in the Nouri barbershop. The man having his black hair trimmed kept his head pointed toward the mirror, but his eyes swiveled to the right where the television sat. It was March 24. The president was about to speak. The barber kept snipping but was clearly listening as he worked.

"Now we are living through decisive days in which fighters and the great Iraqi people are doing exceptionally well and for which they deserve victory and satisfaction from God, as he promised the true faithful against the enemies of God and humanity," said Saddam Hussein, if that was really him, wearing his military uniform and speaking with a slight slur. He mentioned specific battles, units, and commanders by name, presumably to dispel any doubts about this appearance being prerecorded. "It is our right, nay, our duty, to be proud as fighting believers who are patient in this epic war."

When the speech was over I asked a couple of the customers what they thought, and while one of them, a 41-year-old soldier having a prebattle trim, swore his undying allegiance to "our father" a big bomb landed in the distance, slightly shaking the shop. Nothing in his face or conversation suggested that he had heard it.

"It's normal now," he laughed, when I mentioned the explosion. "In the night, when there is bombing, my kids play soccer in the street and fly paper airplanes off the roof."

Although I still could imagine only one outcome of this war, each new day made me wonder whether it was all such a good idea in the first place. The Iraqis were beginning to feel that they and their country, not just their leaders, were under attack. I sensed a growing momentum of confidence and unity in Baghdad. State-run television was now showing an American Apache helicopter downed in a field. Families who had fled the city a week ago, including Yousef's, were now returning from the villages. Cars filled the formerly empty streets. A surprising number of shops and restaurants had suddenly reopened.

But to me, the greatest indicator was Yousef. Almost overnight he had lost all confidence in the Americans' ability to win the war. Saddam would stay in power and the future Yousef had briefly glimpsed had disappeared. Only days earlier he had been merrily predicting the rapid collapse of the regime. Now he said that the talk in the drivers' office at the Palestine—his favorite barometer—had turned from a tentative but clear rebelliousness in early March to lock-step nationalism. There was no laughter in Yousef now. He said there were intelligence men all over the hotel. He was silent for long periods as we drove around the city.

"I've never seen it like this before," he said. "Everyone, Shia and Sunni, is coming together. I do not think the Americans will come to Baghdad. A single tiny unit has been fighting the Americans in Umm Qasr for days. They will keep bombing but they will never come into Baghdad on the ground."

"Yousef, they will. I'm sure of it."

"No," he said. "They will never come. Saddam will stay president."

He clammed up and I thought that he must now be regretting all the loose words, all the help he had given us.

I wrote a story that night about this mood change. I logged on to the Internet in my room and found a report that not one but two Apaches had been downed by small-arms fire and rocket-propelled grenades, and that a group of thirty other Apaches had retreated after all of them had been damaged by similar low-tech shooting south of Baghdad. But I never had a chance to file the story. Someone's knuckles were rapping on the door.

2

No Speak

The first inmate I saw in Abu Ghraib prison did not wear a blindfold. He didn't need one. His eyes were swollen ovals of purple and blue. Someone's fists, I supposed, had done that to him. His shoulders slumping forward, he walked behind a guard into the cell block where we were being processed and was sent to stand in the corner like a naughty schoolboy. He wore blue-and-white striped pajamas and turned his face to the matching blue-and-white cinder-block walls, silent and stripped of any dignity. He was quite a big man but he looked like a small person, someone who didn't count anymore.

I'm about to become him, I thought, as I sat on the concrete floor of the corridor that ran between the dark blue bars of the cells. If I'm lucky.

Molly Bingham, a freelance photographer I barely knew, mumbled something to me that I didn't pick up. We had been ordered not to speak to each other. Then I heard her say, "I hope they need us." Without believing a word of what I said, I assured her we wouldn't be harmed: "They're not that stupid."

But they had been stupid enough to arrest us and take us to Abu Ghraib, the last circle in every Iraqi's hell. So they could, in fact, be stupid enough to do anything they chose. I knew that. I just didn't want Molly to know, or the others.

After a night behind me without sleep, and several before that with only snatched moments of rest, my physical strength was all but gone. Now the last of my mental strength ebbed away with my body heat as I sat on the cold floor. Replacing my spirit was a poison of powerlessness, self-loathing, and fear, as if I had spent all night drinking and taking drugs that were now leaving me with nothing but depression and the conviction that I had gone too far this time. And there was nothing I could do about it: I had overdosed on war journalism and now I was going to pay.

I calculated, as much as my quivering brain would permit, what our possible futures were. I knew there could be only one reason we had been arrested: the Iraqi authorities suspected us of being spies. It was wartime. We had no recourse to Iraqi law, to diplomatic appeals, to the Red Cross, to anything. There would be no chance of leniency if they had already decided we were guilty. Our governments—now Iraq's enemies in battle—would be less than helpless. Accompanied by aggressive men with guns, we had passed through two huge perimeter walls, and we were now crouched in silence on the corridor of a prison block with a blinded prisoner for company. Our futures were not ours to decide, and the possibilities were terrifyingly few.

One: immediate execution. That would mean that we wouldn't even make it to the pajama-and-torture existence of the inmate standing in the corner. I thought that it was highly likely that we would be killed very soon. That's what generally happens to captured spies in wars.

Two: torture followed by execution.

Three: televised confessions of our crimes of espionage, which I was already sure I would provide given the necessary coercion, followed by execution. Televised or not, that didn't seem relevant.

Four: torture and miraculous release.

Five: the war, which had suddenly turned bad for the Americans and the British, drags on for months; we are given a very public prison sentence and then released as a gesture of the resilient regime's humanity. This would not even be worth hoping for, but I couldn't let it go.

You make these calculations, these realizations, so fast that you allow yourself none of the indulgence of false comfort. There wasn't a moment when I thought, "Oh, this is all a terrible mistake. We'll be out in an hour and apologies will tumble out as we are led back to our hotel with an armed escort."

I worried also, in those long minutes spent on the surprisingly clean floor, about being raped. Out of the five of us picked up hours earlier from the Palestine Hotel by men in suit jackets and irregular military uniforms, I was the second to be called into a cell that was the reception area of this wing of the vast prison. I was the second to have all my possessions registered and stored, and I was the second to be told to strip to my underwear and put on the same type of pajamas the broken man in the corner was wearing. Moises had gone first and he had sat down beside me in pajamas, utterly stunned at his transformation from photographer to prisoner. Apart from his boxer shorts, he had been stripped in that cell of everything he owned. Every roll of film, every notebook, every pair of socks, every dollar, every picture of his girlfriend had been fingered and noted down in a ledger. His clothes had been searched and put in a transparent plastic bag.

As I started the registration, the stripping, I noticed a condom packet on the floor under the desk of the two men taking down my details. Apart from Molly, I knew there were no women held in Abu Ghraib. At least they practice safe rape, I thought to myself.

The rapping on the door was not the coded knock my friends and I had agreed on. It was forceful and unhesitant. But I wasn't too worried because our satellite phones were already hidden in the room: good hiding places, in an air vent with a removable metal grille across it and zipped up inside a flak jacket. I padded silently toward the door and got a goldfish-bowl view through the peephole. A crew of eight or ten security men stood outside. This was just a sat phone shakedown, I told myself. They would take a quick look around and then leave, looking for bigger catches in the BBC's rooms or with the networks.

Moises was not in our room, 1122, when the men came. Bombs were falling again around the city and he, as ever, was working through the night to find the right view for the right picture. He had gone off with a friend named Cho, a photographer I had not met before, the last person to have visited our room that night.

"Hello," I said.

A uniformed man with a huge belly pushed past me into the room and was followed by several others, most in plainclothes.

"Mister Matthew," said a tall man in a dark suit and tie and a white shirt, "where is Mister Moises?" They knew who I was by sight.

"He's in another room with a friend."

"Which room?"

"I don't know," I said, "perhaps one on the sixteenth floor. No, I remember, he went to visit someone in room 1406. Can I help you?"

"Turn off your computer, please, Mister Matthew."

When my computer closed down, it was 12:58 A.M. and 26 seconds. I did not get a chance to send my story.

"Sit down, Mister Matthew," the man in the suit said, pointing to my bed. I did as I was told and was now gazing up at the men surrounding me.

"Is there a problem?"

"We just want to ask Mister Moises a few questions," the man in the suit said.

I wondered why they had not yet asked whether we had sat phones. They did not search the room. Most of the men left to find Moises, but two waited with me, one sitting opposite me on the other bed, the other standing by the door.

Something discomfiting occurred to me. Perhaps they were not here to look for satellite phones. Perhaps they were here to expel us. During the previous days, several journalists, including the entire CNN team, had been ordered to leave the country. It would be a catastrophe for Moises and me to leave at this stage, after we had worked hard to remain in Baghdad during the war. We had reason to worry about being expelled: other than Cho, the last person who came into our room that night was our friend Marco DiLauro, an Italian photographer. Tyler, Moises, and I had sat and listened and offered counsel as he told us that men from Intelligence had just come to his room to tell him that he was to be removed to Syria the next day at seven in the morning. Should he hide in some tiny hotel or agree to get on the bus? We barely knew what to suggest. Inside, I felt utter relief that we were not faced with the same threat. We had our Ministry of Information accreditation and I was attending all the right press conferences and bus tours and being seen doing my job, like all the other journalists, by the right officials. Now it struck me: Were we being put on the same bus to Syria?

Marco and some others had come in recently on tourist visas. I had briefly met a few of them, including two photographers, Molly and a quiet Dane named Johan Spanner. It's possible, I thought, that the authorities, eager to control the news reports coming out of Baghdad, had decided to winnow away the many dozens of journalists still in Baghdad by expelling anyone who had not come in on a full journalist visa. We might fall into that category seeing as our visas had limited us to covering the activities of the human shields and we hadn't touched that story for at least three weeks now. They were infuriating questions without answers; the men now in my room only smiled when I asked them again what the problem was.

What I did know, however, was that they were not from the Ministry of Information. I knew most of the faces in the press department of the ministry and I had never seen these men before. These were clearly members of one of Iraq's intelligence services. That worried me. "We are no longer in control," anxious ministry officials had been quietly telling journalists for about two weeks now.

"What's your name?" I asked one of the two men who had been left to guard me while the rest went looking for Moises. Balding, wearing a suit jacket and slacks, a paunch hanging over his belt, he sat on the bed opposite me, the picture of relaxation. Of the two, he was the English speaker.

"Why?"

"Just making conversation," I said.

I tried to better his imitation of relaxation. I leaned back on the bed, left my legs and arms uncrossed, showing him I was neither afraid nor hiding anything. Which was a body language whopper, because I was both. I got up and poured myself some more scotch, offering some to the two men. They declined.

"Do you have kids?"

"Three."

"Do they get scared of the bombs?"

"Very scared," he said, smiling. I knew I could not trust that smile, but its comfort was a welcome antidote to my growing anxiety. I wanted Moises to come back so this could all be sorted out, and yet part of me wanted him, for his sake, never to come back.

"This is a terrible, stupid war," I said, lying again. I believed that this was a necessary war, a war fought on false pretexts but one that would finally rid Iraq of the kind of men who knocked on doors at one in the morning and gave no answers. "Bush and Blair are crazy."

He looked unmoved and again I offered him some scotch, which I was drinking fairly rapidly by then. Again, he declined.

The phone next to my bed rang and he picked it up. He said a few words and then replaced the receiver.

"Moises was not in that room. Where is he?"

I wanted this increasingly tiring and uncomfortable situation to end. I was sure that he had gone to room 808, where Tyler and Burns slept. But I couldn't allow myself to direct these men to my friends. I said I had no idea where Moises was.

"He is not my son. I'm not his father," I said, and we laughed.

After a torturous hour, during which I clung to my hope that this was all just a scare tactic, I heard the key in the door. Moises walked in.

"Hey," I said, preempting the men and Moises, "we have some new friends. These gentlemen have come to ask you, or us, some questions."

Moises smiled and looked very relaxed, coming to sit next to the English speaker, who had moved to one of the two blue velour armchairs near the balcony window. As he does when he wants to know from me what's going on, he looked at me silently and raised his eyebrows for a second. He lit a Marlboro Light from the pack I had been emptying fast during the past hour.

And then Moises went into charm mode. He got their names when I had failed. The soft-voiced English speaker was Salem. The other man was Hussein. I noticed a wedding band. Someone loved him. He rarely made eye contact and he was clearly carrying a handgun under his bulky jacket. Ministry officials were not known for carrying guns.

Moises wanted to know what we were waiting for. Again I cut in, trying to share information with him about what had happened while he was away, about what we might be facing.

"There's a man in a suit who I assume is the boss, and he just wants to ask some questions," I said. "Although he wasn't the one who knocked on the door. That was a very big man in a uniform. He had a big belly, didn't he, Salem?"

We had a little laugh.

Moises asked me what time it was and told Salem that if the man in the suit didn't come in half an hour, then that was it—they'd have to come back in the morning. At nine thirty. He was tired now and had to sleep.

Salem smiled and apologized and said that would not be possible.

Over the past few hours, a sharp, chilling wind had swept across the desert picking up dust from the surface of the Iraqi desert. The red storm spanned the country and was pounding the sides of the hotel. It virtually trapped the American and British troops in the desert, slowing their race north toward Baghdad and depositing a thick film of anxiety over those already worried about the faltering progress of the ground troops. It powdered the capital and blasted its way into our room whenever Hussein slid the French doors open to let in some air. Moises and I were smoking heavily and it clearly bothered him.

I don't know when—perhaps an hour more of small talk, cigarettes, scotch, and anxiety later—the men came back. Only this time the man in the suit was not among them. Their leader was a huge, muscled, businesslike man in uniform with a solid rectangular head and a handgun in his belt whom we came to refer to in hindsight as "the gorilla." He spoke a little English in a deep, casual growl and told us to put all our bags and gear on our beds.

"What's this for?" Moises asked.

"Mister Moises, you are both going to Syria," Salem said, shrouding the grim news with the typically respectful "mister" so common in Iraq, now laughably incongruous to me.

It was the blow I had feared. We protested. I stood facing Salem and for the first time felt that I was losing the self-imposed cool I had kept since the knock on the door about three hours earlier. Passivity seemed the correct and civilized approach to security officers who come for a chat. But I would not be expelled without some resistance.

"Salem, we have risked our lives to come to Iraq to cover this war," I said, with a measure of irritation and self-righteousness that was partly genuine, partly designed to put him off-balance. "We are here to do our jobs as journalists. To show what is going on in Baghdad while America bombs it. Do not make us leave."

He smiled and gently told us to keep packing. I turned to the gorilla, who seemed as if he had more authority, and tried the same line of argument, raising my voice a little.

"I don't want any problem," he said and stared at me. That was all he needed to say for me to understand that we had no choice in what was going on. I could tell Moises was furious and ready to argue more but from that moment I knew we were on the bus to Syria, at best. The man's stare and the numbers of men involved in this operation had begun to make me worry that something else could be going on.

The gorilla went through every single thing we had in the room. Bottles of water, computer cables, tubes of toothpaste, our wallets. Another man sat on the bed and took a scrupulous list of everything we owned. The gorilla sat on my bed and noted every dollar I had—how many hundreds, fifties, twenties, tens, fives, and ones. I remembered a few more in my belt pouch and handed them to him. He sighed with frustration; he'd have to redo his figures. This encouraged me. They simply don't want to give us any reason to accuse them of stealing from us when they pass us over to the Syrians, I thought.

One of the first things Moises packed into a bag was his flak jacket, which secretly held one of our sat phones. It was a relief to see it packed away without being discovered. The other was behind the grille in the air vent, and obviously we had both decided just to let it stay there, to sacrifice it. This was, in fact, our one relatively legal phone. Customs had registered it at the border and we had the documentation for it. But it had never been sealed, unsealed, and kept at the Ministry of Information, as the rules demanded. (Normally, all sat phones had to be sealed at the border and unsealed only by officials at the Ministry of Information in Baghdad, primarily so that the ministry could extort enormous daily fees for use of each phone. Once unsealed, the phone could not legitimately be removed from the building.) We did not want trouble and so, silently, we agreed to abandon the phone in the vent.

When we had finished packing, the gorilla and the other men left us alone with Salem and Hussein again. A bus would take us to Syria at 7:00 A.M., said Salem, ever smiling. That matched what Marco had told us. A bus to Syria at seven.

Moises and I stared at each other silently, frustrated and angry but unwilling now to cause trouble.

"You got those pills?" he asked, referring to our Valium supplies. I felt the same way. I just wanted to sleep all the way to the border, blacking out the depression of being taken away from Baghdad.

Salem and Hussein spoke to each other and laughed.

"What's he laughing about?" Moises asked Salem.

"He says that in one hour there will be a surprise for you."

"A good surprise or a bad surprise?" Moises asked.

"A good surprise."

In our situation, there was no such thing as a good surprise.

I lit another cigarette and Hussein opened the balcony door. The wind rushed in again. It was one too many times for the slatted metal cover of the air vent. The wind must have been dislodging it every time Hussein had opened the French windows, millimeter by millimeter. It crashed to the floor and Moises and I sat in our blue velour chairs and tried not to look at the rectangular hole where our gray satellite phone was now clearly visible. We didn't look at each other. Oh God, I thought, please don't look up there.

Hussein picked up the grate and slowly raised his eyes. He gazed at it for a few seconds.

I jumped out of my seat.

"Oh, thank God," I said. "We forgot our satellite telephone. Thank you. My boss would kill me if we'd forgotten that. It's worth a lot of money."

Salem and Hussein looked at me, unimpressed.

"Why did you hide it?" Salem asked.

"The manager of the hotel told us we should put it there to prevent it being stolen," Moises lied, and I felt a chill because it was a lie that could easily be checked but would have to be maintained.

Hussein stood on a chair and pulled out the phone, checking to see if there was anything else stashed in the vent. As sat phones go, it was a rather primitive model, but the two men gingerly examined it as if it had been a laser gun or an interplanetary radio.

"We use it to send our stories and photographs to New York," Moises said.

Salem packed it in my bag. "OK," he said, glaring at me, "let's try again." He added it to the long list of items under my name on his clipboard.

It was all going badly. And none of our friends knew this was happening. They would not know where we had gone and they could do nothing to help. I had to find a way of speaking with someone. And then I remembered my flak jacket, which I had left in Burns and Tyler's room. I did not want to lead these men to their room, but if I asked to go and pick it up I could use the coded knock, give them time to hide their sat phones, and then tell them that I needed my

flak jacket because we were being taken somewhere by these men—
perhaps to Syria. I was sure this would work. The men were obses-
sive about our taking absolutely everything, down to the last bottle of
water, even though we assured them over and over that we just wanted
to leave much of our countless belongings in the room. We would not
need car batteries, kerosene lamps, a generator, two microwave ovens,
boxes of food, and dozens of bottles of water in Syria. But they insisted. So I thought they would agree to let me fetch my flak jacket.

"No," Salem said. And that was that.

We waited and waited and shortly before 7 A.M. more men came
to the room. The hotel's manager came and we checked out, paying
him the $307 we owed. He looked cowed and in a hurry to be gone.
He gave me a receipt.

Two porters arrived with trolleys, and the intelligence men
insisted that they carry out every single thing we owned. When we
had checked out of the Palestine at the end of our previous visit to
Iraq in October 2000, I had left a bottle of scotch for one of the
porters. We would often shake hands and laugh about nothing. But
this time he would barely meet my glance. I put my hand into my
jeans pocket and pulled out a $20 bill that I had kept in my pocket
without telling the gorilla. I slipped it to him when the men weren't
looking, hoping he would tell one of our friends what had happened—whatever was happening—and he grabbed it and gave me a
look of what I thought was concern and sympathy and helplessness.
He seemed to know something that I didn't, and he was perhaps
even more scared than I was. It was not comforting.

It was time to go.

More security men I had not seen before appeared to escort us
along the corridor, to the freight elevators. There seemed to be dozens
of men involved in this operation. They clearly did not want anyone
to see us leave through the main entrance. Men in suits stood on either side of us, smiling but eerily silent. The elevator doors opened
and we walked into the basement parking lot and storage area, a cavern of darkness and concrete. It seems like a good place to shoot someone without witnesses, I thought. And from that moment on, even in

my sleep, I never lost the vertiginous feeling that my life might not go on for much longer. Someone was dangling me out of a window by one ankle, and at any moment he could let go.

If we were being taken to the border, it would likely be in a bus or in the orange-and-white Chevrolet Suburbans or GMCs that worked as taxis between Baghdad, Damascus, and Amman. Instead, two white pickup trucks stood outside the loading bay at the side of the hotel. My stomach contracted. In one I could see Molly staring at me with a sort of passive horror. In the second truck sat other figures. From the side I could see that one of them was Johan. Marco was not there. Security men in the vehicles guarded them. Others stood around. Some carried machine guns. From the belt of one, whose young face was sharp and without many traces of mercy, hung a pair of silvery steel handcuffs. On the rear of the pickups were emplacements for machine guns. This was not the sort of transportation you take to Syria. These were the vehicles that had taken over the streets of Baghdad in the past weeks. They belonged to the security services. But perhaps, I still hoped, they were going to take us directly to the border to make sure that we did in fact leave the country.

I walked up to the young man with the handcuffs, the one who worried me the most. "We go to Syria?" I asked him. He looked at me blankly for a few seconds. He clearly spoke no English, so I used the Arabic pronunciation. "Suria?"

He paused, nodded, and turned away to Salem.

I understand a little Arabic.

"What's this about Syria?" the man asked Salem.

"I told them we're taking them to Syria," Salem replied quietly.

I turned to face Moises and spoke into his left ear. "We're in big trouble," I mumbled. "We're in big trouble, man."

I approached Salem.

"Salem, are we really going to Syria?" I asked him.

"No, you are going to another place in Baghdad. A safe place."

A few minutes later, Salem and the man with the handcuffs walked over to us. By this time, all our bags and belongings had been loaded into the back of one of the white pickups.

The sharp-faced man, his thin beige sweater tucked into his trousers, took the handcuffs off his belt. He unlocked them with a key and cuffed Moises's left hand and then my right. My hand was twisted the wrong way around. It was the first time in my life I had been hand-cuffed, and I managed to get it wrong.

"Mister Matthew, Mister Moises, you are under arrest," Salem said.

"Why? We are *journalists*," I said.

"I know." Uninterested in what I had to say, he turned around and walked away.

Moises and I were directed into the front seat of the pickup Johan was in. I couldn't see who else was in the backseat. Three men. I assumed they were all under arrest.

"Has anyone explained to you what's going on?" I asked quietly, without turning around.

"No speak," said a voice over my shoulder. I turned around now and saw that Johan was in the middle. To his right was a security man. To his left was a bearded middle-aged man I had never seen before. He had dark hair and I couldn't tell if he was a Westerner or an Iraqi.

The gorilla got into the driver's seat with his assault rifle by his side. It was a tight fit and my left shoulder pressed cozily up against the gorilla's right shoulder. My hip was against his, my leg leaning on the gear stick. He didn't seem to mind or think it strange to be so physically close. I forced my leg away from the gear stick and we set off through the deserted streets of Baghdad in the predawn darkness.

Moises and I had got ourselves into a spot of similar trouble once before. It was in Afghanistan in December 2001, in the days after the fall of the Taliban. We had driven out from Kabul to report an inconsequential story on the same road where four journalists had been executed by pro-Taliban forces only the day before. I don't really believe in second-guessing the risky decisions journalists make all the time, but that was perhaps the stupidest thing I have ever done in my life. When three gunmen hijacked our car, our translator talked our way out, persuading them that it would be un-Islamic to kill us.

So in the days leading up to the bombing campaign in Baghdad, Moises and I had worked out a coded conversation that we would have if we again found ourselves in a vehicle with armed men who might kill us.

I would ask him, "Where's your leather jacket?" Moises did not own a leather jacket. That meant: Should we take out our Leatherman knives and try to take these guys?

He could reply, "I left it in the hotel." That meant, let's go for it. Or he could say, "I left it in New York," which meant forget it.

As we drove along the highway leading out of central Baghdad, with only two security men in the car and four prisoners, I thought about initiating that coded conversation. With my left hand I could pull my Leatherman out of my belt pouch. But I realized then that what keeps regimes like Saddam's in power is sheer and simple physical force. Guns, muscles, cars, radios, walls. In other words, if I had been lucky, I could have stabbed the gorilla in the throat and grabbed the wheel while Moises and Johan dealt with the other security guard. But then what? The vehicle behind us would have seen what was going on. Molly could have been executed on the spot for convenience. And as far as I knew, we were at least fifty miles from American troops, and we wouldn't stand a chance of getting through the checkpoints and lines of defenses.

So my fantasy of empowerment, of escape, faded and gave way to my first attempts at coming to terms with death. "I have lived a full thirty-three years," I told myself. "If they kill me, that's OK. Many people die younger than I do and have lived less fulfilling lives. It hasn't been all great, but I've been lucky." I was so panicked I could barely get those sentences completed in my mind, and once I had finished them, I didn't believe them, barely knew what they meant. I repeated them and still they made not a dent on my terror. I was not ready to die.

"Where are we going?" Johan asked the security man in the backseat.

"Kill, kill," said the man, laughing, and I turned in panic and saw him either making a gun with his hand or just pointing to Johan and the other man in the backseat, whom I did not know.

"You can kill me if you want," said Johan, in his American-accented English, his voice gentle and even; I knew, of course, that he was acting, like all of us. "I don't care if you kill me."

"Are you going to find a place where you can dump our bodies in the desert?" asked the other captive man. His voice was American and tinged with sarcasm. I would find out later he was a peace activist named Philip Latasa.

"No, no," laughed the security man.

"Why are we being held?" I asked.

"Just a small problem with passport," he said.

I looked in the side mirror. Molly was behind us in the other white pickup. Its headlights shone in the first light of day. She was alone with her Iraqi captors.

"Killing," resumed the man in the backseat, laughing again.

I looked at Moises. We asked the gorilla if we could smoke and, coordinating our handcuffed wrists, we fished out a pack and a lighter and breathed in the smoke heavily. We made sure to give one to the gorilla.

We turned off the highway and on the off-ramp we passed an Iraqi army unit moving two antiaircraft batteries around under the semi-cover of darkness. Then I saw a road sign, in English and Arabic. Abu Ghraib.

Moises turned his head and looked into my eyes. We were driving toward the biggest, most feared prison in Iraq, perhaps in the Middle East. Having been there in October, we knew what happened inside its walls: torture, execution, indefinite detention.

After a drive of about forty minutes, the gorilla turned off the main road that ran alongside the northern wall of the prison into the front gate. The young guard was clearly not expecting new inmates so early in the morning. He slouched out of the rectangular guard house on the left and sullenly approached the pickup. He argued with the gorilla for a few seconds. It looked like there were no orders to herald our arrival. And then our driver said a word in Arabic that finally told me who it was who had us, and it was the most awful word I could have heard.

"Mukhabarat," he told the guard, and the young man hurried to open the gates and let us in. Never before had I heard an Iraqi use or even hear that word without immediately lapsing into a tense silence. As he said it, this man was entirely nonchalant.

We drove past some low buildings and into the compound. It was huge and surprisingly empty in the center. Roads angled through land that had been dug up and turned over and left like filthy fallow fields. Straight ahead and to the left were large squat buildings. Alongside the road were yellow brick benches with concrete shelters, like bus stops. We drove straight and then right, through the wasteland, until we came to an enormous, solid, white metal gate that was an entry-way into a high-walled compound within the compound of Abu Ghraib itself. None of us said a word.

The gorilla leaned on his horn, but the gate did not open. He got out and banged on it, but still no one came. So he reversed the pickup and drove back around these internal walls to another, smaller en-trance. There was a sign in Arabic that I could not read over the en-tranceway. Again, the gorilla honked and eventually a guard opened the door.

Salem and the handcuffer reappeared from a third pickup that I had not noticed in our convoy. The sharp-faced officer unlocked our cuffs and took them off. Salem led us inside to an anteroom decorated with murals of Saddam with a dove of peace, Bedouins resting at a tranquil desert oasis, and verses from the Koran. We sat on a tattered couch next to one wall and smoked some more. The sharp-faced of-ficer joked around with another man's pistol, arming it and pointing it toward the door.

"Come," Salem said after a while, and we were back at the pick-ups, taking all our bags and belongings off and carrying them through the anteroom, down a pathway, through a large doorway, and into the compound. At first glance, the place looked incongruously bucolic. I had only seconds to look around as I grew weaker with each heavy load that we carried into a blue-and-white-painted cell block and dumped in its corridor. But sure enough, there were sea-blue concrete benches lined up under a shading roof. There were neat rows of vegetables planted alongside the walls. There were flowerbeds to avoid stepping in as we staggered in with our boxes of water and leaking car batteries and microwave ovens.

"Sit," one of the guards told us.

We crouched and slumped on the floor and on bags and watched as guards slowly appeared from cells that were clearly their bedrooms, looking sleepy and unwashed, most of them only mildly interested in the five Westerners sitting on the floor as they walked past to the block's bathroom. Others were more intrigued and asked where we were from. A few of them snickered when they heard that Molly and Philip were from the United States and I was from Britain.

A guard appeared at the door to the block with the beaten prisoner following him like a drone, turning his battered eyes to the corner.

"We're in the worst prison in the Middle East," I whispered to Molly, when no one was near us. She didn't hear me and I didn't hear what she then mumbled. Later I would find out that she had been trying to share with me the only cheering piece of information that any of us could possibly have: Her roommate, Nate Thayer, had seen her being arrested. Someone knew we were there.

Molly was new to Iraq, I knew, and what I had told her wasn't exactly comforting. But I was desperate to push back rising horror, knowing that we were in the depths of a prison that Saddam had deliberately cultivated as both a weapon and a symbol of his rule of terror, and I hoped that perhaps by sharing the knowledge it would dissipate my terror a little or at least bring us all a bit closer together. Already I felt almost completely cut off from the other four by the prohibition on talking, even though they sat just next to me.

"Come," said a young guard in a crisp khaki uniform. Moises stood up and entered the cell that had been turned into the reception office, the processing room. We sat and smoked and passed around a bottle of water. Moises came out in pajamas. Then it was my turn.

That was when I first met Abu Ibrahim, although I had not yet overheard this honorific nickname. Father of Ibrahim. Every Mukha-barat agent was known as father of someone as a way of making sure that detainees never heard their true names. Wearing civilian clothes, Abu Ibrahim sat behind the plain white desk and spoke some English and understood more. Like nearly all Iraqi men, he had a moustache. A few strands were graying, the rest black, and his hair was retreat-ing a little from his forehead. I put him at about 40 years of age. He was, unlike many of his ursine fellow intelligence officers, slim and graceful in his movements. His hands moved without hesitation and without rush over the paperwork on his desk. It was no bother to him to stop his work—checking us in to prison—to tell a humorous story to the surrounding officers. I could tell he was a good storyteller, build-ing up the narrative gently but with real momentum until he and all his listeners crescendoed into laughter. But perhaps people always laugh at the jokes of men who are more powerful than they are.

It must have been about eight o'clock by this time—an early start to the day—but he seemed wide awake. He must sleep here too, I thought. Abu Ibrahim insisted on writing down on a list every single thing that belonged to me, just as the gorilla and his assistant had done only a few hours earlier in the hotel room. And as we finished with each bag—opened, searched, and then closed after certain things like notebooks and electronic items had been placed to one side—I had to carry it to the back of the room and pile it up.

He asked me in his gentle, slightly high-pitched voice to put on the white undershirt and the pajamas another man handed to me and the beige flip-flops that I took from a transparent plastic bag. Like Moises, the only possession I had left was my boxer shorts. My watch was gone, and any accurate sense of time began to float away.

When the registration was over, the young guard in his dark, neatly pressed khaki uniform grabbed my left hand with both of his. His name was Mohammed, as I would overhear later. With one hand he yanked my thumb painfully away from my other fingers and pressed it into a blue ink pad. He lifted it up and jammed it into a space on the bottom of the list of my possessions, again curving my thumb in a way it is not meant to curve, as if he would sometime soon be interested in testing its breaking point. Or mine.

Abu Ibrahim laughed at me. He pointed to my pajama bottoms. They were very long and baggy. His laugh was easy, not jeering, as if we were sharing a joke about an oversized fancy-dress costume.

"Would you like to change?" he asked, his eyebrows coming together in concern.

"No, no, they're fine," I replied, wanting to keep as much clothing around me as possible because I could already feel the cold of the morning adding to the shivers that ran through my body. "Really, thank you."

The flip-flops weren't fine. They were too small and the left one dug into the upper part of my foot. But I chose not to complain and turned out of the cell into the corridor to wait for the others to check in and change into their uniforms: I knew that having undersized plastic footwear was not likely to be the most challenging problem I was due to face.

Mohammed grabbed my right arm and pushed my pajamas up to my elbow. He looked at a piece of paper and then took a red ballpoint pen and wrote the number 276 on my forearm.

"In here, your name 276," he said. "OK?"

"OK," I said and let my pajamas fall to my wrist again. I sat on the floor and waited.

In the shock of arriving at the prison, of beginning the long period of knowing that I could be killed at any moment, I had barely looked around. A large part of me did not want to see, did not want to witness anything or anyone. The less I saw and knew, perhaps the safer it would be for me. In late November, I had taken a course in how to survive hostile environments. One observation that our trainers, ex-British soldiers, had told us came back to me now: Be worried if your captors let you see their faces. Be worried if they don't blindfold you or put your head in a bag. That means they don't care if you see their faces. That means they might already be planning to kill you.

I could see their faces. And I could see where we were.

Carrying the two blankets we had been given and as much of our bottled water as we could manage—our captors' one act of generosity so far—we began the walk to our new home. Out of the block, left and then right, toward the largest section in the compound.

"Welcome," shouted out a guard, laughing at us as we shuffled along a pathway in our flip-flops. "Welcome."

Between the single-story cell blocks, painted white, were surprisingly charming gardens. Roses looked ready to bloom in the early spring. Flowerbeds, carefully tended, stretched between the buildings. Under leafy bowers were benches and tables—even a Ping-Pong table and a pool table. Some walls were decorated with murals of Saddam Hussein; others depicted ancient cityscapes and floral gardens. Eucalyptus and willow trees grew alongside some of the pathways.

All of the walls were made of cinder block. All of the windows had bars, either metal or thick concrete lattice, painted blue or white. We walked past a blue-painted wire fence, turned right, and walked past a water cooler into the large cellblock. I barely had time to look around. One by one, we were allotted cells on the right side of the concrete corridor. First was Moises, then Johan, then me, then Molly, then Philip Latasa.

Mohammed and another guard showed me how I should use my blankets. He folded the very dirty beige one—covered in stains and curly hairs, dead insects and dust—and laid it across the cell. I folded the cleaner one, dark brown wool hemmed with synthetic material, and lay down between them.

"Number, you," Mohammed said.

"276," I said, and he wrote something down on a piece of paper that he taped to the wall next to my cell door.

"Sleep," Mohammed said. He padlocked the door and turned away, his shiny leather shoes clicking steadily down the corridor.

I did not know it then, but I had a friend in this corner of Abu Ghraib—a man I had written about in my newspaper in October. Saad Jassim—Sam Jason to his American friends—had spent three years living in the cell next to mine, the one Molly was now occupying. Only days earlier he had been ordered to clear out his cell and move to another block, across the garden area. His story and his friendship would, weeks later, help me understand this world I suddenly found myself in.

That morning, Tyler called Jim Dooley, *Newsday*'s director of photography, and left a message on his answering machine. Tyler's call was the first of many extraordinarily brave efforts of our friends at the Palestine to find out what had happened to us and how to help. The call prompted the start of an effort by *Newsday*'s staff, our friends, our families, and people I have never met that will forever humble me.

"I imagine you are probably aware that Matt McAllester and Moises Saman have—I'm not sure exactly what happened, but they are no longer here at the Palestine Hotel. I saw them as of last night—both of them—everything was OK. And today their room is empty. There have been a lot of expulsions overnight. People are being taken to Syria. We think they may have been among that group of people. Although we haven't had any contact with them . . . I spent a better part of the day talking to people and trying to figure out where they are, but we haven't had any contact with them. If you have heard from them, it would be great if you could drop me a line and let me know so we can relax about that."

It was the kind of call that I prayed people were making as I lay in my cell.

3

Amnesty

October 2002

Two days after Saddam Hussein ordered Iraq's prisons to be emptied of their inmates, I paid a visit to the old American Embassy, which was now manned only by local staff and Polish diplomats, who represented American interests in Iraq. Inside the consular section of the embassy, where American diplomats had not worked since 1990, two Iraqi women were speaking to the clerk through the thick glass window. Around the waiting room were posters of the Statue of Liberty and other scenes from Iraq's greatest enemy. It struck me that the women's very presence at the embassy was an act of bravery, or desperation. Some strong motivation must have propelled them through the constant wall of surveillance that surrounded the building.

As the women were leaving, one of the Polish diplomats came out to the waiting room to chat with me.

"Do you know who they were?" asked the Pole, a cheery and

helpful man who spoke to me on what was an absolutely standard condition of anonymity for diplomats speaking to reporters in those days.

"No," I said.

"That was the sister and another relative of an American citizen who was not released on Sunday," the Pole said. "And there's another one who also didn't come out."

"You're kidding. There are American prisoners? I thought everyone was released."

"No, there was a clause in the amnesty," the Pole explained. "Foreigners convicted of spying for Israel and the United States were the only people it didn't apply to. These two are dual-nationality Iraqis and they did not come out. They were in the Arabs and Foreigners Department of Abu Ghraib, and we don't know where they are now. Probably still there."

Moises and I drove west toward Iraq's notorious gulag.

For the gatekeepers of one of the most intimidating prisons in the world, the uniformed men at the front gate of Abu Ghraib seemed rather young and skinny. The two guards eased themselves out of their seats in the concrete sentry posts that stood on either side of the road.

"We've just come to take a look around," I said, speaking through my Iraqi government minder, who acted as my translator. Upon arrival in Baghdad, every journalist registered at the Ministry of Information and part of the process was to be assigned one of these official guides whose primary job, besides translating, was to prevent you from seeing or doing anything unsanctioned by the ministry and to write reports on you for the Mukhabarat. I had not told my minder, Louai, why I really wanted to come out to the prison. It was two days after the presidential amnesty had emptied Iraq's penal system of its tens of thousands of inmates. On the day of the amnesty I had been interviewing someone and had missed the mass rush to Abu Ghraib that the Ministry of Information had organized for visiting journalists. I told Louai that I just wanted to take a look around the famous Abu Ghraib.

"It's closed," said the young guard in charge. An assault rifle hung over his shoulder. He looked about 17 years old.

Iraqis driving by Abu Ghraib did their best to keep their eyes on the pavement in front of them. But to the unwitting passenger, it wouldn't look particularly intimidating. If you hadn't known what you were looking at, Abu Ghraib would have struck you as just another of the walled military bases that lined the main roads leading out of the city. It was surrounded by watchtowers and high, dust-colored walls, but so were dozens of these installations. The walls were not particularly high, even. Just high enough to prevent passers-by from seeing the concrete buildings where everything that was wrong with Iraq secretly found amplification in the cells and corridors.

"But there have been hundreds of journalists in here in the past two days and we'd just like to take another look around," I said. "It's no big deal. We're just curious."

"Well, now it's closed."

Only the steel bars of the gate that spanned the single-track road stood in our way. The prison looked so poorly protected, so easily accessible, for a place with such a horrifying reputation for keeping men inside for decades, for torturing and executing prisoners without recourse to any normal concept of law. Here was a prison where healthy men would beg tuberculosis patients to spit into their mouths so that they could contract the disease and get a comfortable bed in the tuberculosis ward. Inside these walls was a system of spying and paranoia and punitive violence that was a distillation of the society that lay beyond the walls. But like the Iraqi security agencies' nondescript detention centers all over the country, there was very little to indicate that Abu Ghraib was anything particularly remarkable. Even the multicolored portrait of Saddam to the left of the entranceway was relatively modest in comparison to many of the vast murals and statues in Baghdad.

"Just a few minutes," I said. "Please."

"No. You must leave now."

I turned to the cowed and endearing Louai, who was really just a low-level, middle-aged government clerk who happened to speak

English and therefore had been press-ganged into working as a minder by the Ministry of Information during this busy period.

"Tell him that we must go inside because there are two American citizens being held in the Foreigners Department and I want to see them," I said, changing my tone a little.

The young guard looked at me quietly for a couple of seconds before answering.

"The prison is empty," he said. "There are no prisoners inside."

"Yes, there are," I said. "I know for a fact that there are two Americans here."

"No, there is no one."

"Where are they then? Because they haven't come home to their families like everyone else did on Sunday. Where have they been taken?"

I am not an American citizen but the guard didn't know that. I hoped he would feel the sort of pressure that can sometimes open prison doors for diplomats demanding to see imprisoned citizens of their countries. He apparently felt nothing of the sort.

"You must leave," he said. And then he looked to Moises, who was about to shoot some pictures of the front gate. "No photographs."

And so we left as ordered, driving back along the straight road that leads into the heart of Baghdad and away from the two men I believed to be among the last prisoners still held in an Iraqi prison.

It was on Sunday, October 20, 2002, that Saddam had issued his extraordinary decree. Iraq's prisoners, including political opponents, could go home. Many had spent more than a decade inside what human rights groups considered one of the least humane prison systems in the world. All over the country, as the surprise news spread, guards unlocked cells where prisoners had cowered and lived through years of torture. Nowhere was the spectacle more amazing than at Abu Ghraib, the one place that Iraqis feared more than any other in the country. And when the tens of thousands of men held there were suddenly released, so too were feelings of fury. The prisoners, in an act of unprecedented spontaneous protest, ripped the prison apart as much as they could before bursting through its gates in crushing waves. As the news spread, hundreds of cars raced out to the prison, blocking the roads all around as family members rushed toward the main gate in search of their husbands, brothers, and sons. Prison officials tried to release the men in batches but eventually gave up, and prisoners poured out of the gate, haggard, elated, and carrying anything of value they could find.

I wrote about Saad Hamid Jassim and Mohammed Samir Fakhri Jihad, the two American citizens and convicted spies. And then the next day, I forgot about them. I had other stories to do. Besides writing about them, I thought to myself, what could I possibly do to get them out?

But there was another reason that I forgot about them so easily, a reason I did not recognize until recently: I did not know then what it was like to be in Abu Ghraib. I felt not empathy but sympathy, and sympathy can crumble quickly, leaving nothing but a short newspaper story hibernating in a database.

The almost 700 prisoners inside the 20-foot-high walled compound that was the Arabs and Foreigners Department of Abu Ghraib were permitted televisions in their cells if their families had the money to buy one for them.

Sometimes another prisoner would come into Saad Jassim's cell to chat for a bit. Then he would suggest watching Saad's TV for a while and would quickly reach over to the small desk where the TV sat to turn it on before Saad could. The prisoner would "belong" to one of the guards and would be looking to see if Saad had been watching the banned antiregime channel that the Iranian government had recently started broadcasting into Iraq. Even in the department, the Iraqi Intelligence Service recruited spies.

The other two channels were permitted viewing. At least the prisoners could keep up to date with official state news and sports on the main channel and the Youth TV channel run by Saddam's oldest son, Uday. The luxury of television, unusual in Iraq's prisons, hardly compensated for the punishing beatings that were part of daily life in the department, but seeing the outside world, even if it was through the distorting filter of Saddam Hussein's regime, could sometimes ease the loneliness, boredom, and fear.

On the morning of October 20, it brought the best news that a prisoner could ever hear. Al-Sahaf appeared in an unscheduled address. Saad sat in his cell and stared at his television.

"The first announcement of the amnesty was quite clear. All the prisoners. Nobody excluded. That's what al-Sahaf said exactly. He did not say anything about Iraqis, Arabs, foreigners. He said all the prisoners are good to go, you know. Like the Americans say."

Al-Sahaf stared into the camera and read: "The amnesty covers all crimes, no matter what the kind and level of crime."

Saddam knew that war was coming soon. For months he had been trying to secure the support of the population he had terrorized for thirty-four years. For him to have any chance of surviving an American and British attack, the Iraqi people would have to side with their president. And so he sent money and guns to tribal chiefs. He doubled the monthly food rations around the country. Cars and pay increases came the way of soldiers and intelligence officials. A few days before the amnesty, he had staged a referendum to extend his term as president of Iraq for another seven years. All 11,445,638 eligible voters made it to the polls, the government announced, and all of them voted yes. The amnesty was billed as Saddam Hussein's thank-you present to his loyal and loving people.

The reaction to al-Sahaf's announcement was extraordinary. The hundreds of prisoners in the five sections of the Arabs and Foreigners Department erupted. They let out huge roars of relief and delight. They danced up and down in their overcrowded cells and hugged each other. Some had been there for half their lives, far away from their loved ones, locked away in one of the most hopeless corners of Saddam's Iraq: Turks, Indians, Iranians, Arabs from all over the Middle East, and Iraqis who had given up their passports for citizenship of other countries, like Sweden and the United States.

Saad had spent seven years in prison—as long as one of Saddam's so-called presidential terms.

"After ten minutes, half an hour, we were called to attention and told there was going to be another announcement on TV. Boom, here comes the TV announcer and says the amnesty only included Iraqis. So in our section everyone just had a major, major nervous breakdown. We know as prisoners that we had to analyze every single word the TV said. We all knew right then that we were excluded from that amnesty. . . . We had some prisoners who had spent nineteen years in that jail. They just went to their room and fell down on their beds, pretending they were sleeping—but they were actually crying."

It was a different kind of torture than usual for the men in the blue-and-white cell blocks of the department. It was the worst kind. And it continued.

"They waited for two hours. 'We have another announcement for our brothers, the Arabs.' Then the prison came back to life again. Everyone started dancing and cheering again. Sahaf came back, and he said, 'We thank the Arabs, our brothers, blah blah, we give amnesty to all the Arabs, except the Arabs who were charged with spying for America and the Israelis.'"

Saddam had released every single prisoner in Iraq apart from these twenty-eight men and the Iranian prisoners held in the department. Among the twenty-eight were twelve Turks and two Indians; the rest were Iraqis who had citizenship in other countries, including the Americans, Saad and Mohammed.

As they watched their cellmates run out of the high side gate and the tunnel-like room that was the main entrance of the department, the remaining prisoners did the only thing they possibly could. They knew it was pointless, but they appealed to their guards. These men may have been officers in the Mukhabarat, but they had no leeway when it came to presidential decrees.

"You guys know and we know if Saddam Hussein and a few guys from Intelligence find a real spy, you either trade him or hang him," Saad pointlessly reasoned with the Mukhabarat officers. "That's the way you guys deal. But charging a person for spying and putting him in jail means he is innocent. Whoever is innocent is sentenced for twenty years."

That was Saad's sentence—plus another eight for illegally entering the country from Jordan in the early 1990s. While murderers, rapists, and men who genuinely had tried to overthrow the regime were walking through their front doors and enjoying home-cooked meals, Saad had another twenty-one years ahead of him. When I came to the front gate of Abu Ghraib, facing the denials from the guards of his existence, Saad was sitting in his cell several hundred yards away, two days into the next twenty-one years of his stolen life.

With each day that followed the amnesty, families of those prisoners left behind in Abu Ghraib slowly began to realize that their sons and brothers were not on their way home. One woman wrote to her brother in a letter that he kept for months but left among the abandoned cells of the Arabs and Foreigners Department when Saddam's regime fell:

> *My dear brother, I was so happy and delighted hearing the amnesty news. I also cried at the same moments because I was really keen to see you. So I kept watching TV, searching for you among the crowds of men who were released. . . . And whenever the telephone or my mobile rang I wished it were you. . . . I wonder if you have received the money that I sent you. . . . Anyway, it's not that important. I went out to buy the newspapers to see the names of the people released after the amnesty. So I saw your name in the paper and then I understood the reasons that kept you from calling.*

4

Closer to God

FEBRUARY 2003

It was an almost wordless coming together. Out of the three hundred worshippers massed in the courtyard, the men and some of the boys quietly stepped across the cooling tiles into lines, forming concentric squares under the stars that had only a couple of days earlier been hidden by a dust storm. In the innermost square stood seven drummers, who began to beat time on animal hide stretched over round wooden drums. Opposite and next to them were the dervishes, Sufi holy men. Their long hair, unshorn since their first communion with God, and usually tied up, now hung down their backs. It was eight o'clock on the night of Thursday, February 27, and the three hundred men, women, and children at the Sufi temple known as the Takyia Kasnazan in this quiet neighborhood of west Baghdad were about to begin their most important weekly ceremony.

Swaying their heads gently from side to side and calling out *Ya Allah* in time with the drumming, the Sufis began their journeys toward, they hoped, a trance that would allow them a closeness to God. Although they were all standing together in the same courtyard trying to take that journey, each man and boy was ultimately on his own. For some, it wouldn't be their night. They would sway and nod their heads in vain, reluctantly anchored to the material world. Others would find their escape quickly. One teenage boy was writhing on the floor within three minutes, immediately oblivious to the hardness of the tiles, to the rigidity of his government, and to the vast military force stationed only a few hundred miles away that was now preparing to attack his country. To be that close to God was to be far from Saddam.

He squirmed on the ground, alone at the end of the outer line of the gathering, as if he had been tipped over and battered by centrifugal force.

In the center of the concentric squares, the older dervishes—most of them between 20 and 40 years old—were now swirling their heads and their long, dark manes around at speed. They reminded me of head-banging heavy-metal fans from the early 1980s, blanking out the agonies of suburbia and adolescence. Now and then a dervish would shout out, or moan, or lose control completely, falling violently to the ground or pointing aggressively at nothing in particular. By now the noise was great, and I gazed with some pity at the neighboring houses.

"Soccer players need exercise and training so that they can play good soccer," the regal Ali Abu Tiba had told us over dinner before the ceremony, his black eyebrows meeting in the center to form a V over his kindly face. "The heart also needs exercise so that it can love religion. These ceremonies are exercises for the heart, to be closer to God."

Throughout our long chat over a cross-legged dinner of chicken, beans, rice, and the delicious flat bread of Iraq that's always best when it's slightly burned, the senior Sufi cleric never once brought up politics, or railed against the American aggressors, or volunteered his fealty to His Excellency, President Saddam Hussein. I had never encountered any holy man from the much larger Sunni and Shia strands of Islam who did not skip past the tiresome topic of faith straight to furious denunciations of the United States and Britain. All of the clerics that journalists were taken to see by the regime's minders were appointees, terrified men who lived under the constant watch of the ruling Baath Party—but sometimes lived well for their efforts.

Abu Tiba offered no direct comment on his president or on the hostile forces amassing on the borders of his country. Instead, he spoke only of healing, love, brotherhood, togetherness, and peace. Less a head banger than a hippie.

The section of the ceremony that followed the drumming and whirling shifted from the metaphysical to the distinctly physical. Sufi men took off their shirts and kneeled in front of me while others forced skewers through their chests, jaws, and cheeks. One man dined on about a dozen Chinese-made razor blades, one of which he gave to me to check before he crunched it up in his mouth as if it were a square of fried bread in a *fattoush* salad. Even the man who took two very sharp daggers to his tongue, slashing it so excitedly that blood droplets began to spatter in front of me, was clearly performing an act of selfless worship to the miracles of God (even if some of these miracles were just hammy old circus tricks). The only jarring moment, the only political moment, came when a member of the congregation stood up and took the microphone to urge his fellow Sufis, his fellow Muslims, his fellow Iraqis, to fight with all the fury and strength they had against the evil American invaders when they came. I knew at the time that no public gathering could pass without an obligatory denunciation of the enemy, but unlike in the mosques of Baghdad, this outburst came and went without comment or cheer. There was no ensuing outburst of *Allahu Akhbar* from the congregation. The man finished his speech and sat down again amid silence.

This, I thought, is an Islamic Iraqi community that truly hopes to transcend the ephemeral nature of politics and war. It puts its faith not in the technology of war and political theory but in a mystical idealism.

Weeks later, I would see how wrong I was.

*   *   *

I had been in Baghdad for less than three days when Moises and I visited the temple. We hoped a visit to a Sufi ceremony on a quiet Thursday night would provide an insight into a little-noticed part of Iraqi life, an opportunity to meet ordinary Iraqis and a way of discussing their feelings about the coming war. The Sufis also held another attraction for us. Being outside the Shia and Sunni divide in Islam that threatens the continuing existence of Iraq as it does no other Muslim country, I figured that the Sufis might provide a different and perhaps more neutral outlook on Iraq. But mostly, we were at that early stage in our visit to Iraq when we were just looking for a colorful story that was not overtly political and would not, therefore, get us or anyone else into trouble. It was not even our idea. Our new driver had suggested that we might like to see the ceremony. No Iraqi driver I had ever known would volunteer a story idea that would put him in danger.

Moises and I had our own particular reason to keep out of trouble. We had been applying for regular journalist visas for months at the Iraqi embassy in Amman and had received no response, even as hundreds of other journalists were approved. I don't know what the problem was. I can only suspect that my stories from my last visit to Iraq, in October 2002, had once again landed me on the Ministry of Information blacklist that I had been put on after a trip to Iraq in May 2001. On that first trip I found it hard to maintain the journalistic reticence that was so often the route to future visa approvals for journalists. "You are aggressive," my obstructive minder told me on that first trip. "You were aggressive," he reminded me when I saw him in October 2002. I can only imagine how much more frank was the report card he prepared for ministry officials and the Mukhabarat once I had left. So I had been banned from coming back until a hardworking connection in Amman persuaded the Iraqis to let Moises and me in to cover Saddam Hussein's referendum in October 2002.

This time, as war approached, there had been no change in policy: we absolutely could not get visas. It was late February and it looked like the bombing and invasion could start any day. We had been planning this for months, and we felt that we had to be in Baghdad to record the American-led attack from the Iraqi side. Nearly every journalist I spoke to in Baghdad felt that we could not leave it to the embeds and the Pentagon to write the history of this war. While the journalists accompanying—embedded with—the American and British forces would perform crucial roles in reporting on the war, by the very nature of the arrangement their stories would be one-sided. They wouldn't be speaking to many Iraqis on the receiving end of the American-led attack.

In the lobby and dining room of a damp, dirt-cheap hotel in downtown Amman, three of us took turns camping out at what had become the headquarters of the human-shield movement. Philip Sherwell of the *Sunday Telegraph* had been a close friend and workmate of mine since my first days as a foreign correspondent in the Kosovo war. We would meet in messy places and often end up working together on stories. Moises became good friends with him in Afghanistan during the war there in late 2001.

It was Phil's idea, and I would still say that it was a good one under the circumstances: we would take our chances with the Iraqi authorities and enter the country as journalists limited to covering the activities of the human shields. We knew we would not restrict ourselves to that one story, that we would be breaking the rules in a country held together by the fear of breaking the rules. But journalists tend to break rules—and sometimes even the laws of countries whose actions are themselves illegal. In Iraq, journalists always broke the rules, trying not to push so hard that we did not suffer what we all considered the ultimate sanction—to be barred from future visits to the country. People used satellite phones in their hotels, brought in more cash than they declared, bribed officials, and moved around after hours without minders for surreptitious and, hopefully, frank conversations.

We set off in the early afternoon from Amman in a group with four other journalists.

The drive in and out of Baghdad is the best car journey I know. There can be few smoother, straighter roads than the desert highway that during the embargo years would take the full oil tankers out of Iraq and come back empty from Jordan. I love the road, especially the main Iraqi section, because I usually sleep and wake only when the driver of the big orange-and-white GMC four-wheel-drive decides to fill up with gas or empty out his bladder.

Phil, Moises, and I made it to the border quickly and waited for the blue-and-white chartered bus carrying the human shields. For once, the usually venal and thorough Iraqi customs officials seemed half-asleep and uninterested in our equipment. They knew we were journalists but barely searched our many bags. We gave them a list of our electronic equipment, and whereas they usually copied out the manufacturer's name, model type, and serial number of anything with an electric pulse, this time they waved us away as we offered them radios and tape recorders and other gear. We registered one satellite phone—like all journalists at the time, we had others hidden in our luggage—and they did not, as they were meant to, wrap it with string and seal the string with lead. Partly by default and partly by design, we were breaking rules.

When we arrived shortly before four in the morning, the city was deserted, its yellow streetlights illuminating the wide boulevards and elevated highways that in places give Baghdad the feel of a Middle Eastern Los Angeles. We drove past metal-shuttered appliance stores, kebab and roast chicken restaurants, women's beauty salons with their painted portraits of heavily made-up brides, and money-changing offices whose signs often showed American dollars overlapping with the mauve image of Saddam on the Iraqi 250 dinar bills. The streets, as ever, were spotlessly clean. Modern office buildings, nearly all of them government ministries, directorates, or military offices, kept watch over the street-level businesses. The employees in the ministries who were lucky enough to have offices with a view would be able to gaze out over the looping, murky Tigris and the urban peninsulas spotted with sand-colored riverside villas for the rich, that the ancient river carved out of Baghdad. Date palms and bulrushes lined the banks. And those parts of the city that seemed all palms and greenery were, everyone knew, not parks but the vast grounds of the first family's palaces. There were never any boats or swimmers in the central section of the river. The punishment for swimming too close to a palace was to have your head pushed under the current until you drowned.

All of the hotels designated for the human shields that we tried were full, so Moises and I checked in to the towering, shockingly ugly Palestine Hotel, where we had stayed in October. Phil stayed with Julian Simmonds, the *Telegraph*'s photographer. He had driven in a bus with the shields from London to Baghdad, a journey rife with internecine battles and clashing egos.

The following day I walked out of the Palestine and went looking for a driver, a rather random venture in which the successful candidate would nearly always be an English speaker with a slightly rebellious air about him. In October we had used a jolly Shia Muslim driver named Ali. He was nowhere to be seen. Instead, a balding man of about 40 strode out of the driver's office holding a cigarette in his hand and hailed me in English.

Drivers are usually crucial to the successful work of any reporter overseas but in Hussein's Iraq, drivers were something else. You couldn't trust your minder. They were there to report your every move and question and comment to the Mukhabarat. But when the minders had gone home for the day, or in private moments, English-speaking drivers could take risks if they chose, risks that could be incredibly helpful to you and horrifyingly dangerous to them. The first driver I had in Iraq told me that he had spent two weeks being tortured by the Mukhabarat because he had helped German reporters on an unsanctioned story. The driver's brother was a general who had fired Scud missiles at Israel in 1991, but his family connection offered him no protection from the all-powerful Mukhabarat. At the same time, many drivers were also obliged to report to the Mukhabarat themselves. Trust came in tiny measuring cups.

My new driver's name was Yousef and I had never heard an Iraqi speak as he did. His candidness was exhilarating, and also unsettling. Was Yousef too good to be true? This is what I wrote in my diary that evening.

I was astonished today when I found a new driver and he very quickly began to speak openly about the government, about Iraq's ethnic tensions, about the security services, about how I should come over one evening when it's dark and drink whisky at his house and—this has never happened within my earshot before— about Saddam himself. He was, my driver said, a "difficult man." If you're overheard by the wrong person saying that in Iraq, you're dead. My driver and his friends have recently started talking about the post-Saddam world in groups, he said, and he promised me that we would talk about it all at length when I brought round the Famous Grouse.

He's not looking forward to the war, though.

"The problem is," he said, speaking in English that he learned from his policeman father, who spent two years training with Scotland Yard before the days of Saddam, "that this time, unlike in 1991, the war will come to the city."

We drove past some sandbags piled up in the grassy divider. Behind them was a small trench.

"There, look. There are lots of them now. We didn't have that in 1991."

And they are, indeed, all over the place, these hopeless efforts at stopping what will be an American tidal wave of military strength.

"Let me tell you one thing," he said, as we drove on. "The only people who fight will be the Special Republican Guards, the Republican Guards, the Baath Party members, people like that. And they will not fight because they hate the Americans or the British or because they love Saddam. They will fight because they know what will happen to them at the hands of their neighbors. So they have no choice. If they manage to keep Saddam in power, then they will be all right. Any other way, they will be killed."

Are people secretly looking forward to a world without Saddam, then?

He glanced right at me with a look rather lacking in excitement and hope. But then he casually added to his already long list of sacrilegious comments. We were gently rounding a block. He is a care-

ful driver, rarely honks his horn. "The government is always say-ing that Iraq is a rich country, that it has the second biggest oil reserves in the world. Well, where is the money? They spend it on weapons."

"And on palaces," I said, seeing as we had just driven past one of Saddam's biggest.

"Yes, on palaces."

"Perhaps someone is keeping it in an account in Switzerland," I ventured.

"Yes. And they give it to the Palestinians. Why do they give it to them?"

"Suicide bombers?" One of the sacred cows of the Arab world, the noble martyrs of Palestine, the killers of Israeli civilians.

"Yes. Why don't they give it to us? We don't care who comes and takes over Iraq. The Americans, the British, the Israelis. Who cares? Even if they gave us one quarter of the oil money, we'd all be driving around and living like Kuwaitis. But I'll tell you what we really fear. If the Shia take over. They're a majority, you know? Sixty-five percent. If they take over it will be like Iran. We prefer Saddam Hussein over them."

He leaned out of his window to speak to a parking lot atten-dant.

"I'm serious. We'd prefer to keep Saddam."

I thought about telling him that I've been to Iran a few times, and that it's an immeasurably more liberated and liberating coun-try than Saddam's Iraq, but I thought better of it.

My driver is a Kurd on his father's side and a Turk on his mother's side. In a country where the official line is that there are no economic or social inequalities between Sunni, Shia, and Kurd, the driver was having none of it.

"Let me explain one thing to you. In this country there are the first-class citizens—the Sunni Arabs. Then there are the second-class citizens—the Shia Arabs. Then there are the Kurds."

Because he's a Kurd, he said, he was never sent on trips over-seas when he worked at one of the government ministries, unlike all his Arab colleagues. His father lost his job as head of the police in Baghdad when the monarchy ended in 1958 and the Sunni Arabs really came into ascendancy. Before then, he said—seeing the past with what the history books suggest are rather rose-tinted lenses— there was no discrimination in Iraq between Sunni, Shia, and Kurd.

Chance laid on a rather immediate, petty example of the kind of ethnic tensions that officially don't exist but have led to intermittent slaughters in Iraq over its eighty-year modern history. On our last trip to Iraq, we had used a Shia driver from the same hotel company. He was charming but a regime loyalist—or at least an everyday person too afraid to say boo—and he spoke almost no English. In other words, he had nothing going for him against the new driver. Ali, the old driver, happened to stroll by when the new driver and I were standing in the street. We shook hands and kissed on both cheeks, and about two seconds later Ali asked whether he should pick me up the next day.

"Uh, no, sorry," I said. "I'm working with this new man. He speaks English, you see, Ali."

Ali wasn't happy, that was clear. But I didn't expect him to try to force the new man out of his job, which is what he tried to do— vaguely threatening him. Ali even turned up at our hotel in the evening to try his luck again.

When he had left the street scene, the new driver started muttering about "Arabs." Oh dear, I thought, as we play out the last days of Saddam's enforced, illusory ethnic harmony. What might be around the corner in this artificially constructed country? Perhaps Saddam might not be so bad after all.

It is impossible to exaggerate how much of a risk Yousef was taking in speaking to me as he did in that first meeting. In describing Saddam as "a difficult man," he had committed a capital crime. To insult Islam or God in Iraq would bring about a hefty prison term. Law 25A makes it clear: Slighting the president would result in a visit to the hanging chamber in Abu Ghraib. I know of an entire team of engineers at Saddam International Airport who were imprisoned after one of them was overheard making a joke about a member of Hussein's family. They got off lightly: each served five years in Abu Ghraib. Yousef and I were already bound by information that could lead in only two possible directions—trust or betrayal.

With his good English, understanding of journalism, and willingness to push the limits of what was permitted, Yousef became our key to Hussein's Iraq in its final days. Before long, he was not just a "difficult man." He was a "fucker man."

The following night, after we had settled into a more comfortable hotel, the Al-Hamra, I wrote in my diary about how strange and exhilarating it was to be working in Iraq without a minder and, apparently, without government monitoring:

> *I don't really trust it though. In Iraq you can never really be sure that you are having a private moment. And even the possibility of intrusion, the doubt about the genuineness of the moment, destroys it. That's the core power of totalitarianism, just as fear and not violence is at the heart of terrorism. Even when you are sure, if you can ever be, that you are talking privately to someone absolutely trustworthy, the moment's fleetingness and the rush toward a future of renewed surveillance tends to take the joy away rather. It's no wonder that people just give up and lose themselves to fear and loyalty. It's just not worth the effort.*

> *But the more time I spend with Yousef, the more I sense that the end is coming fast and many people are profoundly excited in a way that they have perhaps never let themselves be before. Yousef says they are. Some of the drivers at his company are spending their down time sitting around the office talking about the end of Saddam, he says. He's only worked there three weeks, but he seems to trust them enough to have conversations that, if leaked by one of them to a neighboring Baath Party member or intelligence official, would more likely than not end up in his disappearance.*

> *"People are afraid of their own shadows," he told me in a loud voice as we crossed a street today, and yet he doesn't seem to be able*

*to control his urge to talk about the coming change and the future.
It's because it's perhaps the first new future he's known since Saddam became president in 1979.*

*"That was a terrible year," he said today, walking with me
through the bazaar, surrounded by people buying duct tape and gas
stoves in preparation for the shattered windows and power cuts that
would come with the war. I had to remind him to keep his voice
down; you never know who could understand English and overhear. "Saddam came to power in the later part of the year, and by
the next year we were at war and we've been at war ever since.
That was a dark year."*

*Saddam was already the power behind the throne during the
Bakr years, but with his own ascent to the presidency he unleashed
his imperial ambitions by starting the war with Iran that would
turn affluent, vibrant Iraq into a country devastated by its own
version of the First World War—trenches and poison gas attacks,
years of pointless attrition, a generation of young men devastated,
and a conclusion that left both countries basically territorially the
same. During those eight years, the Iraqi government became more
than ever a family business, and if you didn't happen to be a distant cousin of the peasant boy from Al-Awja village near Tikrit,
then the next best way to curry favor was to join the Baath Party.*

*"You may not believe it, but I was a member of the party
once," Yousef said with a grin as we crossed Rashid Street. We had
moments earlier passed the spot where the young Saddam had been
part of an unsuccessful assassination attempt on then-president
Abdul Karim Qassem. "It was during the war and I was working
in the helicopter directorate of the army. They came in one day and
said that we had two choices. We could either stay in our job and
join the party or we could go to the front. I joined."*

*So for about six years Yousef read the right books and attended
meetings with his other suddenly enthusiastically Baathist colleagues in the helicopter base near Baghdad. Finally the war
ended.*

"Then I became a bit forgetful about going to meetings. Or sometimes I had other commitments. They just gave up on the likes of me, and I left."

In some ways, Yousef's family spans the history of modern Iraq. There is, in his house, a secret that has stayed concealed for decades.

"This is top, top, top secret," he says, and he can't help smiling, desperate to tell me. "Hidden in my house is an order to arrest Saddam Hussein."

"Excuse me?" I thought, but then remembered who his father was; the former chief of detectives in Baghdad during the last years of the monarchy. His father's signature, Yousef says, is on the arrest warrant for the young, revolutionary, pan-Arab, socialist, nationalist, murderous troublemaker. He doesn't tell me where it's stashed away but promises to show me one evening, when he invites me over. His father is 80 years old and still has the English he learned during his two years in England. I get the impression that he's a little frail and that I can expect the conversation to be rather short when it happens. "He will be so happy to meet you," Yousef says. I look forward to it immensely.

Bonhomie is not the only thing fueling my end of this friendship with Yousef. I have been thinking for months about the dangers of being here when the bombing starts and when the regime feels that its days are over. I am scared of American bombs and Iraqi chemical and biological weapons, but I am most afraid of vengeful members of the regime. Yousef says I'm right to be afraid. And so I have been working on contingency plans for a while, the most valued among them being making contacts with trustworthy Iraqis in whose homes Moises and I might be able to hide during the most dangerous hours. In Amman last week I persuaded a recent air force defector to give me a name and number of a man who has promised to come and pick me up in a white Chevy at a certain place when I call and say my name. I'm pretty sure he's a Shia military officer. One option is not enough, though. I had asked yes-

terday, rather too early in the relationship, for Yousef's home number. He declined and said I could call him at the cab office. I said I entirely understood.

"I'm going to give you my home number," he announced, while driving today. "But . . ."

"We only use it as . . ."

"The change is happening," he said.

"That's a promise," I said. "I don't want to do anything to get you into trouble. Thank you."

We didn't discuss it further, and I didn't actually ask for his number.

Yousef's home sounds rather well prepared for a long war. He's got flour, oil, water, whisky, and fuel stockpiled. He's dug a well in his garden. They'll boil the water, he says. All his neighbors have done the same.

That evening we went to the temple. Yousef warned us that many Iraqi Sufis, long persecuted in countries around the Muslim world, had found a degree of protection in Saddam's Iraq by cooperating closely with the regime. The congregation, Yousef said, would be full of Republican Guard officers and security officials. I didn't quite understand then how that jibed with the Sufis' protestations of universal love and apparent lack of interest in politics. But I let it pass. Yousef had a plan: he would drop us a few blocks away and blend in to the crowd during the ceremony so that he could keep an eye on us and gauge whether the Mukhabarat was around. When we left, he would be waiting in the car on a street corner and we would quickly drive away.

And that's how it went. At one point during the ceremony, I saw Yousef, a woolen cap pulled over his balding head, standing in the crowd. He winked at me. I looked away and tried not to smile.

5

Barefoot in the Trench

In the tiny kitchen of her crumbling house, where the family's chickens walked in through the front door as freely as her nine sons, Mesheeda al-Garawi was serving up a late lunch of rice and potato sauce for those of her large brood who happened to be around. Musa and Mohammed were shaving. Fariq was taking a shower. Sadiq was on the roof where he kept his bird coop, feeding the creatures he so doted on. The four brothers were all in their twenties or thirties and they had just come back from fighting in the disastrous war in Kuwait.

Outside in the street, a roughly flat stretch of earth covered in garbage and rutted by thin canals of sewage that filled the air with a constant stench of human waste, 8-year-old Ahmed was playing marbles with his friends from the neighborhood. He crouched down in his jeans and his blue-and-white striped shirt and rolled the little glass globes toward those of his opponents, the marbles taking unpredictable routes through the obstacle course of putrid debris. The jeans were hand-me-downs from another brother, Saddam, the name written on the inside of the denim by a tailor who had once repaired it. Mesheeda and her husband Bakr al-Esawee had once loved their president so much that they had named one of their sons after him. The Shia of Iraq, including Mesheeda's family, had long since changed their minds about their leader.

It was a tense day in Hilla, a predominantly Shia town of about one million that sits an hour and a quarter's drive south of Baghdad. A few nights earlier, in the middle of March, the Shia uprising that followed the end of the war in Kuwait had reached the town and the local rebels, desperate to overthrow the Saddam regime, had seized control. Suddenly most of Iraq was in the hands of Shia or Kurdish fighters. On February 15, President George H. W. Bush had publicly asked "the Iraqi military and the Iraqi people to take matters into their own hands—to force Saddam Hussein the dictator to step aside." Bush's message was broadcast all over Iraq and the Shia and Kurds had taken it to mean that the U.S. military would support their uprisings against the Baathist regime. But it did not. When Saddam realized that Bush was not going to prevent either his ground or air forces from putting down the rebellions, he unleashed a strike of astonishing brutality on his Kurdish and Shia citizens.

It was really more of a lesson than a counterattack that Saddam had in mind. His people had betrayed him, and he had to teach them the price of that betrayal. It was not enough to squash the revolt and kill and capture those who had participated. The communities, the families, had to understand what the consequences would be if their men ever did such a thing again. When the punishment came, it didn't matter that some of the men of Mesheeda's family had just spent months in Kuwait fighting for Saddam in his elite Republican Guards. In the arbitrariness of Saddam's lesson it didn't really matter, either, that they had a political stain on the family: Bakr had been suspected, correctly, of membership in the outlawed Shia party called Dawa, and in 1987 officers from General Security had cut off his right foot. And it didn't matter that Ahmed was 8 years old. The only thing that mattered to

Saddam in these days after the Gulf War was that Iraq's Shia and Kurdish people, who together made up the considerable majority of the population, be reminded where their loyalties lay. For them to really understand that, Saddam decided, many, many of them would have to die.

The red Nissan bus pulled up outside the house at about half past three in the afternoon. Wearing khaki uniforms, officials from the local Baath Party and Special Security stepped down from the front door of the bus. Some of them had kaffiyehs wrapped around their heads so that only their eyes, dark eyebrows, and the bridges of their noses showed through a thin crack. They carried machine guns, which they fired into the air. Already inside the bus were about thirty people, blindfolded and with their hands tied behind their backs.

Ahmed was playing with his next-door neighbor Samir Matrud and some other boys. When they looked up and saw the bus, the boys scattered, realizing what it meant. But the bus had stopped directly outside Ahmed's house on the corner of the street and he had nowhere to run.

"Please, help me," he screamed, as one of the men grabbed him. He was only 8, but a family photograph shows him to look older than his age. He was a fast runner—had some trophies for his efforts—and he had inherited his butcher father's musculature. In the photograph he has a longish face, a strong chin, and thick, dark hair.

His mother dropped her spoons and dishes when she heard her son's screams and rushed out of the kitchen, through the living room and into the street.

"Just leave him," she begged. "He's a small kid."

One of the men kicked Mesheeda in her belly, and she fell back, gasping for breath and unable to move.

"We're only taking him for interrogation—questions and answers— and then he'll be back," a Special Security man told her.

Other men had burst into the house. At gunpoint, they seized Musa, Mohammed, Fariq, and Sadiq. Another brother, Akil, was also there. He was 11. He pleaded with the men that he was just a kid, and they, true to the random spirit of Saddam's project, let him go. While they were in the house, the men in khaki smashed up the refrigerator, the freezer, and four televisions. They stole all the money they could find, along with the gold jewelry given to the brides of the married brothers on their wedding days, and took away a couple of cassette recorders. They did their best to smash up the family's ragged couches and chairs.

Three brothers were away at the time, visiting relatives or friends. Another was dead, a soldier killed during the war with Iran. Two weeks earlier, their father, Bakr, had died of natural causes. He was spared the sight of five of his sons becoming part of Saddam's vast lesson to his people.

His widow, Mesheeda, lay in the garbage outside the house and watched the red bus drive away with her boys. Blood rose to her mouth from some internal damage caused by the kick to her belly. To this day, every two weeks or so, her insides release a little blood and her mouth tastes as it did the last time she saw Ahmed and his brothers.

Ten miles north of Hilla, on the road to Baghdad, is a village named Muhawil. It is surrounded by salty marshes, deep irrigation trenches bursting with bulrushes, and fields of wheat. The buses drove north and then took a right turn down an unmarked, dusty track lined with the occasional squat date palm and, on the right, banks of rushes from which the breeze summoned a mournful rustling.

At about nine in the morning, Jaber Husseini was in his fields alongside the track when the first three buses arrived, churning dust behind them: Two buses carried about forty people and another held about twenty. There was a mechanical digger there too. The farmer tended his flock of sheep and watched as the digger sliced into the land where he harvested corn and watermelon, carving out a trench. Then the men in khaki offloaded their passengers and led them to the edge, pushing them into the ditches. Getting a solid footing, the men squeezed the triggers of their Kalashnikovs, filling the quiet of the marshes with a violent staccato for a few moments. The digger filled in the holes, the men got back on the buses and drove away, and again there was only the sound of the wind in the rushes.

Jaber knew what had been happening in the area. He knew there had been an uprising, that it was still going on. But he had never expected to see what he had seen, civilians taken to his fields, bound and blindfolded and executed. At about two in the afternoon, the buses returned. And again at five. It happened every day until April 6. He saw people about to be put to death who could never have participated in an armed insurrection: a man on crutches with one leg, women in black *abayas* holding their infants, little boys in clothes dirty from play.

The men in khaki shouted at Jaber and his sons, who also repeatedly saw the killings, to go away. During the weeks of killing, the Muslim holy month of Ramadan began. Often the family would break their daily fast in their nearby farmhouse as the last shift of the day's killing echoed around the flatlands.

"We are innocent, we have done nothing," Jaber's son Akil heard some of the victims shouting before the gunshots began. He was 12 years old at the time, watching across the fields as other Shia 12-year-old boys obediently lined up in the trenches to be executed. Sometimes their killers threw stones at them before firing, to get them all into line.

"God bless their souls," the boy intoned quietly as he walked back to his house. When the air was still, the shouts of the innocent reached the farm.

More than four months after the war, a man with intimate knowledge of the killings at Muhawil, whom I cannot identify, showed me a set of photographs. He would only tell me that he had obtained them from "his sources," but they were clearly taken by someone involved with the killings. These men liked to have mementos of their moments of violence.

It was just as Jaber described. Men in khaki or wearing *dishdashas* had wrapped kaffiyehs around their heads to hide their identities. In one picture, three of them surround what appears to be three men, a boy, and a woman who all lie curled up in the bottom of a trench with their hands bound with black plastic. It looks like they are still alive because there's no blood to be seen and one of the men is stretching out his fingers in the sort of pointless effort to live that some people cannot help making even as they know they are surely about to die. All the people in the trench are barefoot: They seem to have lost their shoes along the journey.

In another photo, there are six people and two of them are clearly still alive. They sit on their knees, their hands bound and heads bowed. They look more at peace with what is about to happen than the man with the outstretched fingers.

Two other snaps indicate that the act has been done. This time the victims are not in a trench but on the flat ground. There is a different hue to one area in the blackness of a woman's *abaya*, suggesting dark blood seeping into the material. Next to her lies a boy under the age of 10 with a red blotch spreading out in the whiteness of his *dishdasha*. Preening themselves behind the bodies are four men. Two point at the eight bodies; two others give the V for victory sign for the camera. The familiar electric towers and sparse trees of Muhawil stand in the blue sky behind disgorged piles of earth.

Another shot features a woman lying in the foreground next to a young boy. A man is bending down and has his hand firmly on the shoulders of the boy, who stares at the ground. Two other little boys gaze from the side at the contact.

The photographs betray more than the last moments of the Muhawil victims, of whom nearly 2,700 were finally dug up after the war, when Jaber led people to his very own killing fields. To document murder was standard for the Nazi-like Baathist regime, convinced equally of the need for order and the inevitability of its own survival. History had to be recorded, and those who made that history would never have to answer for it because they believed that, just as they controlled the present of Iraq, they would control the future. What we consider self-incriminating photographs of a crime were to them, I suppose, a record of a moment of resurgence and strength. I wonder whether they felt proud of what they did, proud of the pictures they could pull out of a drawer for friends and guests over the years.

After the war I got to know a senior Mukhabarat officer, a loyal regime man named Abu Thar who also happened to be Shia. We would drink whisky and eat lunch, and one day I asked him about the uprising. He had been sickened by the Iraqis' betrayal of their own government, he said, but even this man who had served in Saddam's security services for twenty-seven years acknowledged that he had gone too far this time. "The way the government dealt with the people—it should have behaved in a more reasonable way. Not taking innocent people with the criminals, with the people who did the uprising."

Although in September 2003 the Muhawil grave remained the largest discovered so far in Iraq, it was just one of dozens.

When the killing ended in early April, when the buses and the digger stopped coming, Jaber and his family returned to work in the land around the flattened area—about three acres—that now looked like just another fallow field. They did not replant it. They did not graze their herds there. Jaber and his sons said quiet prayers and mumbled passages from the Koran as they walked or drove past the spot. And they kept the secret of the field and the voiceless earth that pressed down on the bodies. The Husseini family knew they could share their knowledge with no one.

It was knowledge for which the surviving members of the Al-Esawee family, and thousands of other families, would have paid dearly. When the security man had told Mesheeda that her son would be back home soon, she had believed him. What else could she do? Her sons almost certainly died on the same day that she last saw them, but a mother does not let go of hope so easily, especially in a country where for years the security services had picked up men randomly for interrogation. Often they came home, bruised and cowed, but they came home nonetheless. How was Mesheeda to know that March 1991 was to be a time different from all the others?

The family began to sell its belongings, including three cars, to gather the money they knew from experience would be required if they were to get any information about the five brothers from the security services. They made contact with General Security officers and local Baath officials and gave them bribes; in return the officials periodically gave them details of the cases against the brothers and how their investigations were proceeding. The brothers were in detention, in prison somewhere, the officials said, as they pocketed every dinar the family could get together.

When Saddam issued the amnesty in October 2002, the brothers did not come home. Instead, local party officials arrived at the house and once again asked for the full names of the brothers so that they could issue the family with death certificates, a bizarre formality entirely in keeping with the warped sense of order and propriety that typified the regime.

At last the family could begin to mourn. But still they did not have the bodies. They had no idea where the brothers had gone on that day in March 1991.

When the new American war began in March 2003, the Shia of Iraq did not rise up. Saddam's twelve-year-old lesson had been effective. And the first President Bush's betrayal had left the Shia no reason to think his son would be any different. Like nearly everyone else, this time the Al-Esawee men stayed at home and let the Americans do the fighting themselves.

"Big Bush helped Saddam Hussein stay in power," Mohammed al-Esawee told me after the war. He was the brother who was given the name of his president but he had since changed it to Mohammed. "We blame Big Bush more than Saddam Hussein. Big Bush was able to get rid of Saddam Hussein. Why? We blame him so much. But the son fixed what the father corrupted. Little Bush is gifted from God to feel about human beings. But if I could I would take his father to a military trial. He and Saddam Hussein should be kept in the same cell. Little Bush should be crowned. We thank him."

Mohammed was watching television after the war when news broke about the grave at Muhawil. Jaber Husseini had unleashed the secret that he had had to keep for over a decade. Mohammed was one of the first at the scene.

As we spoke in late August, Mohammed and I realized that we had met before. It was at the grave in May as he helped orchestrate the digging. The families of the dead had brought a digger, much like the one that had buried the bodies, to unearth the remains of their loved ones.

The huge machine scooped out the earth, turning slightly and tipping out the contents. With each load four or five bundles of bones and clothes would spew onto the ground. Volunteers scrambled to pick out the remains with their bare hands, trying to discern which ribs belonged with which skulls and which shirts. Cradling the dead, they would shovel them into transparent plastic bags and another volunteer would reach in to search for identification cards, rings, or anything that might give a clue to the identity of the dead. Beyond the digging site were clusters of bags sitting in the sun, hundreds and hundreds of them, glinting dully in the sunlight.

What we were watching on that May morning was what journalists in Iraq, other than those who had reported in the relative freedom of Kurdistan after 1991, had never seen. Human Rights Watch estimates that about 290,000 Iraqis were killed during Saddam Hussein's regime. This was where some of them ended up. The scene at Muhawil was testimony not only to the dead but also to the stunning superficiality of the reporting done by most journalists in Saddam's Iraq. It was not our fault. We would have spent our time looking for Muhawils if we had been allowed, but it was simply impossible to work with much meaning in that period. In May 2001, I had driven within a few miles of Muhawil on my way to Basra. I had no idea what lay across the flatlands at Jaber Husseini's farm. On that trip, my minder and local Baath officials in Basra made sure that I saw nothing and spoke to no one who did not corroborate the regime's view. There had been no uprising, I was told, over and over. The pathetic highlight of that whole two-week trip was when a doctor mumbled something vaguely anti-government to my friend Sandro Contenta, of the *Toronto Star,* while I kept our minder busy. I've been to a few oppressive countries, including the horrifying Burma, but nothing I have ever experienced touched the total control and fear exerted by Saddam's regime.

My experiences of reporting in Saddam's time were, I believe, largely typical. We knew we were being duped, blindfolded. For example, I remember asking to visit a mental hospital in October 2002 and being told repeatedly by officials that there were no psychiatric patients in Iraq, especially none suffering from the kinds of war trauma that I was interested in. After the war, journalists quickly discovered the country's rundown psychiatric hospitals, full of patients suffering from inhuman neglect. In spite of the lies and the walls, most journalists in Saddam's Iraq tried to eke some sort of truth out in the margins of our stories, always knowing that the Mukhabarat would pore over them afterward.

That meant that we could identify no one who had spoken out of line—not that that was a common problem—and that we might never again be granted visas if our stories were deemed too critical. It was a dirty, self-compromising process whose tragedy seemed amply magnified by the piles of bones in front of me now.

As Mohammed labored at disinterring the bodies, he sifted through the bones and clothes to see if he recognized any that could belong to his own brothers. On May 12, his hands filtering a new collection of dirt and bones, he found a pair of jeans wrapped around the skeleton of a boy. Inside the jeans was his own former name, Saddam, written by the tailor all those years ago. He had found Ahmed. "I lost my nerves, I was almost unconscious," he told me. "It was like someone finding treasure."

Around him at the time were female members of the family, and he did not want to present them immediately with the grief that he felt pounding in his chest. Quietly, he put Ahmed's bones and clothes in a plastic bag and gave it to a friend, telling the man what precious bones he was carrying. Then he went back to digging. Six days later he found the bodies of Musa, Mohammed, and Fariq. Two were together, the third some distance away.

Sadiq's body remains lost. Mohammed and his surviving brothers have looked in other mass graves but without luck. They know that somewhere under the flatlands of Iraq is their last, lost brother. It's possible that Iraqis will be finding mass graves for years to come.

"There are two Iraqs," a family friend said, as we sat cross-legged on the floor in their living room, faded photographs of the dead hanging high on the walls. "There is the Iraq under the ground and Iraq over the ground."

The family took the four bodies they had found and drove with them to Iraq's largest Shia cemetery, in the holy city of Najaf, where they put them back into "the Iraq under the ground": this time, on their own terms.

I asked Mohammed what he would say to his brothers if he could speak to them. "God be with you," he said. "And by the will of God, we will never stop seeking revenge for your blood."

As we sat in the family's living room, someone put on a crudely recorded video compact disc and the television burst into life. Two men in uniform stood on what looked like a military parade ground. They each held one end of a piece of wood in the middle of which were two loops. One by one, men who were lined up in the background stepped forward, lay on their backs and slipped their feet into the loops, which were then tightened. A large man wearing a navy blazer, jeans, and black loafers stepped forward and began viciously beating the men on the soles of their feet. I had heard many times about this form of torture, known as *fallacca*, but had never seen it. The worst thing was the screams. These grown men squealed like pigs having their throats slit. I asked what they were saying. They were baying out their love for their president, I was told. "God bless Saddam Hussein," screamed one writhing man, as the stick crashed onto his feet. What surprised me most was the family's explanation of the scene. This was not torture of political enemies or criminals, they said, but hazing in the Iraqi military. The men lined up were new recruits and this was part of their initiation. It was a form of brutalization: learn to do this to other people, learn its effectiveness. This was another of Saddam Hussein's lessons.

The family had bought the disc from the local marketplace. Such discs are quite popular in Iraq now. There are torture and execution discs for sale, copied from films made by the security services that were seized from their offices after the war. They are sold alongside pirated copies of the latest American action movies. Perhaps some of their popularity comes from a voyeurism borne of decades of violence. But for the Al-Esawee family, the disc seemed emblematic of their desire to remember what happened under Saddam's regime and an equal yearning for those responsible to be tried and punished for their crimes. The family can reel off the names of the former officials they believe responsible for the killings as easily as many people in and around Hilla. They have no inclination to forgive or forget. And they complained to me that the American forces were not doing enough to track the men down.

Although it's rarely visited now, the site of the Muhawil killings remains an unfinished story. When I visited the grave in late August I found the area fenced off with coils of razor wire. A trench surrounded the area to prevent water soaking into the sacred ground. Inside, still, were about a thousand graves of those who had not yet been claimed. The volunteers reburied the anonymous bags of bones, numbering each grave and leaving the clothes and any identifying objects on the surface of the raised earth.

I walked around for a few minutes. The smoke from the chimney of the nearby brick factory blew sideways in a gentle northerly breeze. The wind and the shouts of a cowherd across the fields were the only sounds to break the silence. It seemed that the search was over at Muhawil and the unclaimed would remain lost to their families.

A gray houndstooth check suit jacket was the only clue to the identity of the person who lay in one grave. Not exactly hard forensic evidence to prove that the bones below were those of someone's son or father. On another were old boots that looked like they had been washed up on a faraway beach after a year or two at sea. A black comb and the khaki of a military uniform suggested that this was the grave of a soldier, perhaps a deserter. How do you tell one uniform from another? How do you tell if this is your son when there are hundreds or thousands of decaying piles just like this one?

Weeds had begun growing on top of some of the graves. It had the air of encroaching permanence. And then I came across two freshly dug graves, meter-deep holes in the ground that spoke of hope. People were still looking and someone had found their buried treasure very recently.

Akil Husseini sat in the shade of a hut the family had built at what was now the only entrance to the site. He and his brothers took turns guarding the place, partly out of fidelity to the dead, partly because the local governorate paid them to do so. His father was away in Baghdad, he said, lobbying the authorities for the money to build a mosque on the site as a memorial to the dead.

I came back a few days later and found Jaber Husseini at home. We spoke in his *diwaniya,* the room that Iraqi families reserve exclusively for men to discuss matters of the world. It was unlike any *diwaniya* I had ever seen. Usually they are part of the main house but this was a separate structure and, besides the wooden pillars and beams, was entirely made of bulrushes, huge bundles of them twisted and bent over to form an arcing tent of the marshlands.

Jaber was calm; he had told his story many times but was still keen to narrate. "I saw them. Can you imagine a woman holding her one-year-old baby? Is she part of the uprising? A disabled man. An Egyptian. A bride wearing her wedding dress. So you see, to see such a scene, even an idiot could understand that Saddam Hussein was trying to exact his revenge for the uprising on all the Iraqi people."

We talked and something nagged at me all the while, now that I had the time to think it all through. How could Jaber and his sons have witnessed the killings so clearly and repeatedly without becoming victims themselves? There were locals involved, Jaber and others in the area told me, including Shia men like himself. I wondered silently if he had some kind of protection from someone involved in the killings. But all I could do was to ask him why the men in kaffiyehs had not killed him.

"We are a big tribe," he said. "They would not risk having a conflict with the tribe. They could not beat our tribe."

Yes, Jaber, they could, I wanted to say. I left him after a couple of hours and drove back to Baghdad wondering if it was possible to find an Iraqi who somehow did not have the stain of blood on his hands. Or if it was possible that my months in an Iraq still drenched in the contorted suspicions that had supported Saddam Hussein's for so many years had made me see badness even in the best of men.

"All Iraqis have an ability to forget because they have lived in misery all their lives, through wars and sanctions," Jaber had told me just before I left his *diwaniya*. I had asked him how, security and electricity aside, Iraqis could move beyond what had happened in his field and perhaps hundreds of other similar fields. He was hopeful, if vague. "I think Iraqis now are able to adapt and fulfill their lives and make up for the years they missed under Saddam Hussein."

A few days later, still trying to understand how Iraqis were processing the mass killings, I visited the studio of a Baghdad painter named Mohammed Msayer.

Mohammed was courtly and gentle but his paintings were expressionistic outpourings of horror. In 1991, he was in his hometown of Basra when the Shia uprising took place and was crushed. He heard through friends that near his house was a mass grave that families of the disappeared were secretly digging up at night. Mohammed walked up to the top of the sandy hill that had newly appeared near his neighborhood and watched as six or seven silent figures sliced into the ground with shovels, pulling out three bodies.

Once back at home, Mohammed could barely speak. He told only a few trusted friends what he had seen. But he realized that there was a way he could communicate the horror: he could paint it. And in one of the supreme ironies of the period, Mohammed's painting of bodies in the mass grave was selected to be shown at the Saddam Arts Center in Baghdad. He had given the painting an oblique title, "The Death," and presumably the Baathist officials who selected the painting thought it referred to Iraqi civilians killed by the United States in the 1991 war or by the U.N. sanctions.

Since the end of the regime, Mohammed Msayer had allowed a decade of images in his head to come out on canvas. As news broke of Muhawil and other mass graves, Mohammed painted and painted. When I visited him he had completed fifteen pieces and was working on the last for an exhibition to be staged in September. We sat in his oven-hot studio surrounded by his canvases. They all told stories. A blindfolded skeleton with one shortened femur grimaced, his crutch at his side. A skeletal mother folded her arms around her skeletal child. And in another, marbles tumbled from the bony hand of a little boy.

I asked Mohammed where he had heard about the boy with the marbles, thinking of Ahmed al-Esawee, and he told me about a boy from Karbala whom he had heard had been taken while playing marbles.

Mohammed had been painting manically since the fall of the regime. Sometimes he spent all day in his studio. At others, he completed a painting in a few hours. He felt it was his responsibility, he told me, to record the regime's crimes. "It's a warning to all the citizens of the world that they should be careful about allowing another dictator to rise and do what Saddam did," he said. "I feel so afraid that this subject will be forgotten, that it's not given the importance that it deserves. . . . We were the dead in the form of the living. Life at the time had no meaning. Saddam was against all humanity, the environment, birds, fish, land—he was against the whole universe."

In the car on the way back from Muhawil, I thought of the pictures that still hang on the walls of the Al-Esawee living room and of Mesheeda's old face, crumpled by memory and loss. And I thought of her sons' unsated desire for revenge. Was it possible to build new lives while nursing untreated fury? In my own comparatively puny way, I was trying to do the same. My time in prison continued to unhinge me a little at times, and yet I had to go back home to get on with things: overdue tax returns, getting to know my new godson, and the other minutiae that just keep happening to us no matter what else is going on in our lives. When you get back your freedom after suspecting it has gone forever, it's pretty easy to convince yourself that you've had a life-changing epiphany, that you will see only the good in people, that you will tend only to matters of consequence. It's an illusion, one that doesn't last long. And it's quickly replaced with weighty memories of trauma and the featherlight irritation of missing a bus or having bad service at a restaurant.

The only answer I could come up with as we headed back to Baghdad was that Iraqis simply have no other choice than to try to live with both their decades of trauma and daily challenges. It wasn't a comforting answer, I realized, and I felt that when the trauma is the size of a nation, it may linger and erupt again for generations to come.

6

Saddam's Walls

Ghraib—strange, foreign, alien, extraneous (to something), odd, queer, quaint, unusual, extraordinary, curious, remarkable, peculiar, amazing, astonishing, baffling, startling, wondrous, marvelous, grotesque, difficult to understand, abstruse, obscure (language), remote, outlandish, rare, uncommon (word).

HANS WEHR,
A Dictionary of Modern Written Arabic

Iraq, under Saddam, was a country of walls. He built them everywhere. Try finding your way around the palaces of Tikrit, now home to American soldiers, and it's easy to get lost in the apparently infinite number of huge rooms and identical marble passageways. Saddam, ever paranoid about potential assassins, worked with his architects precisely to create this multi-layered confusion of bricks, this maze of stone. He built a lot of prison walls, too. Whether in palaces or prisons, the walls kept people in their places. And then there were the virtual walls, the invisible ones that ran through Iraqi society.

In the stonework of these virtual walls, Saddam's masons built windows and secret passageways. Some of the residents of his country, the security officers, knew a few of the ways through the stone and they could slip through the apparently impregnable walls to surprise their neighbors. But just when they were least expecting it, another Iraqi could appear from a different secret doorway behind them. The only person in this walled country who had a plan of all the barriers and passageways was its master architect, Saddam Hussein. And there he was, sitting in its center. He was unhappy, though, I think. He had realized years ago that he had built so many walls around him that he could never leave his castle and breathe freely. He had so imprisoned his people, so stripped them of any sense of trust or truth, that he became afraid of them. And he knew that in order to stay alive, he had to keep building the walls and hidden doors so that no one else could discover the way into his chambers.

It was easy to get swallowed up amid the frenzy of wall-building and spying. You could be walking along the street and a man would suddenly appear from one of the secret passageways and just because you happened to be passing, he would seize you and pull you with him into the hidden tunnel. And no one would ever see you again.

Innocence and harmlessness became as irrelevant in Iraq as they had been in the Soviet Union of Saddam's greatest role model, Joseph Stalin. The system assumed that everyone was a traitor and unknown numbers found themselves yanked out of their normal lives into the horror. The terror had that random edge to it, but that didn't prevent some from trying to prove their fidelity to Saddam. The only way to prove loyalty was to demonstrate willingness to betray everyone else. Graduates of Iraq's school for spies, first known as the Higher Institute of National Security and later as the College of National Security, ended their three years of study instinctively spying on themselves.

"As an employee in the Mukhabarat you had to give information every three months on what happened in your family," explained a former security agent named Walid a few weeks after the war. Walid was one of the first graduates of the school, which was in the Amariya area of Baghdad. After graduation Walid chose to serve in Iraq's FBI, the General Security Service, rather than the Mukhabarat; but he had constant contact with the Mukhabarat throughout his career. Although ostensibly the Mukhabarat was charged with foreign intelligence matters, like the CIA in the United States, it also monitored domestic threats to the government.

"If you have a newborn child, you should write it in a daily report," he said, referring to the logs that members of the Mukhabarat had to keep on themselves. "If you fail to do so, the party member of your area will inform the Special Security office about you."

The Special Security Service was the most powerful of Iraq's secret police agencies, led by Saddam's younger but more trusted son, Qusay. Its bodyguards were Saddam's last line of defense. Special Security agents had absolute power, even over the enormously powerful Mukhabarat.

"If Special Security compares the information they got from the party member and the information provided by you, and if they find out you have failed to report such a thing, then you are in big trouble," Walid said. "You had to report everything. Sports, visiting a friend, going to a coffee shop, drinking or not drinking alcohol. They had to spy on themselves. If we are a team and we are assigned to a mission, they will pick one of us to spy on the rest."

That kind of spying has a momentum, a snowballing paranoia that never stops growing. It is inaccurate to call it espionage; espionage connotes governments or businesses spying on each other. Spying—anyone can do it. The Mukhabarat trained its agents in espionage, but its forte was spying. And its momentum grew to such an absurd extent that in 1996, the Mukhabarat took over the section of Abu Ghraib that they had themselves filled—the Arabs and Foreigners Department. They could not even feel secure about the men they had already imprisoned. In the whole of Iraq, there was no place where a man could be less of a threat to the regime, to Saddam Hussein, and yet still his spies monitored the inmates.

It was the plots and deception of some prisoners themselves that brought the Mukhabarat into Abu Ghraib. Saad Jassim had been in the prison just a few months when it happened.

"Before the Mukhabarat took over the office, we had prisoners who actually tried to hurt each other. Writing reports on each other. In the reports they'd be making this guy out to be a great spy that the Iraqi government did not discover. They were writing all kinds of things. Such a report, when it reached the Intelligence office, it raised hell, really."

When the Mukhabarat would arrive, Saad and the other prisoners would be sitting outside undergoing the regular head counts to make sure that no one had escaped.

"All of a sudden we would a see bunch of guys in suits. We knew from the way they looked that they are Mukhabarat, Intelligence guys. They would burst into the section, go into one particular room, take the room apart looking for stuff. When they were done they would call one of the prisoners, whose room they searched, and they just make the guy stand, walk over to them, put handcuffs on him, take him, and go. This caused total horror in the prison. This guy was taken by Intelligence, as if he did something real terrible. When he came back after three months of interrogation we found out that there is somebody who wrote a report on him. The reason this guy wrote a report was that he asked for a pack of cigarettes, and this guy refused to give it to him or wanted money for it. Something like that. Really, not something worth mentioning. This story happened ten or twenty times. Eventually they said, 'Wait a minute. We have to know what's going on in the prison. We can't just receive these reports.' So they decided to take over the prison."

On the first day of Mukhabarat control, the new head of the department ordered a head count. As usual, the prisoners lined up outside the five sections of the department.

"Some of you have been writing reports and you have been giving us all kinds of bullshit," the senior officer told the silent inmates. "We decided to take over this place to make sure things like that are not going to happen in the future."

When the lineup was over and the prisoners went back to their cells, they agreed that the arrival of the Mukhabarat was a godsend. They would bring an end to snitching, favoritism, backstabbing. There would be discipline, for sure, but it would be equitable.

That's not how it worked out, though. The new guards, all Mukhabarat agents, reverted to type. Each guard would choose five prisoners from each of the five sections. He would cultivate them, encouraging them and forcing them to inform on the other prisoners in their section. Each inmate soon became "Mohammed's man" or "Jamal's man." The Mukhabarat had brought the world of spying and betrayal with them into Abu Ghraib.

It was sometimes petty, sometimes dangerous. The prisoners would often behave like schoolboys telling tales on each other. For example, two inmates in the department were involved in a dispute. This was a brief Mukhabarat report I found on the incident in the abandoned cells of the department.

Statement
Prisoner/Sayer Abdullah Saeed/Saudi/In for 5 years

Q1. Tell us what happened between you and the other prisoner, Hassan Kamel.

A1. The prisoner Hassan Kamel, as all the others know, doesn't follow orders—especially in the lineup for prisoners. He is always standing in the end row drinking tea in addition to having rude behavior toward the others, and he speaks loudly and doesn't follow the major's orders and he told all the prisoners to address him as "Sir." When I told this to the officer, he said I should put that in a report.

Q2. Do you have anything else to say?

A2. I don't have anything else to say except that I have no enemies.

The guards snitched on each other too, like boarding school prefects jockeying for favor with the house master. Among the papers left in the department after the war was this note from a guard to the security officer whose job it was to coordinate the internal spying on the department's employees.

Memo.

To the security officer of the Arabs and Foreigner Department.

I would like to draw your attention that our colleague Kareem al-Hanshawi came to the section accompanied with three persons from the south of Iraq wearing Arab-style dress, and he asked for our colleague Jamal. They have entered the section without his writing down the names of the guys with him as it seems they had some agreement with Jamal.

Other documents to the security officer from the Mukhabarat guards are full of similar cavils. These may sound trivial, but in Saddam's Iraq they could hamper a man's career and even endanger his life. A scribbled note dated February 15, 2000, complains of a guard named Alaa Hussein who has let his friend come in to take blankets for free. In April of that year, the officer in charge of keeping the prisoners' documents, Ratib Mizaal Hindi, found himself the target of a colleague's secret complaint that Hindi was responsible for losing a Saudi prisoner's passport. The information officer, Hammed Daieh, the man who meets visitors in the reception room of the department's office, should be reassigned, beseeches one of his fellow Mukhabarat guards. He's unhelpful and unpopular, the snitch writes, and he hints that Daieh uses his position for financial gain. He "tries to make intermediate relationships for his benefit."

The reports form a catalog of the spiraling absurdity reached by Mukhabarat agents after decades of self-monitoring. Instead of conducting espionage from embassies in foreign lands, these men had ended up working in a prison, trying to ruin each other by telling their superiors that they were giving out free prison blankets.

When Saddam created the agency in 1968 he envisioned it as his premier spy agency, one that would rival the CIA and the KGB. Using translated textbooks, training tapes, and films from both of these agencies—Iraq was then nurturing diplomatic and intelligence relationships with any country it considered potentially useful—the Mukhabarat built itself into an efficient force, former agents say.

They describe a system of training at the Higher Institute of National Security that might have impressed Ian Fleming. In fact, one of the documents I found among the mess of the department after the war was a Mukhabarat phone book. The first entry, written in English, was for "James Bond."

There were endless lessons in night shooting, diving, aviation, bombing, opening locks and safes, martial arts, foreign languages and the customs of other cultures, diplomatic affairs, hiding secret cameras and microphones, recognizing and using poisons, and, of course, using nearly every weapon ever manufactured. After three years, the men and women came out as efficient, highly motivated spies and killers. One graduate I met after the war, a senior Mukhabarat officer who still saw the hand of the Mossad everywhere, told me he had read the Torah in his spare time.

But when it came to internal discipline, the Mukhabarat had more of the flavor of Blofeld's SPECTRE than Bond's gentlemanly MI6. Saddam passed on control of the intelligence service to his half-brother Barzan in 1975, and the service's agents quickly came to know the price of failure.

Two former Mukhabarat officers and Walid, the former General Security agent, told me very similar versions of the same story. In Barzan's time there was a team assigned to monitor a visiting Iranian official. The Iranian had given one of the men a bottle of whisky, which he accepted. Barzan heard about this and summoned the team's members to his office in the Mukhabarat headquarters. He calmly asked the offending agent to explain himself and then invited him and the others to the gardens of the building. He made the agent stand to one side and then pulled out his pistol. "You would sell your country for a bottle of whisky?" Barzan asked, just before he pulled the trigger.

Everyone was trapped, even those who were as close to the president and his family as it was possible to be.

After the war I met a man who claimed that he could shoot anything out of the sky with his first bullet, every time. But it was not just his marksmanship that led him to become one of the presidential family's most trusted bodyguards—an elite within the elite, the men of Special Security who protected Saddam and his closest relations. It was the man's family background, his genuine belief that Saddam Hussein was the best man to lead Iraq, and his willingness to die for his rulers.

He agreed to talk to me as long as I did not use his real name. I'll call him Salah.

Now 43 years old, Salah has made the observant Muslim's pilgrimage to Mecca, the *hajj*, twice. He no longer drinks or spends his spare time with prostitutes at the Habbaniya Tourist Village, the favorite lakeside resort for the elites of the Saddam years. He is married with children and lives in a quiet, mainly Sunni neighborhood in the north of Baghdad. He wears a white skull cap and a graying beard.

As a bright and athletic high school graduate from one of the prominent families in Fallujah, one of the towns that formed and still form the base of Sunni Arab support for Saddam and the Baath Party, Salah was just the kind of young man Saddam Hussein's family counted on.

Even so, Saddam's people took no risks. "It's not easy to get people to do that job," Salah said. "There were many people in my college course. They took just a few to the family after they had checked our family backgrounds to see if we were trustworthy. During our training they sent people to check out our families several times and in different ways. General Security, Special Security, the party—each one wrote a report. They saw I had a good background and so they sent me to the family directly."

No one will likely ever know the truth about Saddam's father's fate, whether he was killed in the months after Saddam was conceived or whether he abandoned the family. But Saddam grew up without a father. That role was taken by his maternal uncle, Khairallah Tulfah, and there would be no more influential man in Saddam's life. It was to Khairallah's side that the 19-year-old Salah was sent after he finished his six-month training course in 1979. That was the year that Saddam, who had been the real power in Iraq since the 1968 Baathist revolution, became president.

"They were the power," Salah said, sitting in his living room late one afternoon after the war. He laughed as he remembered the vain impulses of his youth, fondly recalling his own good looks. "So I wanted to be with them."

Salah knew that there was no job in Iraq that could give him such prestige, comfort and immediate wealth as being a bodyguard to a member of the family. Of the four main security agencies, Special Security was the most powerful. It was untouchable. Salah loved it. Other graduates of the training course went on to be office workers and drivers. Salah was soon calling Saddam's mentor "uncle."

"Not sir or mister. Not all the bodyguards could do that. Only the close ones."

The power was fabulous. Salah could show up in the office of any minister and drop Khairallah's name, and whatever he wanted would happen immediately. There were few men in Iraq, other than Saddam, more influential than Khairallah. The former policeman had taken in his nephew when Saddam was a boy, unhappy at home with his mother. He had steered Saddam throughout his career, demonstrating the savvy ruthlessness that Saddam would take to new levels. And he was not just Saddam's uncle and virtual father: he was his father-in-law. In 1963, Saddam had married his cousin Sajida Tulfah, Khairallah's daughter.

Khairallah, once his protégé was running Iraq, became legendarily avaricious. There's a story about him that Baghdadis, who had him for their mayor until even Saddam could bear his corruption no longer, like to tell. One day, Khairallah was driving past an attractive building. "Find out who owns that building," he told his aide. "I want it." "My sir," said the aide, "you own it."

To his guards—the men who stood between him and an assassin's bullet—Khairallah was wisely generous. Salah quickly became head of Khairallah's security detail, and so his rewards were especially bounteous.

Saddam's father figure gave Salah land on which he built a house for his own father. He gave the young man a handcrafted 9 mm pistol. And there were frequent cash handouts on top of his generous salary, especially on holidays such as the Prophet Muhammad's birthday.

In return, Salah walked by his side on shifts that were sometimes as long as twenty-four hours, wearing a suit and tie, his Browning pistol at his hip and his Kalashnikov automatic rifle over his shoulder. At night, he would walk through the gardens of whichever one of Khairallah's homes the old man happened to be staying in.

Two or three times Salah and his colleagues received intelligence about attempts on the old man's life. "We just made things even more secure in those times," Salah said. "We looked like wolves around him. No one could do anything to him. If someone had attacked, I would have thrown my arms around him. I was always next to him."

Apart from when Khairallah was meeting with his nephew and son-in-law, that is.

"How are you, Uncle?" Saddam would say to Khairallah, as the two men kissed.

"Hello, Saddam," Khairallah replied. And that was the last Salah would hear before the two men went into a private room that was ringed by the president's guards.

By 1986, Salah had become close with Khairallah's son, Louai, who was five years younger than Salah. At Louai's request, Salah became his main bodyguard.

Then, Louai was studying engineering at Baghdad University. Having bodyguards with him around campus helped him get girls. It made him look important, Salah said. Louai, though, didn't spend much time on campus. Like Saddam's sons, he preferred lounging on boats and by the shore at the Tourist Village in Habbaniya. And pretty soon he became Uday Hussein's second-in-command at the notorious Olympic Committee building in Baghdad. Sure, Uday liked sports and, as the de facto minister of sports in Iraq, it pleased him when his country's athletes did well. But Uday mainly used the Olympic building as a base for his extensive business interests and his enthusiasms for torture and rape. The basement rooms featured implements for torturing failed athletes and anyone else who gave Uday displeasure. Down there was one of his favorite spots for sating his indiscriminate lust for women, some of whom were held as sex slaves. Salah, still loyal to the family, would not tell me whether Louai—or even he himself—took part in the violence at the Olympic headquarters. He preferred not to talk about Uday much.

"They were very good friends. They were always in the discos at the Sheraton and Al-Mansour," he said. "Both had many girl-friends."

A relative of Salah, to whom he has spoken more candidly, told me that Salah may be loyal still, but he is also haunted by the brutality of Louai and Uday. Salah also became scared of hanging out with the psychopathic Uday and the excitable Louai. In the city's discos and riverside restaurants they would drink until they were almost falling over and pull out guns and start shooting. You never knew who they would aim at. Or who would suddenly decide they had had enough and start shooting back. When I first met him, Salah dug up some old photos of his time with Louai. There's Khairallah's son standing on a dam shooting fish with a shotgun. There he is in the Mansour disco, dressed in the same cheap-looking late-eighties suits as his troupe of grinning bodyguards. One of them is wearing a porkpie hat inscribed in English with the words "Al Capone."

Salah wanted out. But taking your leave from the Special Security Service, especially when you have had access to the family, was like telling Capone that you didn't want to be a made man anymore. What reason on earth could a man have for walking away from such power and wealth and knowledge? The very act of asking to leave could brand you as an enemy, a potential traitor. Salah may have had power of life and death over nearly every other person in Iraq, but like everyone else in this country that Saddam had turned into a massive prison, he was not a free man.

"It's very difficult to leave that job," he told me. "No one can leave."

Salah had only one possibility—to bypass Louai and appeal directly to the head of Special Security, Qusay.

"Please, I wish a long life to your father, to you and your son Mustapha," Salah told the second most powerful man in Iraq. "But things are hard for me. I want to leave. You can trust me if you let me leave."

"Why?" Qusay was unhappy at the request.

"You know me very well. I've been doing a good job for thirteen, fourteen years. But I'm tired now."

Salah described the routine of a bodyguard—endless surveillance, being on call twenty-four hours a day. He told Saddam's wily son that he was exhausted.

"Maybe your uncle Louai will refuse," Qusay said.

"Just give me permission and I will take care of that," Salah said. "Give me the order and I will talk to Louai."

It worked. Perhaps Qusay recognized that a tired and unwilling bodyguard is a useless bodyguard, whatever his true motives for leaving Special Security. Salah went to Louai, and Louai asked him to stay as a private employee. But Salah declined. Louai was angry, wanting his most trusted bodyguard to stay by his side. He even used his girlfriend to get at Salah, sending her to flirt with him and woo him to stay. It didn't work.

"I didn't see Louai again," Salah said.

Salah knows he was unusually lucky to win permission to leave from Qusay. "Guards know secret things," he told me. "If Qusay had said no, I couldn't have left."

He took a year off and then started work as a driver between Amman and Baghdad, taking foreign guests of the government into Iraq and back out again, a highly responsible job that not just any old driver could get. At the same time, Salah's brother was the senior Baath Party official in the Iraqi embassy in Amman. So even though Salah had been granted a reprieve from serving as part of the inner wall of the prison, he remained part of the network. There was no such thing in Iraq as deciding to slope off and away from the security machine to live a quiet, apolitical life.

But even if you had never been a part of that machine, you could not choose to be apolitical. You could not keep your head down. You could try, sure, but that would not necessarily make you safe. The mass grave at Muhawil is testimony to that.

The tenants of those graves had been passing by one of the secret passageways in Saddam's network of walls when the hidden door had opened and someone popped out to haul them away from their lives. They were targets because they were Shia and that was enough to establish guilt. Genuine guilt was not a prerequisite. Everyone in Iraq was a potential enemy of Saddam, and even the hint of anything suspicious would often lead to an interrogation room, a conviction, and a final journey—usually to Abu Ghraib. There were guilty men—both criminals and political dissidents—in Abu Ghraib, but there were also countless inmates who were guilty of nothing more than having behaved as a guilty man might.

For Saad Jassim, his own semblance of guilt marked the beginning of his journey to Abu Ghraib. As long as he could remember, Saad had always had what he calls a "European or American mentality." There was nothing shameful, unpatriotic, or unusual about such feelings in the Iraq of the 1970s and 1980s. In spite of the Baathists' lip service to pan-Arab nationalism, vast numbers of Iraqis looked to the West. They gained degrees in British, French, and American universities. They married fellow students from their host countries. They took dual citizenship. And they either stayed where they were or came back to Iraq with a fluent foreign language and a top-class education that enabled them to enjoy fully the extraordinary bounty of Iraq during that era. Oil prices, and the government's generally equitable and generous distribution of wealth, gave average Iraqis what was probably the highest living standard of any Arab middle class in history, excepting the absurdly wealthy citizens of Gulf countries like Kuwait and Qatar, where there are essentially no indigenous middle classes, just varying shades of affluence.

After he finished high school, Saad took off for London. It was 1982, and in those days it was easy enough to get visas. Britain and the United States were backing Iraq in its war with Iran. Relations were good. Besides, Saad's father was a successful merchant, dealing in lumber with traders from Europe. One of them, a Dane, came with the 20-year-old to the American Embassy to vouch for him, and Saad walked out of the building with a U.S. tourist visa, valid for one month.

After a two-month summer vacation in London, Saad took a flight to New York. At Kennedy Airport, the Immigration and Naturalization Service automatically extended his visa, allowing him to stay in the country for six months.

Saad adored the United States. Although he sometimes missed Iraq, he didn't miss being drafted into the Iraqi army, which was then in its third year of the apocalyptic eight-year war with Iran. Saddam had started that war and would send hundreds of thousands of Iraqi men to their deaths for a victory on paper that meant nothing but pain and deprivation on the streets and in the homes of Iraq. Saad wanted to avoid that at all costs.

He made his way to New Orleans, where he had Iraqi friends. His dream was to learn to fly commercial jets. So he enrolled at Louisiana State University in Baton Rouge, and after graduating he attended flight school in Vero Beach, Florida.

Not long after he arrived in New Orleans a friend introduced Saad to his sister, Julia, a cashier in a big wholesale store. The friend thought that Saad and Julia would get along. When Saad talks about Julia now, his words are quaintly Springsteenian. American dream stuff.

"He decided to introduce me to her. We took a ride together, went to her house, you know. She was great. She was nice to me, treated me good."

Julia had a baby boy named Tommy from a previous relationship. (I have changed their names to protect their privacy.) And when she and Saad were married, the boy became "more than a son" to Saad. And so within four years of arriving in the United States, the Saad Jassim with almost nothing had become Sam Jason with an American wife he loved, a child he doted on, and a career in flying jets ahead of him. To cap it all, the INS gave him a green card, the last stop on the way to becoming a citizen of the United States.

The family moved from Florida to Philadelphia in 1988. They

moved around a fair amount, though, after Saad graduated from flight school the following year. It was tough to get work as a beginner pilot. You had to rack up flying hours as an instructor before you could hope to get a job flying commercial airliners. So they drove to new towns in new states as the jobs popped up. A couple of months in Detroit, then off to Los Angeles, then back to Florida. And in between jobs, Saad picked up whatever work he could—fixing and selling cars, helping out a friend with his cleaning business.

In 1990, although travel from Iraq had become more difficult, Saad's mother and brother came to visit. The three of them hired a minivan and took off across country, flying back from Los Angeles. After another week in Philadelphia they all flew to London to see Saad's father, who was taking a trip to England. It was good to be with his family again, Saad thought. And so when they leaned on him and persuaded him to come back to Baghdad for a short while he agreed.

He was traveling on his green card, having lost his Iraqi passport. His father, still a well-connected man, went with Saad to the Iraqi embassy in London and persuaded officials there to give his son a travel document. Their story was that Saad had just come with his father from Iraq to London and had lost the passport there. It wouldn't do to tell the consular officials that Saad had been living in the United States and had permanent resident status there.

"I know a lot of powerful men, so they won't let anything bad happen to you," Saad's father told him. "I promise you that you'll only stay one month. Then you can go back to the States."

Saad believed that Julia perhaps wanted to move with him back to his homeland, in spite of her misgivings about living in a country with such a reputation for oppression. And yet he felt he could not tell her of his plans to go back on this visit. "I couldn't tell my wife. All these years living with her, telling her stories about Saddam Hussein and the Iraqi regime. . . . All of a sudden her husband decides to go back. It would make her go nuts. I didn't have time to explain to her."

When he tells this story, Saad's face suggests that he sees both an internal logic to it and utter madness. I've told him, in words and looks of my own, that he radically misjudged how a Western woman would react to such a lie. He shakes his head at the mess of his own making all those years ago.

The family returned to Baghdad. One month became two months as Saad, now without a passport, had to rely on his father's connections to get him a new one. All of a sudden his father did not seem too keen on helping Saad leave the country. There were all sorts of procedures necessary to obtain a new passport, formalities that his father, with his connections, could have sped up if he had chosen to. "My father did not fulfill his promise. He knew I was stuck and he wanted me to stay. They didn't like the idea of my marrying a U.S. citizen. So they just forgot to help out. They trapped me."

As the days went past, he could not bring himself to call Julia. First of all, he knew she would be furious at him for lying. But what really troubled him was that she would not realize that they could not talk candidly over the phone. She would ask how he had made it to Baghdad without an Iraqi passport and how he planned to get out again. Saad knew that all international calls were taped by the Mukhabarat, but he had never explained this fully to Julia. So he delayed calling. The weeks passed by. And by then he knew that when he could finally no longer bear not talking to her, Julia would be apoplectic and he wouldn't be able to explain on the line what was really going on.

But he called her anyway.

"Honey, I'm in Baghdad."

Julia wouldn't talk to him. He called and called. Eventually she gave him a moment to explain what the hell he was doing there and why he had lied to her and why he hadn't called and why he had abandoned Tommy and her. Saad could explain almost nothing to the woman he loved. Over and over, all he would say was: "Honey, I'm coming to America. I have things to take care of here, and then we'll come back to Iraq together."

To an American woman with a young son, this was not a particularly reassuring line. She had so many questions, and Saad could not even begin to answer them over the phone. Even speaking to her made his stomach clench in anxiety, knowing who was listening in to his calls.

"She wanted an answer and I couldn't give one. So I pretended I was mad at her. I'd curse at her on the phone, yell at her, hang up a couple of times. That's what screwed things up. If I'd answered one question, there would be ten questions following it. If I start answering any questions, the guy listening on the phone will report what he heard. . . . People would come to me. The Mukhabarat would come to me. I had to make the call as normal and simple as possible. She couldn't understand that. You know how things work in Iraq. The only solution here is to jump on her and make her quit calling me till I get the chance to go back to the States. I'll explain to her."

On August 2, 1990, at about eight o'clock in the morning, Iraqi radio and TV reported that President Saddam Hussein had ordered his glorious armed forces into the upstart country of Kuwait and that Kuwait was now under Iraqi control. The Jassim household, like every home around Iraq, erupted in chaos and anxiety. Almost immediately army representatives came looking to draft men of military age, including Saad. The country was at war yet again.

At ten o'clock, Julia called.

"I was in shock because of the situation. She demanded an explanation right then and there. 'Julia, please, wait till tomorrow—you're going to hear the news.' 'What news?' I was afraid to tell her. I was nervous now, thinking there was no way of going back to the States. The borders would be closed, the airports, everything. So I hung up on her. Deep down I knew it was over between us when I hung up."

Two or three days later, Julia called back.

"She said, 'This is it. I can't take it anymore.' She asked me for a divorce. She was a Christian, but she'd become a Muslim when we married. The Muslims' way of divorcing is saying the words and that's it, you are divorced. So she insisted on me telling her over the phone, to divorce her over the phone. And she was really jumping on me, so I told her okay, you are free to go, you are divorced."

Saad could not quite believe how, in three months, he had gone from being a happily married man in the United States to a divorced army draftee in Iraq. He had to get out, get back home and explain things to Julia. Saad's brother gave him his own passport and Saad flew to Amman and then to London.

"So I went back to the States and met her, talked to her, explained things. But it was too late. She said, 'If you treated me like a wife, you would never have left me in the States alone with my kid.' She was right. She is right."

Only a trip to Baghdad would really have explained the situation to Julia, Saad felt. But it was too late for that. He signed the divorce papers in Philadelphia. The last time they spoke was in 1992—about his passport. She had a couple of documents he needed. He found no warmth on the end of the line.

"The one thing I regret in my life is losing her," Saad told me as we sat drinking tea one day after the war, and even though his surprisingly unwrinkled face was filled with the pain of losing a love, it cheered me to hear him say that. After seven years of unimaginable torture and degradation, he still feels the worst thing that has ever happened to him is that he lost a woman. Prison never managed to erode his love and his sense of what matters most.

Losing Julia and Tommy unbalanced Saad. After he signed the divorce papers, he visited friends in New York and then headed across the river to Atlantic City. A month later he had lost a lot of money and started drinking. He flew to LA to visit a friend and from there to Utah and then down to Las Vegas. He continued the losing streak he'd started in Atlantic City. Every place he chose to visit was somewhere he'd been with Julia. He'd see her in the carpeted casinos and on the sidewalks of LA.

"Saad," one of his friends told him, "this is not helping you. You are blowing your money away. You can't think right. You're talking about her all the time."

All his Iraqi friends told him the same thing: Go back home and get married. Build a new family, an Iraqi family, and stay in Baghdad.

Eventually, on February 27, 1992, the day after he was finally issued his American passport, he flew to London. He was in such a hurry to leave that he'd forgotten to sign his passport. The airline check-in clerk had to remind him. Within days, Saad was back in Baghdad.

On April 15, less than two months later, Saad married his first cousin.

"I didn't really know what I was doing. I found myself married with a son after a year. I couldn't stop thinking of my wife. Whoever suggested anything to me, I say OK, yes, fine. Just like that. It's like I was in shock. When I woke up I found myself married with a kid."

One of the other things Saad's family told him to do was to go and manage the farm that his father owned twenty miles southwest of Baghdad. It wasn't the life of an American aviator, walking in a navy blue uniform to the steps of the jet on a runway in a sparkling new Midwest airport. Saad was now raising chickens, breeding cattle, and farming fish in huge tanks in a dustbowl country that was run by a dictator and cut off from the trading world by a blanket of UN sanctions. The way Saad tells it, a mixture of Iraq's byzantine and corrupt bureaucracy and the sanctions regime did him in. I suspect he never really wanted to succeed as a farmer. He was in a life and a place he hadn't chosen. A man with a "European and American mentality" isn't going to suddenly learn to enjoy feeding tanks of fish in a country where temperatures climb over 120 degrees in the summer and every time you call overseas you're taking your life in your hands.

To obtain all the licenses he needed to expand the farm, he had to visit every ministry in Baghdad, it seemed. And then the inspectors would come out to the farm for breakfast and a stroll and then lunch and then they'd come back for another look, another breakfast, another lunch, and a handful of dinars to make all the problems go away.

"I had to pay and kiss ass at the same time."

He'd negotiate to buy dairy cows at 100,000 dinars per head. By the time he had his licenses from the various ministries and directorates, five months had gone by, the economy had become worse, and the price was now 300,000. It was hopeless.

Memories of the United States did not fade. If anything, they sharpened under the dusty sun of Iraq. "Inside of me was always a comparison. I always compared things in Iraq and America. Everybody knows in the Arab world there is no meaning for time. Back in the States, time is money. Technology—I missed that. Deep inside of me I wanted to go back to the States and live there."

Not a sentiment any Iraqi would be wise to express in the 1990s. But it wouldn't go away. In 1993, married only a year, Saad took off. He spent six months in the United States, sure that he was going to prepare a new home for his new wife and son. But something had happened. Being back around his three brothers and five sisters, his parents, his nephews and nieces and dozens of cousins had reminded him of what Iraq had to offer him that the United States never could. So Saad went to Detroit to stay with friends and he traveled around, feeling unsettled, confused, torn between two countries that he considered home and that considered each other the enemy.

In the battle inside Saad's heart, Iraq won. He headed home in 1994. With the farm a failure and his father's money tied up in an account in London, Saad had to think of a new way to support his family. His idea was to export oil, in violation of the sanctions, through contacts in the southern city of Basra to the Gulf countries. To set up his company, to establish the confidence of the buyers in the Gulf, he needed a letter of credit from a solid bank, a necessity for smugglers in those days. Iraqi banks, cut off from the outside world, were useless. Amman's banks became the intermediary financial institutions for Iraq's smugglers. So Saad drove through the desert and arrived in the Jordanian capital.

It was a bad time for an Iraqi to be in Amman. Bill Clinton had just brokered a peace deal between Jordan and Israel, ending decades of war between the two neighbors. Jordan, which had sided with Iraq during the Gulf War, was trying to make amends.

Amman has for years had a big Iraqi population. There are legal residents, secretive refugees, opposition émigrés. Downtown there is a hectic bus station where Iraqis gather and catch rides back home to Baghdad. It was the obvious place for the Jordanian government to order a random sweep of Iraqis, just to show their American and Israeli friends who was in charge of Jordan and how they really felt about Iraq nowadays. The peace deal with Israel was anathema to Jordan's Palestinian majority. Saddam was their hero, and now their king was shaking hands and sharing cigarettes with Israeli prime minister Yitzhak Rabin.

Saad was downtown when the police came with two buses that they filled with Iraqis and then took to jail. It was Saad's first time in a cell. Eventually he bribed a guard 20 Jordanian dinars to make a phone call to the U.S. Embassy to let them know that he was being held. A consular official came and promised that Saad would be out soon. There was a problem, though: The Iraqi visa in Saad's American passport. As soon as Saad had his new papers he had declared his change in citizenship to the Iraqi authorities—only a suicidal madman would keep his American citizenship a secret in Iraq—and he began traveling in and out of the country on his American passport. But since 1991, it had been against U.S. federal law for American citizens to travel to Iraq. Now there was the visa in his passport to prove that he had broken the law. It did not endear him to the consular official.

"You'll be out in a couple of days, and there will be a quick trial but the judge will dismiss the case," the official told Saad and left him in jail.

One of Saad's friends bailed him out. And in a couple of days, as promised, he went to court for what he thought would be a formality. But the investigating officer didn't show, so the judge postponed the case for fifteen days. The same thing happened at the next hearing. And at the third and fourth. Saad knew the official was never going to put in the appearance that would enable him to be cleared. So he skipped bail, leaving his passport with the Jordanian authorities, and smuggled himself back into Iraq, hiding under a huge pile of bread in the backseat of a GMC four-wheeler driven by a friend.

Saad headed home to Baghdad. He came back to a family in crisis. His older brother had also failed in business and owed a lot of money—100 million Iraqi dinars. Even with the currency horribly devalued from its prewar peak of $3 to the dinar, this was a lot of money. And the family didn't have the means to repay the debts. Men started coming by the house, demanding their money back, and soon one of them began to threaten to tell the government that Saad had entered the country illegally if they weren't paid. That was what turned Saad's mind. He would take advantage of the incredible opportunity his American citizenship offered him. He would take his wife and child to the United States.

But now he had no passport, only a certificate of naturalization; his wife and son were also without passports or visas, and the Polish diplomats who staffed the defunct U.S. Embassy in Bahgdad were unable to issue them. Saad knew, though, that up in Kurdistan there were Americans. Since 1991, this northern Kurdish slice of Iraq had been essentially its own state, and yet Iraqis from the main part of the country could travel there with relative ease.

Perhaps Saad was a little naïve. The Americans in the hilltop town of Salahaddin were primarily employees of the CIA working with the Kurds and the opposition group called the Iraqi National Congress. Together, they were plotting to overthrow Saddam. It was an open secret. Everyone, including Saddam, knew the CIA and the INC were there. To Saad, they were just the most obvious people to go to for help—the only Americans in the neighborhood. He had heard that they helped people get out of Iraq. So he went to see them and they told him that they would check his claim of citizenship with the embassy in Amman and that he should go back to Baghdad to get his marriage certificate and his son's birth certificate. Come back in a month, they said.

A month later, Saad headed north again, along with his cousin, Maher Jassim; a Kurdish friend of his cousin's named Abdul Rahman; and the driver of the truck they had rented for the trip.

It was about nine o'clock at night when they reached a checkpoint north of Mosul on the way to Kurdistan. Armed and uniformed men surrounded the GMC. A man in a suit, one of three plainclothes officers, came to Saad's car door.

"Saad," said the man, whom he had never seen before, "get out of the car."

The man grasped his arm and led him through the night to a Toyota. "Please get in the back," he said. Another officer ushered Maher in the other side. A uniformed guard sat in the passenger seat and trained his rifle on the two men.

"Get your heads down in front of you and put your hands on the seats in front of you," he told them. "Do not look up."

The officer behind the wheel drove smoothly and slowly through the night back toward Mosul. In a car behind them were the Kurd and the driver, also in custody. When they arrived, the men led the four detainees into a large building and then into a broad, quiet hall. A guard told them to sit on the ground.

After a few minutes in silence, guards came and took the three others away, leaving Saad sitting alone.

A tall man in a silver-colored suit came into the hall and walked over to Saad. He was in his late forties and had a polite, gentle manner.

"Saad, do you know where you are right now?"

"No, I don't know," Saad replied, although he had a pretty good idea.

"You are in the Mukhabarat," the man said. That, Saad knew, was synonymous in Saddam's Iraq with "You are a dead man."

"We know everything about you," the man said, in his kindly way. "We've been following you. How was your trip to the north of Iraq? Okay, tell us one thing. Did your trip have anything to do with intelligence?"

Saad did not yet realize that there is only one answer to questions like that. He gave the wrong one. "No," he told his first interrogator.

"Look, you're going to tell us the truth, one way or another," the man said, looking resigned and a little tired.

"No, sir, this trip had nothing to do with intelligence. I don't know what you're talking about. I can tell you my story in full detail."

"Well," said the man who now had control of Saad's future, "I'm all ears."

Saad told him his story. The interrogator told him to take a pen and some sheets of paper and write it all down.

"The next day it was like all the Mukhabarat officers in Mosul came to that building. It was like a huge celebration to them, catching an American. You can hear their footsteps, you can tell from the guards that it was like excitement in there. They called the Kurdish guy, the driver, and my cousin, and there were actually two officers interrogating one guy, they were all interrogated at the same time. I can hear them beating the hell out of them. Everybody trying to gather information at the same time. Later I understand that the chief of that building was leading the investigation, so everybody had to kiss ass. That's why two officers at the same time interrogated one suspect."

Then the officers came for Saad. They blindfolded him and led him back to the large hall.

"Man, you can't believe it. When I walked in there I can only see my legs. I can see only the floor. I saw there were thousands of shoes sitting there. It looked like thousands to me. Everyone waiting to see me. They made me sit in the middle of the room. They were nice enough to bring me a stool, didn't make me sit on the floor. I was still blindfolded. They were shooting questions here and there. I was talking to this guy and one behind me throws a question. . . . Listening to his question, trying to answer. Another guy fired a different question. I had to stop and answer this one. It's a way of fucking with my brain, you know."

After an hour of this, they took him back to his cell. Later the interrogator came back with five other men.

"The story you wrote on the paper is no good," the man said. "You have to tell us a different story, the real one, the truth."

"The truth? This is all I got," Saad replied.

That's when the first blows came. Cables swung from the hands of the guards crashed into Saad's back.

"I didn't know which way to go or how to protect myself. I receive a hit from my right, I turn to my right, four hit me to my left. They make me spin around the room. First I was in the seat, then on the ground, standing up, falling back again. I've got my hands tied in front. Big black cables with wires inside, a meter long. I could see it under the blindfold. It was probably two or three minutes, but four or five guys hitting at the same time really, really felt like forever."

When the beating stopped, the interrogator tried again, in the gentle tones that are customary among experienced Mukhabarat officers.

"Saad, you are going nowhere. You have to tell us the truth."

"Write whatever you want and hand me the pen and I'll sign it. Just don't beat me."

"No, it doesn't work this way. You have to tell us the truth."

"I already did."

"No, tell us what you did in the north of Iraq."

Saad told his story again. The interrogator tried a different tack, asking direct questions, feeding the terrified, compliant Saad his lines.

"Did you spy on military things or civilian things or what?" the man began.

"Military things."

"Did you spy on Al-Rashid military base?"

"Yes."

"Did you spy on Al-Taji military base?"

"Yes."

"Have you been into Al-Rashid military base?"

"No."

"What?"

"Okay, yes, yes, yes. The same with Al-Taji."

The interrogator was writing down all Saad's answers.

"Did the Americans send you?"

Saad paused for a moment, knowing how fast he was plummeting into an abyss, and how much pain he would face if he did not voluntarily take the leap into self-accusation.

"Well, yeah. Yeah, the Americans sent me."

"That's more like it," said the smiling interrogator.

The man put the finishing touches to the statement and told Saad to sign.

"And I signed," Saad told me. "That was the end of it. He happily took that statement and went to his boss and said, 'We got ourselves a spy.' "

There would be another four and a half months of torture and dehumanization before Saad found his way to Abu Ghraib. But the hand had already reached out from one of Saddam's walls and started pulling him to the heart of the prison state. He was innocent. But he looked potentially guilty. That was enough.

7

Hiding in Plain Sight

FEBRUARY–MARCH 2003

Moises and I had also begun to look potentially guilty. And that was enough to further our own unwitting journey toward the center of Iraq's system of terror.

We continued to work without a government minder and without registering at the Ministry of Information. We stayed in our suite at the Al-Hamra Hotel, which Yousef said was barely monitored by the Mukhabarat, which was kept too busy by the hordes over at the Al-Rashid and the Mansour. We spoke to Iraqis and used Yousef as a translator when necessary. Some people clearly thought that he was a minder. I tried to choose stories that would offer me a window into the country without attracting attention to myself on the streets.

In these weeks leading up to the war, Baghdad was suffused with a passivity occasionally spiked with lip-service defiance. All over town, sandbagged bunkers multiplied on street corners and in the central meridians of main roads. They struck me as purely symbolic, as signs of the coming human resistance against the most powerful military force in history, rather than as physical defenses that had any chance of being effective. When asked, Baghdadis told me that of course they would fight the Americans. Yousef sneered and told me that this was *haki fadi*—empty talk. Everyone would lock their doors and stay at home, he said.

There were plenty of subtle but clear signs that people were expecting "the change," as Yousef called it. Even as the final bunkers were being carved out of the ground, Iraqis were making defensive preparations that indicated they knew all too clearly who was going to win and what chaos would likely follow—as indeed it did. Store owners bricked up their shopfronts. Men who had never owned a firearm before bought Kalashnikovs on the black market. They knew that if the government fell, criminals and looters would have a free hand.

I stood in the parking lot of the Al-Hamra one day and talked with Yousef in the morning sun. On his way over to the hotel he stopped off in the coffee shop he owns with another man. The regulars there knew he was working with foreigners, and they talked about it in a way they would not have dared to a year ago.

"Do they say there's going to be a change?" one man asked.

"I don't know," Yousef said, "I just drive them and they work. That's all."

"Well, let us know if they say anything. Listen, did you see him on television yesterday?"

Everyone knew what "him" referred to; Dan Rather's interview with Saddam was being shown repeatedly on Iraqi television.

"Yes," said another man in the group, "he was saying we're going to defend Basra and fight off the Americans. What's he thinking?"

Yousef stayed quiet during the discussion; you never know who's in a group like that ferreting out threats to the regime while pretending to be a voice of dissent. But he said later that everyone there appeared to want the end of Saddam desperately, and simply felt they could voice that urge in a way they had never been able to before.

And then Yousef looked at me and said, as he had several times before, "Do you think it will happen? Do you really?"

And I said, with confidence, "Yes."

"If that happens, I will give you a big gift," he said, bursting into laughter.

The economic indicators, such as they were, all pointed to a widely held conviction that Saddam was finished. The stock market continued its climb. People were betting on an influx of foreigners and their money. Iraqi companies would enjoy new opportunities, the market was clearly saying. Real estate agents saw prices climb, especially in the wealthier neighborhoods. The foreigners would need somewhere to live. Less hopefully, high demand had also driven up the price of a Kalashnikov. A few months ago they cost about $150 apiece, said Yousef, but in Saddam City, the huge Shia suburb of Baghdad rife with poverty, repressed antiregime fury, and weapons, he had recently bought one for $300.

In the small business center of the Al-Hamra were two computers that had Internet access. You could send emails from there but all emails in Iraq were channeled through the Ministry of Information. Free web-based email sites were blocked and highly illegal.

Moises was in the business center one day when the young woman who worked there, Dahlia, whispered to him, "Do not tell anyone, but there's one site you can use. It's like Hotmail. It's called coolgoose.com. It's top secret."

She also told Moises not to delete all his pictures from the official email account—as he had been doing—because the security men who came by to check the files would want to see some proof of what was sent.

On the evening of Sunday, March 2, Yousef took his biggest risk yet: he had us over for dinner. A modest event in most countries, a private dinner in an Iraqi home without a government minder present was a rare thing. I had never experienced it.

"Try to remember the route," he said, as we drove past the Sajda, one of the newest palaces, with its four vast molded busts of Saddam.

We burned the directions into our memory in case we needed to escape to Yousef's home without his guidance.

Happily, Yousef's house had a covered driveway and high walls around the front yard. I was keen that the neighbors not see us.

"Look," Yousef said, when we were out of the car. He pumped the handle of the well he had dug in his front lawn. They would boil the water they got from it, of course.

His home was two stories, a dust-colored brick house with a flat roof, a common design in Baghdad. His wife Shafika, wearing pants and no headscarf, greeted us at the door. She was a former Arabic teacher who quit work five years earlier because the tiny government wages made continuing a waste of time. I asked if I should take my shoes off, which is customary in many parts of the Muslim world.

"No, no, we're normal here," Yousef laughed. "No one prays here. Except my father."

The main room was heated by an electric burner and there were cracks in the walls. The yellow paint had last looked fresh years ago, I guessed. All of the picture frames, the couches, the carpets looked tired and worn; there was no vibrancy in the colors, even in the obligatory portrait of Saddam that hung prominently on the end wall. I had met middle-class Iraqis selling their last bits of furniture to survive but I had never seen the reduced means at home. Only now that Yousef had started work as a driver had their prospects looked better. This family got by better than many, I realized, but life was still a struggle compared to the boom years of the 1970s, when the price of oil shot up and the Iraqi government spent generously on its people. Those were years of astonishing progress for Iraq, which had been in economic and cultural decline for centuries. The Baath government had nationalized its oil industry shortly before the 1973 oil boom, and money suddenly poured into the state coffers. It was an extraordinary and unprecedented opportunity for a socialist-minded Arab regime to prove to the world, and to fellow Arabs, that it could take care of its people without relying on a superpower. Throughout the decades, literacy rates rocketed, health care became among the best in the Middle East, women's rights flourished. All over the country the evidence of industrialization sprang up: massive highways, electricity pylons, towering hotels. The government gave out free televisions and refrigerators. Gasoline was available at negligible prices. Foreign workers, including thousands from proud Arab countries like Egypt, flocked to Iraq for the money they could earn as waiters and cooks. Newly rich Gulf Arabs from dry, Islamist countries would head for the discos of Basra for alcohol and women.

The hand of President Ahmed Hassan Bakr was firm—and behind him Vice President Saddam Hussein controlled most sources of power—but with such affluence, the authority seemed largely beneficent to families like Yousef's.

Although Yousef was half Kurdish, half Turkish, his wife was from a prominent Sunni family with close connections to the regime. They lived in a predominantly Sunni neighborhood, the Green Area. Formerly known as the Police District, it was still home to many members of the security services, army, and police. It was a good, safe place to live, and the 1970s was the best time to live there.

Yousef and his oldest daughter, Doa, took out a box of family photographs, and I saw him in a 1970s outfit—lapels and collars committing fashion misdemeanors—doing his work as a surveyor, young and slim and Western-looking. There was a big gap in the photographs while he worked in the aviation directorate during the Iran war, but then came his wedding photos, snapshots from a trip to visit relatives in Turkey, and pictures of his first two babies.

Then Saddam invaded Kuwait and Yousef's life changed.

"They called us all back to the army and told us they needed certain people to go here, certain people to go there. They told me to go and stand in one group, and we were all sure we were being taken off to an airport where we would have a quiet war. Instead they took us in buses and we joined the Republican Guard."

So not only was Yousef once a Baath Party member but he had been in the much vaunted, "elite" Republican Guard that had been touted the great nemesis of the allied forces in 1991. The recruiting officer gave Yousef one of the red triangles that distinguished the

Guards; they reminded me of cub scout proficiency badges. He sewed it onto his uniform and followed orders to a desert hideout, to the west of Baghdad, near Lake Habbaniya. A red cotton triangle does not transform a man into a precision killing machine.

"The American planes would come low, flying slow over our position," Yousef said. "We just stayed inside and they never found us. We covered our positions with green material and sand. We'd only go out when they weren't there. There were about ten thousand of us."

His unit never saw a moment of action against the Americans and their allies. But as the war ended and the Shia and Kurdish uprisings erupted, Yousef's unit was pressed into service. This was the last thing Yousef wanted, to fight against other Iraqis, especially if he was to be sent north to fight the Kurds. So he went to his commander and asked him whether it might not be best to have a group of men stay behind to guard the company's munitions. Good idea, said the officer, and asked Yousef to find seven other willing men. Which was not hard to do. And so as his Republican Guard comrades rushed first south to battle the Shia rebels and then north to crush the Kurdish uprising, Yousef sat in the desert and watched over a stockpile of weapons. That was his war. Then the Republican Guardsman went home to his beautiful young wife, his two babies, and the swing chair that sits on his front lawn.

When we came to dinner, I brought the Famous Grouse, but not without a certain sheepishness: more than half of it had disappeared at a dinner the night before. Yousef seemed a little unimpressed by this and asked whether I would like some Jordanian whisky.

"That would be lovely," I said, and he opened a new bottle. A bit frightened by the prospect, I tried not to look at the label—it may have been called Black Mark—but in fact it was drinkable.

Yousef's father, Mohammed, appeared. He was a handsome man, once the top detective in Baghdad, a man with five college degrees. Even though he was past 80, he was still teaching at the police academy twice a week to stave off boredom. He read all the time, Yousef said.

In remarkably decent English, he spoke of his times in London in the 1950s and 1960s. He recalled London street names, mentioned British friends as if he had seen them yesterday, and told us how he had lost touch with a girlfriend called Gloria, who lived in Leicester.

"The first time I went I accompanied the king and his uncle," he said. "They were received at Buckingham Palace by Queen Elizabeth."

He also spoke of how, when the king and his family were killed in the bloody revolution of 1958, the new authorities threw him in jail for three months. "They thought I might try to take vengeance," Yousef's father said, and given his lingering feelings of affection for the monarchy, that might have been a reasonable call. Let the young man calm down a little in the slammer.

Yousef brought out a copy of a 1956 report by the British police on their Iraqi trainee. It was a hilarious self-parody of condescending, colonialist praise with a couple of barbs at the end. Read literally— or by any Iraqi without an extremely acute understanding of British imperial lingua franca—it looked like a glowing report. To my eyes, it was a microcosmic example of why it was all for the better that the British did not still run Iraq, or any other part of the Middle East for that matter. I thought of my times in refugee camps in the West Bank and Gaza when old men, hearing that I was British, unleashed decades of fury about how Churchill, Kitchener, Balfour, Lloyd George, and their colleagues had so disastrously carved up the Middle East during and after World War I. The original sin, for these older Arabs, was British, not American. Mohammed Aziz's letter also made me worry whether I might, in two or three years, see versions of the same letter from the new occupiers: An assessment, say, by a former senior New York police officer of a new detective in the reformed Iraqi police service suggesting how well the recruit was doing, considering who he is and where he's from.

As I had suspected, Yousef's father didn't stay long. As soon as Yousef brought out the whisky he was off back to his room, citing ill health. In fact, he is an observant Muslim and declines to be around when there is drinking going on.

Once his father had left the room, Yousef brought out the arrest warrant. What it was, in fact, was a photocopy of a Baath Party newspaper article published ten years ago about one of Saddam's glorious antigovernment actions before the 1968 Baath revolution. There was a display in the story of several warrants for Saddam's arrest. One of them had Yousef's father's signature on it.

"Oh dear," the old man had apparently said on the day it was published, "do you think they will come looking for me again?"

There was an amusing irony between Yousef's father's personal feelings about the government and his lingering role as a teacher of the police, and perhaps the most delightful point came up over dinner. He is the author of many books, Yousef said, some of which focus on criminal investigation and other policing matters. They are still in circulation among the security services today, Yousef said. His books help train generation after generation of Saddam's ubiquitous and merciless spies, his Baathist enemies before the revolution and now.

We heard stories of Yousef's time visiting California when he was a young man. He was meant to go to North Hollywood to marry a young woman from the host family and settle in the United States, but "when she appeared I saw that she was very fat. I was surrounded by all of these beautiful American girls and I just couldn't marry her. So the family said, you can go now." He tried to get a green card by enlisting in the U.S. Navy, but the recruiting officer explained to him that the green card had to come first. Every two or three days he was on the phone to friends in Baghdad, hearing about Ahmed and Ali and Barzan playing chess down at the coffee shop and smoking their water pipes, and he was homesick. After three months he returned home to Iraq.

Shafika had prepared delicious steaks, marinated in herbs and barbecued outside. We had huge plates of *mezze*—Arabic salads—and Yousef produced a bottle of Italian red wine.

Each time I brought up anything political, I saw his wife—who was relaxed, welcoming and sophisticated—look uneasy. Perhaps they worried that their house was bugged or perhaps they didn't want their children to let something slip out at school. When I thought about it, I realized Yousef was also avoiding politics when the kids were within earshot. I was sure Shafika had similar political views to her husband,

though. When various members of the ruling elite appeared on television after the Manchester United versus Liverpool game was over,
she said: "Same old thing. They say the same old thing." And she
smiled through her cigarette smoke.

I liked her a lot. I offered to help at one point, and she said:
"Iraqi women don't need help. We are as strong as the man."

She was studying parapsychology, she said, and was able to see into
the future. She was too tired to read the grains in our coffee cups, but
soon, one afternoon, she would do it. But one thing seemed clear: neither Moises nor I would ever marry our girlfriends. Moises was ruled
out of matrimony just by a vibration, apparently. I had to explain my
rather complicated situation a little bit more, but then Shafika delivered a firm verdict that I would never marry this woman.

We must take Eastern wives, Yousef said. That way we would
have women who stay in the home and look after the children and
do the cleaning and cooking. I had heard this so often from men in
the Middle East that I didn't hold it against him, but it was a little
disheartening to hear it from someone so well educated, urbane, and
solidly middle-class.

The kids were charming and extremely bright. The two older
children already had their futures mapped out for them, futures that
depended on "the change." They were to go to medical school in
London.

We took our leave and thanked them all profusely for their generosity and hospitality. And, as they had done several times over the
evening, they told us that this was our home now and they were our
family. That we were to come to them for anything. Anything at all,
at any time.

In the car on the way back to the hotel I wondered if Yousef's wife
really understood what she was saying in that goodbye and whether
Yousef had discussed it all with her.

"Oh yes," he said. "She knows."

They have made a calculation, I told myself. They are gambling
on the change and on months of future employment with *Newsday*.
It could help secure their children's education in London, it could

help them repair the cracks in the walls. I did not mean to question their genuinely hospitable impulses, but when having two Western journalists round for dinner can get you killed, there has to be something in it for you.

One quiet morning, still trying to keep a low profile, we went to see Saddam's favorite propaganda weapon, the Al-Amariya air-raid shelter, where two American Tomahawk cruise missiles killed 408 women and children in one night in 1991. I had resisted going—though minders would suggest a visit if there was even a bit of down time—but the coming war made the visit seem relevant and fair. It might give Moises and me an idea of what was about to happen in this city.

The place of greatest emotional impact in the shelter is the place where the missiles had the greatest physical impact: the unaltered holes in the reinforced concrete roof and the floor that were torn open by the two cruises before they erupted in fire.

Since 1995, one woman had managed the place and given the tours. Her name was Intesar al-Samarai, and she was warm and beautiful, with high, sculptured cheekbones. We were her only visitors, and we got a tour that she clearly gave by rote. Her bored, politicized commentary sucked the emotion right back out of the shelter. So I started to ask her about herself, and she relaxed, as if she'd never been asked before what it was like to spend every day in an enclosed sarcophagus where her friends and neighbors had been incinerated as they slept.

"Every day I see these people in my dreams," she said, pointing to the Pompeii-like shadows on the floor that marked the places where bodies burned at hundreds of degrees centigrade. Plexiglass covered the burn marks and what she told us was dried blood. "I walk along this carpet and I find these people here. That's why I had people put those glass covers over them. I got people to take samples of the blood and take them to a laboratory to find out who exactly they were. I found out that they were the same people in my dreams."

The shelter was "like morphine" to her, she said. "I can't do without it. . . . Always my daughters are angry at me. 'You love the shelter better than me,' they say."

Intesar said she planned to carry on working at the shelter during the coming war. My foreign editor at *Newsday* had just passed on a message Pentagon officials had given our Washington bureau chief: They strongly recommended that all journalists be pulled out of Baghdad. The bombing would be horrendous, and civilians were guaranteed to be among the dead, was the message. I didn't tell Intesar this, but I did tell her that the shelter might be the safest place in Baghdad. I doubted the Americans would hit it again.

When we left I tipped her, and we shook hands warmly, even though she was wearing a modest *abaya*—usually an indication that a woman will not shake hands with a man. A few weeks later I would wonder whether her warmth and willingness to talk about herself was just another regime-produced pretense, whether her handshake was one of deceit and betrayal of our brief intimacy.

In anticipation of the possible chemical or biological dimension to the coming war, I bought a canary at the Friday animal market. If the caged bird wasn't singing, I would know why, and it would be time to put on my protective suit and gas mask. I strongly hoped that he would never have to fulfill the duty for which he was brought into the household and that he would live a long life and die a peaceful, painless, and natural death. I also bought the canary for company. From what I had learned, at a course taught by former British soldiers to journalists about how to survive in war zones, if the canary fell off his perch because he was breathing in VX gas or sarin, that meant it was already too late for me and Moises.

The Friday markets, the bazaars, are the commercial heart of Iraqi society and in many respects the quintessence of the Arab social world. I had been before to mingle with the impoverished students combing the book market, the smiths who made the copper market clang and ting with their ceaseless hammering, the mercilessly fast barrow-haulers who ruled the narrow alleys of the textile market, the hawks of the covered antique market who would ply Westerners with sweet tea and inflated prices, and the indifferent and down-to-earth vendors in the electrical goods market. I had not yet

been to the market where you could buy animals for pets and sometimes to eat or to pit against each other in wagered fights.

This bazaar was spread out across a few backstreets and parking
lots and sometimes into the street, slowing down the already
pedestrian-speed Friday morning traffic. Above the hum of male
voices and car engines you could occasionally hear the vicious bark
of a dog, the chirping of the caged birds or the gurgling of fish tanks.

In the dog section the rather unhappy Iraqi relationship with dogs
seemed all too clear to me. Dogs have one main use in Iraq—to guard
homes and businesses. Boys selling puppies from boxes pinched and
slapped the big-pawed creatures, getting them roughed up and snarling
at an early age. All the adult dogs were held on chains, and it was best
to keep away from them. They leapt and snarled at anyone who came
within range. Mainly German Shepherds or mixes with Cerberus-like
demeanors. What really caught the attention of the male-only crowds
was when two owners could persuade their dogs to copulate. They
stared in silent fascination.

If the dog market suggested the seam of violence that writers,
kings, governors, tribal sheikhs and ordinary Iraqis themselves have
long noted cuts through Iraqi society, the other two main parts of
the animal market spoke of the tenderness that so strangely accom-
panies the violence. A narrow alleyway led away from the slavering
dogs into a boxed-up oasis of bubbling aquaria, where thousands of
tropical fish shimmered in the dull morning light on this last day of
February. Large men stood transfixed at the grace of the angel fish,
the glory of the goldfish, the mysterious colorlessness of the tiny
coalfish.

"More and more I am thinking about ways that Iraqis escape
from their political surroundings, how they find beauty amid the
strictures and the horror of Saddam's Iraq and Bush's coming war,"
I wrote in my journal that evening.

And I thought of what Ali Abu Tiba, the Sufi leader, had said:
"We believe that people need to exercise their souls and hearts and
minds as much as their bodies. We all need art, music, poetry,
books, dancing. We all need beauty."

These fish provided beauty and so did the birds that I came across next: parakeets, budgerigars, canaries, parrots, all perching in cages, their feathers bursts of clean color, their song always upbeat and pretty. Living beings that don't cause hurt and only provide beauty. No wonder Baghdadis are so keen on birds and fish. Many weeks later I would sit in the tatty home of a forcibly retired Mukhabarat agent with fierce eyes and listen to unforgiving, unapologetic stories of his career. Throughout the long talks, his budgerigars sang sweetly from their cage just outside the living room window.

One night, I sat in a car and listened as the young man sitting in the backseat next to me sweetly sang George Michael songs a capella.

Nadeem Hamid's voice, raspy when necessary, creamy the rest of the time, was a gift but in Saddam's Iraq, it was all but worthless.

After he had finished "Kissing a Fool," he said: "I heard that Robbie's signed a huge new contract." Robbie being Robbie Williams, of course, Britain's current George Michael.

"Yeah, I think it's for eighty million dollars," I said, passing Nadeem a cigarette.

"I'd give up smoking for that," he said.

"I'm not sure of the details, but I think he gets a certain amount per album. Like, ten million or something."

Realizing I wasn't being very comforting, I tried to look on the downside of being Robbie Williams. "It's not all guaranteed, I don't think. There's a lot of pressure involved in getting the records to sell, I think. And I read recently that he gets very bad depression."

"For ten million dollars, I could deal with that," Nadeem said and gazed out of the window at the passing Baghdad streetlights, exhaling a cigarette that suggested he didn't give much of a shit about his voice in reality. If the head of a Western record company were to appear in his living room as if by magic offering him $100 million for five albums he would have to decline. So why give up smoking?

He turned to me again. "Ten million dollars?" I nodded and he blew out another lungful of smoke and looked out of the window again.

I had just spent the evening with him and three other members of

Iraq's first and only English-singing five-member boy band. Their name was a horrible double negative that smacked either of outrageous hubris or glorious hopefulness, I couldn't decide which. Unknown To No One were, however, known only to a few thousand Iraqis. Their first album, *From Now On,* had been out since the summer and it had not sold well, a couple of thousand. And even Iraq FM, the pop music radio station owned by Uday Hussein that favored English-language songs from the West, barely played what was perhaps Iraq's only home-grown English-language pop.

But a small miracle had happened in those months, something that connected the band and their manager, Alan Enwia, to the outside world in a way that was as innocent as possible and yet, because the connection was with the West, was as precarious as possible. Wanting to check that the band's name was not already in use and to stake a claim to it now, Enwia had gone onto the Internet and had registered with a massive online service that catalogued band names. The company, owned by an English pop entrepreneur named Peter Whitehead, encouraged unsigned bands to send in their music. Enwia had managed to ship a CD by land to Jordan and from there by mail to Whitehead in London. Whitehead was intrigued. Here were five boys on a CD cover, wearing gray-and-black almost-matching tailor-made boy band outfits, moodily gazing into the camera and living in a city that might be bombed and invaded by American and British military forces in the coming months.

Whitehead put the CD in his player. They sang in English and they sounded good. Particularly striking was a song called "Hey Girl." It would need to be re-recorded to make it in the British and American markets, he knew, but he was convinced that this was a song of the quality that would make it onto a Justin Timberlake or Robbie Williams album. For now, Whitehead included it on the latest in a series of compilation CDs of unsigned bands that he had been releasing for several years.

His interest, expressed to Enwia through the emails that were, as always, monitored by the Ministry of Information, gave the band the kind of hope they had only dreamed of. That tiny dash of interest from the West had so enthralled them that the band took the risk of meeting with foreign journalists who were not accompanied by minders. First, with Phil and Julian from the *Sunday Telegraph*, then with Moises and me.

We met at the CD store—Melody Records—that Alan owned on the posh Arasat Street on the eastern side of the city. His family name is Enwia but he goes by Alan Melody usually. We drove through the streets to the studio where they had recorded the CD.

Diyar Dulare couldn't make it, the band members apologized. He had to look after his mother, who was sick. (This was a lie. Diyar's father, I learned after the war, had been so scared of the consequences that he had forbidden Diyar from meeting Moises and me.) So I sat in an armchair in the office of the studio's owner, and they perched on a couch and laughed and enthused and finished each other's sentences in fluent English as if they had been put together by a boy band guru in Orlando. Perhaps a little older than your ideal boy band members—they were all now in their early twenties—they nevertheless had a sort of postponed teenage energy.

Their tastes varied widely, from Michael Bolton to Linkin Park, and so did their ethnic backgrounds. A Kurd, a Sunni Arab, a Shia Arab, and two Armenian Christians, they were a walking advertisement for religious and ethnic harmony in a country where the fear of ethnic strife never went away.

It was a fun evening but a little odd. We had to talk around the whole nature of this new hope that had brought us together in this apartment-turned-studio with posters of Sting on some walls and Arab singers on others. We couldn't talk about why I was there and why they were there. We all knew what it was, though. There was a war coming that would likely put an end to Saddam—that would give them a formerly unthinkable opportunity to take this link with Whitehead and turn it into success. Travel. Concerts. Videos. MTV interviews. Girls. As long as Saddam Hussein ruled, these boys were going nowhere. Certainly not into the heart of the Western pop culture machine.

Eventually, I just had to ask.

"I know this is a difficult and perhaps impossible question," I said, "and I'll entirely understand if you simply can't answer it. But do you think that your opportunities would open up if there was a big change in Iraq in the near future?"

A moment earlier the boys had been bouncing around as if they had been drinking a few too many Cokes. Now they were silent and gazing at the floor. Or looking at me with huge disappointment.

"What do you mean?" one of them asked.

I mumbled, embarrassed, through a different version of the question and still they sat quietly, glancing at me as if I had started speaking Icelandic. Eventually, one of them hit upon an answer that could work for all of us. If the UN lifted the sanctions, he said, it could be easier for the band to work overseas. In Saddam's Iraq, you couldn't go wrong in telling journalists that every ailment to befall the country was the fault of the embargo.

As the war approached, tension among Iraqis and journalists rose.

"It's late at night and I'm scared for the first time," I wrote on March 10. "I'm really scared. I've largely kept away from the incessant rumor mill, but I heard one tonight that makes me very anxious. And that is that all journalists are going to be rounded into the Al-Rashid Hotel and that some are going to be used as human shields. Our plans to disappear [to Yousef's house] make us vulnerable to the nightmare situation—being caught and accused of not playing by the rules."

Friends had held a party the previous night in the Al-Hamra. It had become unusually drunken, and all that most people could talk about was whether to stay in Baghdad or to leave before it was too late to do so. Two reporters begun shouting at each other, batting loud obscenities back and forth. Another almost got lynched by colleagues. Someone threw a glass across the room. There was an air of desperation about the evening.

It was becoming harder to sleep. I was forever calculating the risks involved in staying and in not being registered at the Ministry of Information. When we needed to say something important Moises and I would signal to each other that it was time to go out onto our balcony. There, under a huge, humming white neon sign that radiated the name "Al-Hamra" across the city, we would quietly talk about our tactics and concerns. One incident had increased our anxiety enormously. Moises and I had agreed to keep our satellite phones locked in my suitcase when we were not in the room. Sometimes we slipped up and forgot. One day Moises asked me if I knew where his Thuraya was. We searched everywhere, but it was gone. Someone had bypassed our more valuable computers and photography equipment and had taken one of our illegal satellite phones, a piece of equipment that would be monetarily worthless once we had quickly terminated the account. Financial gain was clearly not why the thief had taken our phone. The Al-Hamra may not have been quite the wired spook's nest that the more famous Al-Rashid was, but it was clearly under surveillance. And so, apparently, were we.

For a few Baghdadis, life continued as if nothing unusual was afoot. "This city is about to have the shit bombed out of it, and still they're selling children's plastic tricycles on the sidewalk outside shops," I wrote that night.

But for most, there was something clearly amiss. "The mullahs in the mosques are calling for holy war," I wrote, "telling their congregants that they will go to heaven if they kill foreigners or die fighting. In one mosque on Saturday, the mullah told his people that they could sign up for getting a Kalashnikov. Apparently everyone present put his name down. Are they true fedayeen or are they God-fearing people who don't want to stand out in the crowd by not putting their names down?

"On television, two mullahs appeared today dressed in combat gear and carrying Kalashnikovs at some army base. It seems like Saddam is trying to use Islam to encourage his people, to garner support, to make this truly a war between Muslims and infidels.

"We watched *From Russia With Love* tonight on DVD to take our minds off things and to relax after last night's revelries."

But once the movie was over, talk turned as always to who was staying, who was going, and what were the risks of staying.

March 11

Yesterday we discovered that staying at Yousef's house is a bad idea. Over lunch, I asked him about his neighbors. This seems like something I might have asked earlier. It turns out that the neighbor to his left is a lieutenant colonel in the missiles part of the army. He has five sons, four of them carrying Kalashnikovs. To the right is a neighbor from Ramadi, the loyalist heartland of Saddam's world. Across the street is another lieutenant colonel. Added to which, Yousef's water pump in his front garden will likely be used by different neighbors trooping in and out all day long. There may also be house-to-house searches. I blame myself for not asking these questions before, but I confess to being rather lulled by Yousef's astonishingly relaxed approach. He keeps laughing and singing "I love you every day" to Moises. He jokes about the ministry of popcorn and the governorate of potato chips. As I asked him these questions, he acknowledged that our staying in the house could be rather dangerous.

So we've all but ruled that out and have opted, for the time being, to stay here at our new little hotel, the Al-Dar, with a group of Christian activists who are old and American and plan to be here for the bombing. We have kept our suite at the Al-Hamra, in case that ends up being the safest place. And we are now five minutes walk away from the Palestine Hotel, which is the new ground zero for hackistan [a journalists' hub]. The networks have been told by the Pentagon that the Al-Rashid will be hit, and so everyone has decamped, although no doubt still keeping the rooms.

There are rumors that there will be a sweep of all hotels by intelligence agents looking for sat phones.

We have decided to do nothing, to lay low as before. It's worked so far, and even though the stakes get raised with each day, we hope it will continue to work.

We are spending nearly all our time on this stuff, worrying about it, talking to people, trying to calculate the impossible. It's almost a waste of time trying to work out the safest but most flexible arrangement because no one will ever know until the moment is here, but seeing as our lives and our freedom to work depend on making the right moves, it's hard not to obsess.

Yousef says that he is going to volunteer for the civil defense force, a group of civilians who do not carry guns but go around helping when the bombs land. This should enable him to drive freely around the city when the promised curfew is imposed by the government.

The Iraqis are glued to the radio and gossiping in coffee shops. One antiques store we visited was packing up its contents so that there would be nothing for looters to take.

The restaurants and juice bars—including our favorite Meshmesh on Rashid Street—are turning into mess halls for senior officers, wearing dark green uniforms and carrying pistols in their belts. I try to smile at them and make eye contact whenever possible. Sometimes they smile back, sometimes they turn away.

On more and more street corners there are bunkers and piles of sandbags. There is a rumor that there will be an antiaircraft position on the Al-Hamra's roof, which is our ceiling. Nearby the hotel is an unfinished building. The other day a group of soldiers were going in and out, perhaps preparing to move in when the bombs start.

Two days later, Yousef insisted that we come to his house again, this time for lunch.

"But what if the neighbors see us?" I asked. He told me not to worry about it.

Shafika cooked us delicious chicken biryani, koubeh, and salads. We brought pastries, red wine, and, this time, a full bottle of whisky. We talked mostly about Yousef's attempts to move his family to Syria before the bombing started. Even in the middle of lunch, Shafika could not resist dialing her brother on the green rotary phone to see if he had used his connections to secure them a joint passport. The lines at the passport office were impossibly long, and the only way to get one in time would be through knowing the right people and giving them the right amount of money.

"No?" Shafika said, her face falling, a cigarette dangling from her right hand. "And they want more money?"

She looked at her husband. "Here, you talk to him."

After a short conversation, Yousef put down the receiver and came back to the table to finish his lunch.

"We're all going to have to stay here and die," he said, laughing with the kind of desperate humor that some Iraqis were now using as a comfort. His wife and children didn't laugh.

Lots of other middle-class Iraqis were leaving town. Their fatalism of early March had given way to fear. On Salihiyah Street in downtown Baghdad, buses with chipped paint and well-worn tires parked each day on both sides of the busy road. That's where Yousef's wife and three kids would go to catch a ride to Syria if only they could get the passport.

"I don't want to leave," Shafika said. "I don't want to be without my husband in Damascus."

Yousef shook his head quietly.

"I want to go," Doa said. "I'm afraid of the bombs. I won't be able to sleep at night." She put her hands over her ears.

"She just wants to go because she wants to see another country," Yousef said, trying as ever to inject levity into this matter of life and death, trying to keep his family's spirits up.

When Shafika was out of the room after lunch and the kids were watching television, Yousef pulled on a cigarette and told us again that he had one regret in life.

"I love my wife and children," he said, "but getting married and having children was the biggest mistake I ever made. I got married after the war with Iran and no one thought we would ever be in a war again. But there has been war ever since. I try but I don't feel I can do the best for my family."

It was around this time that Moises and I asked Yousef for a favor, a request that I now find hard to forgive myself for making. We were terrified that if the Americans used the E-bomb (this was the mythical device developed by scientists at the Pentagon that was going to hit Baghdad and emit an enormous electromagnetic pulse that would hurt no one but turn every electrical circuit, even those hidden deep within Saddam's bunkers, into unfixable junk; that could, of course, include our computers, digital cameras, and satellite phones), we would be cut off from communicating with the outside world. Reportedly, this new weapon had an effectiveness range of only 300 meters. If our remaining Thuraya was in a distant place, it would be fine. We told Yousef that we were about to ask a favor that he must feel willing to decline, that it could be extremely dangerous for him. Would he hide our Thuraya in his house?

He thought about it for a few long moments and then agreed.

President George W. Bush, British Prime Minister Tony Blair, and Spanish Prime Minister Jose Maria Aznar met that Sunday in the Azores to decide when exactly to attack Iraq. When they had finished their meeting, they gave Saddam and his family 48 hours to leave Iraq. Almost instantly, the Iraqi government poured scorn on the ultimatum and declared that the president would never leave his country. War was now inevitable.

Like nearly all journalists, Moises and I moved into the Palestine Hotel. The Ministry of Information preferred it that way—it made it easier for them to keep tabs on everyone—and we had decided that we were safest with the crowd. We also were trying to strike a tricky balance. We wanted to be seen around the place by ministry officials, so as to dampen any suspicions they might have, but we didn't want to risk trying to get accredited, because the ministry was still expelling journalists from the country. "Hiding in plain sight," was how John Burns put it as we stood in the hotel lobby one day.

Moises and I had room 1122, a dark blue cavern that was aesthetically stuck in about 1978 and was as gloomy as every other room in the hotel, thanks to the concrete spiderweb that flanked every balcony and did an efficient job of keeping out the daylight. We kept the Al-Dar room as a nearby bolt hole. The front door of the Al-Hamra was now bricked up. We memorized room numbers in the seedy, crepuscular halls of the Palestine: some old friends, some newer, all invaluable. We all dropped in and out of each other's rooms as freely and frequently as freshmen at college for the first week of fall semester, sharing news, good vantage spots should the bombing begin, and good places to hide sat phones. And we shared rumors and anxieties and excitements. It was as generous a time between correspondents as I can remember. We knew we were entering a period of extreme danger, a time for looking after one another as much as ourselves.

As the ministry ejected CNN and told other journalists to leave, the room searches for sat phones intensified. No one was sure whether the men who were showing up at people's doors at random were ministry officials or Mukhabarat agents. To give ourselves moments to hide the phones, should the knock on the door come, a group of us agreed on a coded knock to avoid the panicked rush of stashing away the contraband that we were starting to go through with stressful regularity.

Anxiety would always rise when someone decided to leave for Jordan. They would miss the war, for sure, but they would be safe, we mumbled to ourselves incessantly. But always, we would end up inverting the sentence: They would be safe, but they would miss the war. So in a conference call a few days before the war began, Moises and I did what nearly every journalist in Baghdad was doing at the time. We put the case for staying to our editors and they finally agreed that we could. The commitment to staying among some of us was pretty fierce: there was some talk about quitting and staying anyway if our bosses tried to pull us out.

With the shops closing up for the war, Moises, Phil, Julian, and I realized there were two things we had yet to buy: door wedges and microwave ovens.

Moises and I already had wedges, but Phil and Julian still needed them—one for the top and one for the bottom of their hotel room door—for that moment when things turned bad and someone tried to bash it in. The theory was that they would be frustrated by the wedges and move on to the next room, at least buying you some time. Moises and Yousef took Phil to a carpenter friend of Yousef's to get the wedges, while Julian, his driver Bassem, and I headed for the Karada neighborhood in search of an electrical appliances store that was not yet closed up behind steel bars. From Kosovo to Kabul to Baghdad, I had always found Julian to be an especially determined shopper, never yet foiled in bids to find the right denim shirt or electrical adapter.

"I always like shopping for white goods before a war," said Julian, as we jumped in and out of the green Pajero asking if anyone had any microwaves to sell.

Of all the rumors that would not go away, the one about the E-bomb was perhaps the most persistent. So for weeks nearly every journalist in Baghdad had been worrying about how to protect equipment from this demonic bomb that we feared more than the explosive variety. Some people bought massive lead boxes, confusing electromagnetic pulses with radiation. Others were convinced that wrapping their stuff in aluminum foil would foil the Pentagon's best brains. But several television techies seemed convinced that the only way to protect their gear was to stash it inside a microwave and ground the oven's cable. I don't really know the difference between an amp, a volt, and a watt, but this seemed as good a theory as any. And as silly as any.

"It's ridiculous," Julian said, as we drove around in the fading light swigging scotch from a hip flask, "but it's also one of these things that if we don't do it and it turns out that our stuff is fried, we'll hate ourselves."

At last we found a man who knew a man who had microwaves. Four workers were inside his shop, building a brick wall down the middle of the sales floor to deter potential looters. The owner climbed over the wall, which was about four feet high and getting higher with each minute, and handed over the biggest ovens he had. We'll take four, we said. In room 1122, I cut the plugs off and stripped down the earth wire. I attached one microwave to the plumbing of the bidet and another to the pipes under the bathroom sink so that they would be grounded.

The days crawled by as the forty-eighty-hour deadline approached and then passed. Phil and Julian had been ordered out at the last minute by their newspaper. Others left too. A group of our friends had received similar rulings but had made brave decisions that both countered corporate commands and left them in the danger area: it would be too dangerous now to travel on the road out of Baghdad to Jordan, they told their editors, a line that kept some of the best reporters and photographers in Baghdad for the war.

Now the bunkers around town were manned twenty-four hours a day by uniformed men with Kalashnikovs and, occasionally, bigger machine guns. The Iraqi parliament gathered to announce their solidarity with their president and their willingness to fight and die. Trucks carrying antiaircraft guns and soldiers giving the V sign drove down the city's roads. And as civilian traffic died down, the streets were given over to the white pickup trucks of the Mukhabarat and other security agencies. They ignored red lights, and other drivers gave way to them at all times. Always secretly in charge, they now had Baghdad openly in their hands.

8

American Locks

Two hundred and fifty years ago, a tribe of Bedouin nomads called the Zoba walked out of the Arabian desert toward the lands they had heard had not one but two vast rivers flowing down through them. With their herds of sheep, their tents that could withstand the desert's blasting dust storms, and their fierce loyalty to little but tribal unity and Islam, they arrived between the Euphrates and the Tigris and ended their years of wandering. Only a fool would pass up these green flatlands for the thirsty stretches of the Hijaz, where generations of the Zoba tribe had lived, always in search of another of the region's meager pastures. And as the land they found themselves in coalesced into modern-day Iraq, through the Ottoman and British occupations, the monarchy, the 1958 revolution, and finally the Baathist coup of 1968, the Zobas became an important Sunni tribe in the newly independent country. The two main families, the Dari and the Al-Faris, were large landowners in one of the most fertile parts of Iraq.

The tribal influence, however, did not help them when the new military government took over in 1958 and decided to seize land for government use. West of Baghdad, the Dari family was forced to relinquish a large amount of land that they still yearn to reclaim. The new government had decided that what Iraq really needed to become a country of solid law and order was a big central prison. The Zoba land, which housed a village called Abu Ghraib, was to be the site of this prison. The tribe was furious, but it knew it was powerless in the face of Iraq's ascendant and first genuinely independent government.

"It was theft and we're still angry about it," Sheikh Barakat Bargesh al-Farisi, the head of the Zoba tribe, told me one Friday morning in early July, three months after the war, as we sat cross-legged on the cushions laid out around the sides of his *diwaniya*. I had asked dozens of people how Abu Ghraib came by its eerie name—Father of the Strange—but no one seemed to know: Neither did Al-Farisi, the ancestral owner. (One more prosaic suggestion was that Ghraib can also mean "west": The village sits to the west of Baghdad.)

A law graduate and former member of Saddam Hussein's National Assembly, Iraq's rubber-stamp parliament, he was particularly galled that his tribe's land had been used as the site for a prison in which many Zobas were held. Al-Farisi had a suitably lawyerly approach to his tribe's land problem. "It depends on the formation of a new government. If there is a new property law, we will try to reclaim our land."

The following day I had an appointment at the home of one of the men who kept the Zobas and other Iraqis behind bars. Tamim Taher al-Jader, a former general director of Abu Ghraib, is now a lecturer in criminal law at Mustansiriyah University in Baghdad. He met us in his driveway and led us to his house through the kind of midsummer Baghdad day that makes you feel like an electric bar heater is an inch away from your face at all times. Doctor Tamim, as he is known, served us ice-cold Pepsis and began to talk about the history of prisons in Iraq, which is something of an enthusiasm for him. After three years in the job, he resigned in 2000 in protest at the conditions at Abu Ghraib and the government's willful negligence. Saddam made sure to demote him, comparatively light punishment for such defiance. He has no feelings of loyalty to the regime he served as chief turnkey.

Abu Ghraib was not the first prison in Iraq, he began. The Ottomans had small holding centers, finally building a proper prison in Baghdad named Al-Qala. It sat on the site now occupied by the vast and recently bombed Ministry of Defense.

After World War I, which marked the start of the British occupation, the new rulers of Iraq decided that the country needed more prisons. They built three, one each in Baghdad, Mosul and Basra. They were named the Seem prisons, after the wire fences that ran around their perimeters.

Over the years the buildings degraded and by the time Abdul Karim Qassem seized power from the British-supported King Faisal II in 1958, they were in a state of considerable disrepair. For prisoners and guards alike, they were places of misery. So the new government decided that if Iraq were to join the advanced nations of the world, as the oil-rich country strongly believed it ought, it must build a central prison that met international standards. This aim was formalized in 1959, when the government passed a prison reform law mandating the construction of a prison system built along the designs of Western prisons and large enough to accommodate 0.5 percent of the total population, which Tamim said was the international standard at the time. In the early 1960s, work began on Abu Ghraib in Baghdad and Badoush prison in Mosul.

After the Baathists grabbed control in 1968, they finished the project, and on March 17, 1970, the prison opened for business. Inmates in the decaying British prisons now had shiny new cells and a program of reformatory activities designed to turn them into rehabilitated and skilled citizens when they were released. Across the main highway, for example, was the prison's farmland. Only a few guard towers stood among the fields where short-term prisoners would hoe the earth and plant vegetables as a privilege designed to keep them in touch with the world of work and normality they had recently left.

From across the highway, they could look back and see the vast-ness of the new prison. Its perimeter wall was over four kilometers long and dotted with watchtowers. Its buildings covered over 50,000 square meters. There were separate compounds for long-term inmates, political prisoners, short-termers, and women. There was a rehabilitation department and an investigation section, where offi-cers would look into crimes committed inside the prison. Run by the Ministry of the Interior, the prison was built to accommodate an absolute maximum of 5,000 inmates.

With Badoush opening a few months after Abu Ghraib, nearly all prisoners in Iraq now found themselves housed in these modern reformatories. They would sew uniforms, build furniture, attend academic classes, study mechanics. It was a time when the Baathist government was using the massive increase in the price of oil to build a country that fast became something of a model state in the Arab world. Although ruthless, the government of Ahmed Hassan al-Bakr was not yet the isolated, xenophobic regime of Saddam Hussein. Then the power behind al-Bakr, Saddam could not give full vent to his megalomania and brutality. In fact, he was a driving force behind the spending of vast amounts of money on literacy programs and making sure that Iraq's people, many employed by the government, had a share in the wealth. Many Iraqis look back at the 1970s as the golden era of the modern-day Iraq. Abu Ghraib was some-thing for the country to be proud of.

As the years passed, and after Saddam ascended to power in a carefully devised palace coup in 1979, Abu Ghraib began to fill up. Prisoners had to double up in cells built for one. Guards squeezed new inmates into group cells already full to capacity. But it was after the 1990 invasion of Kuwait that Abu Ghraib's role in Iraqi society began to change in earnest. Suddenly designated a rogue state, cut off from much of the outside world by UN sanctions, Iraq became a place of enormously increased paranoia and intrigue. The regime now saw enemies everywhere. Saddam gave his security agencies more liberty to track down spies and political opponents. After the postwar Shia and Kurdish uprisings of 1991, Saddam's already passionate obsession with suppressing political opposition deepened. It wasn't enough to execute unknown thousands in mass graves. General Security and the Mukhabarat had to be on constant lookout for subversive elements. And most of those they arrested who were not immediately killed were taken to Abu Ghraib. The prison that had been built to benefit Iraqi society, no matter who was in power, now became an implement of oppression and the ultimate symbol of Saddam's paranoia and brutality. As Saddam and Iraq changed, so did Abu Ghraib.

The prison's nominal governors, from the Ministry of Labor and Social Affairs, soon found that Saddam's security agencies were taking a special interest in the property. General Security took over Khasa, the special section for political prisoners. Tamim told me that the Mukhabarat took over the women's section in 1995 and turned it into the Arabs and Foreigners Department, but all other sources, including Mukhabarat officers and prisoners who were there at the time, persuasively insisted that it was General Security that had control over the newly established department and that it wasn't until a year or two later that the Mukhabarat took over. Saddam's top agency, the Special Security Service, also had a small section of their own. The whole prison officially remained under the auspices of the ministry, but now the prison's own governor was not permitted to enter large sections of his domain. "They used the ministry as a cover," Tamim told me.

At the same time, the economic hardships caused by the sanctions and Saddam's exploitation of them led to a significant increase in crime. The prison population soared to at least 20,000, Tamim said. Others said it reached 40,000.

Most of the men sent to Abu Ghraib were guilty as charged, Tamim believed, but their sentences were often absurdly long. "You'd get a guy in for twenty years for stealing a sack of onions or a bird," he said.

One incident typified the stupidity of the regime's obsession with controlling and punishing the population, Tamim said. Without warning, an official showed up one day with busloads of beggars and insisted that they be incarcerated immediately. There were a thousand of them. Tamim showed me a photograph of himself standing in his uniform, a look of resigned exasperation on his face, amid a huge crowd of ragged men, one on crutches, another holding himself up with a walking stick. He set them free the following day.

Time and again he implored the government to increase his budget, to expand the rehabilitation programs, to build more cell blocks. Using Japanese prisons as his model, he planned out several new blocks that could be constructed on the huge tracts of unused land in the compound, then "demanded that they establish new prisons so that this prison could respect the rights of the prisoners." He was ignored.

Only in 2002 did work begin on the new blocks. You can see the foundations today, frozen by the collapse of the regime.

The rot had also set in among the prison guards. Tamim preferred to punish prisoners who had misbehaved by sending them to solitary confinement or denying their right to have family visits or receive letters. Some of the guards opted to beat the offenders. "The guards were not very well educated," Tamim said. "They had lived this way all their lives. They had learned bad ways. And also, some guards had applied for the job in the first place to exploit the prisoners for financial gain."

It was all too much for Tamim, and he resigned in protest. In his place came Saad Majid Ali, whom Tamim described as a man who knew nothing about reformatory practices and was only appointed to do the regime's bidding.

I had tracked down Ali earlier the same day. He was now working as a low-level official in the American-controlled Ministry of Social Affairs. He sat behind a desk in a sauna of an office and did everything he could to avoid an interview. I declined to leave, and eventually he asked us to sit down.

Ali would no doubt object to Tamim's description of him as a regime appointee who was uninterested in rehabilitation. To me he listed all the worthy programs that the prison ran during his one year in charge, but he, too, acknowledged that "the prison was not a priority for the government." And it was not long, he said, before he was clashing with the General Security officers who really ran the prison over their treatment of prisoners. And so they framed him, he said, charging him with "job carelessness."

I had heard about Ali's fall from power at Abu Ghraib before. But the story I had heard was that he had been stealing from the prison's funds. Whatever the truth, the former governor of Iraq's worst prison suffered the same fate as many of his former inmates. General Security held him for seven months in a cell in their detention center. "You can use your imagination about what they did to me," he told me.

"Well," I said, "I can but I'd rather you told me."

So Ali put his left hand up to his mouth and slid out his front upper teeth, which were false, and then slipped them back in. "They took out all my teeth, one way or another," he said. He preferred not to talk about it any more.

After the torture and the isolation, they took him to a special court where his rights were negligible. The judge gave him twenty years, and the guards took Ali back to the place he had run for a year.

The state-of-the-art locks that kept the inmates secure in Abu Ghraib were American. In fact, the whole prison was American. An American partnership, Litchfield, Whiting, Bowne, Panero, Severud, designed it. With branches in Italy and Iran, the company also had an office in Mineola, Long Island. That's a few miles from *Newsday*'s offices in Melville, where my editors and colleagues spent every waking moment during our incarceration trying to get us out. When I called my foreign editor, Dele Olojede, on July 16 to tell him that a Long Island company had taken part in the building of Abu Ghraib, I had to hold the phone away from my ear to accommodate his laughter. The partnership was disbanded a long time ago, but the Sidney Bowne Company, a civil engineering firm, is still based in Mineola. One of the older partners, Robert Stanton, told me by phone that no one could remember much about the project but that the prison had been designed by Litchfield, Whiting, an architectural firm that joined forces for a while with Bowne and the others in the partnership. The Abu

Ghraib project, Stanton recalled, was run out of the company's Rome office.

Kevork Toroyan, a young Armenian engineer with the Athens-based Consolidated Contractors Company, one of the largest Arab contractors, worked on the project for two years, first as deputy project manager and then as project manager. Now living in New Canaan, Connecticut, the semiretired engineer recalled the prison's construction as a master class in inefficiency and absurd mismanagement. "It was a never-ending project," Toroyan told me on the phone from his home. "It just dragged and dragged and dragged." By the end, Abu Ghraib cost about 5 million Iraqi dinars, which was a large amount of money at the time, the dinar being one of the strongest currencies in the world, at roughly $3 to a dinar.

Litchfield appointed an Italian named Luciano Tedaldi as the resident engineer. He was a superstitious man. Not once did he set foot in the execution section, nor would he allow it to be mentioned in meetings, Toroyan recalled. His assistants took care of it in silence. Tedaldi was also a "bit shy," and that did not help him fend off the incessant interference from the Iraqi engineers who were officially under his control. "On paper the resident engineer was a top man, but effectively they blocked him," Toroyan said.

Following the 1958 revolution, Iraq tripped through a series of unstable military governments until the Baathists seized power in 1968. The Abu Ghraib project staggered along under various presidents and their henchmen.

"It was a typical example of how not to run a country. It was such an experience. It was incredible. At one time they needed American locks urgently, so we air-freighted some of the locks from the States. It took us three months to clear it from the airport."

A minor translation problem—the locks were described as hardware—led the customs officials to keep the locks under lock and key. "You know, you could tear your hair out it was so bad. I hate to say that only after Saddam came things started moving again. He was a terrible man and all that, but he started things moving, no question about it."

When the socialist-minded Baathists took over, the engineers were suddenly forbidden to use Western components. Toroyan once needed to import transformers but was told that he could not buy them from European countries or the United States, the very countries that made the best transformers. It drove him mad.

But the project was a worthy one, he said. "Their prisons were so bad, so overcrowded, no facilities. They were in terrible shape. This was going to be a modern and comfortable prison in comparison to what they had." All of the sections had exercise areas. The cell blocks had remote-control locking systems from the United States. Officials liked to come and visit to see the progress of this great symbol of Iraq's modernization. Once, the new Baathist president, al-Bakr, took a tour with Toroyan as his guide. As they strolled round the prison complex, Toroyan explained to al-Bakr that they were now in the political prisoners section. Al-Bakr and his aides, well aware that men historically didn't last long in their positions, looked alarmed at the isolation cells. "You could see bubbles in their heads," Toroyan said. Al-Bakr then nervously asked if the cells had air-conditioning.

Events went al-Bakr's way, however, and he never had to sit through a Baghdad summer in the political prisoners section.

Toroyan moved on from the project to Abu Dhabi and lost track of the prison's use, as engineers do when they shift to new projects and new countries. But over the years, he heard that the "civilized" and modern prison he had helped to build had turned into a sort of hell.

"It was designed for 4,200 inmates, total. I was disturbed later that they put something like 20,000 in there. . . . I could well imagine what state it would be in. Well, the whole country was going to the dogs."

March 20, 2003. Fire and smoke rise from Iraqi government palaces being hit by bombs and missiles during the heaviest coalition bombardment since the beginning of the war.

March 22, 2003. Smoke rises from burning oil trenches set on fire by Iraqi defense forces in the hope of interfering with the navigation systems of American and British bombs and missiles.

(All photographs, unless otherwise noted, by Moises Saman, © 2003 by Newsday, Inc.)

April 22, 2003. View of the corridor in the Arabs and Foreigners Department of Abu Ghraib, where Moises Saman and I were held during the war.

April 22, 2003. Less than two weeks after the regime fell, an American soldier walks by a defaced mural of Saddam Hussein painted on a wall inside Abu Ghraib.

April 22, 2003. An American soldier walks through the part of the prison where a few weeks before the Mukhabarat had welcomed us to Abu Ghraib, taking all our belongings and making us change out of our clothes into blue-and-white prison uniforms.

April 22, 2003. A view of the building's entrance from a cell on our block; the doorway opens into the garden area of the Arabs and Foreigners Department. We would pass through that door on the way to interrogations. The murals were painted by prisoners.

October 15, 2002. Referendum day in Tikrit. Iraqi women in a polling station in Saddam's hometown celebrate after casting ballots in favor of another seven-year term for the president.

October 15, 2002. During the referendum, an Iraqi woman casts her ballot marked with her own blood at a polling station in Tikrit. Saddam received 100 percent approval for extending his rule; according to government announcements, every single eligible Iraqi voted.

February 27, 2003. Sufi dervishes at the Takyia Kasnazan in Baghdad swirl their heads to the rhythm of drums during a ceremony before the war. It was after this ceremony that the Iraqi intelligence service began to follow Moises and me in earnest.

February 27, 2003. A young Sufi appears to be without pain even though another worshiper has lanced his cheek with a skewer during the ceremony.

February 28, 2003. A few days before the war, Baghdadis were still buying pets—mainly fish, birds, and dogs—in the Friday animal market in the center of the city.

March 6, 2003. Members of the only English-language Iraqi boy band, Unknown To No One, pose outside their recording studio in Baghdad less than three weeks before the start of the war. *From left to right*: Art, Nadeem, Shant, and Hasan. The fifth member, Diyar, was missing; his father, terrified of repercussions from the regime, had forbidden him from coming to the interview.

March 22, 2003. During the war, Iraqis gather in Tahrir Square in central Baghdad to pray for an end to the bombing of their city. Portraits of Saddam look down on the vigil.

October 14, 2002. Iraqi security forces monitor events at a pro-Saddam rally at al-Sha'ab Stadium in Baghdad on the eve of the presidential referendum.

May 2003. The remains of hundreds of dead Iraqis unearthed from the fields of Muhawil.

May 2003. A woman looks for her missing husband among hundreds of sets of human remains laid out at the Mussayed Youth Center, converted into a temporary morgue to house remains found at a mass grave near Jurf al-Sakhir. The remains belong to thousands of Iraqi Shia killed during their uprising in 1991.

May 2003. At the newly uncovered mass grave at Muhawil, family members examine an identification card found with the remains.

May 2003. Women weep after finding the remains of a family member in the Muhawil grave.

March 23, 2003. With the war raging around the country, Iraqis take to the streets of Baghdad during a Baath Party–organized demonstration to show their loyalty to Saddam Hussein.

March 23, 2003. With bombs falling on the city almost every hour, Iraqi soldiers and militiamen burn an effigy of George W. Bush during a protest in Baghdad.

March 23, 2003. Iraqi militiamen and soldiers carry a portrait of Saddam Hussein through the streets to show their defiance of the American and British forces now bombing their city.

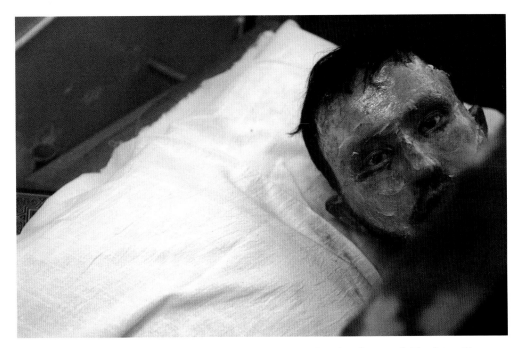

March 22, 2003. An Iraqi civilian lies on a hospital bed at the al-Yarmuk Teaching Hospital in Baghdad after suffering severe burns all over his body during the nighttime bombing of the city.

May 1, 2003. A woman searches desperately for her two children who have disappeared amid a gigantic fire at an illegal gas station in central Baghdad.

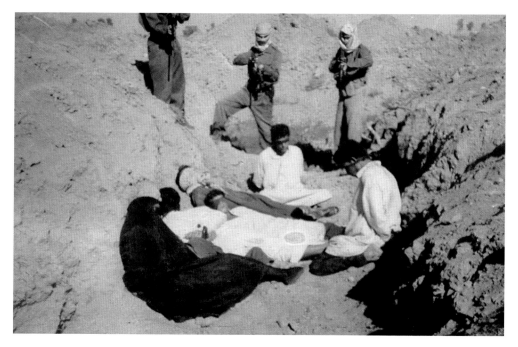

These images, given to me by someone with intimate knowledge of the killings in Muhawil in 1991, show executions taking place. The identities of the executioners and the victims in this picture are unknown. (© 2003, *Matthew McAllester*)

Men identified as Iraqi security agents and members of the ruling Baath Party stand over the bodies of civilians killed at Muhawil in 1991. (© 2003, *Matthew McAllester*)

March 23, 2003. After hearing reports that an American pilot had parachuted into the Tigris in Baghdad, hundreds of Baghdadis gather on the banks of the river to watch the search.

March 23, 2003. During the search, an Iraqi security officer points his gun toward a sign of motion in the bulrushes on the river's banks.

March 23, 2003. Iraqi soldiers and volunteers beat the waters for the downed pilot, who remained elusive.

May 30, 2003. A man weeps as he carries the remains of his brother out of the temporary morgue at the Mussayed Youth Center.

April 30, 2003. Relatives and friends of 30-year-old Saleh al-Jumaily participate in his burial ceremony hours after he was killed by American soldiers in the city of Falluja, about sixty kilometers west of Baghdad.

May 7, 2003. An Iraqi family walks past an American soldier aiming his rifle toward an area where a suspected sniper has just shot at an American army vehicle.

In the weeks before the war, Iraqis found time to carve out moments of normality before the bombs and soldiers came. Here a man feeds birds from the Al-Ahrar Bridge in Baghdad. After the war, Iraqis mourned the calm certainty of those days and yearned for the old sense of security to return, but few wanted the return of the man who had provided the enforced stability, Saddam Hussein.

9

Absent in the Spring

Alone for the first time since the knock came on my hotel room door less than twelve hours earlier, I wanted nothing more than to sleep, to escape into unconsciousness. But my whole being throbbed with fear, the kind of fear that keeps you awake even if you've been up all night under conditions of stress. And besides, the person telling me to go to sleep, Mohammed, was the only person so far who had hurt me, albeit mildly. Fear kept me intensely, pointlessly alert; no amount of protective animal instinct could do me any good here. Fear is one of the most useful assets to have in a danger zone, I had found in the past. It had often made me run away, hide, alter my tone of voice. But it is useful only if you have somewhere to run to, somewhere to hide—if it operates in an environment where there are choices and some degree of freedom. In a prison, whether it be a building or a country, fear is just a constant and painful reminder that you have no choices. People with terminal illnesses speak of the boredom of pain, a pain that is no longer doing its duty of alerting the human body to danger, only to its own disintegration. My fear was like that: unwanted, relentless, useless, and boring. I tried to calm myself by looking around the cell and imposing order on my scrambled thoughts. Perhaps I could force out the fear of the future by cold observation of the present.

My cell is light blue, I told myself. It has a strip of darker, sea blue paint around the bottom rung of cinder blocks. They are going to use electricity on me. My walls are fourteen cinder-blocks high. There is glass in the upper pane of my window but not in the lower. They are going to tear my fingernails out. I wonder what the Arabic words on this torn poster above my blanket mean.

I forced myself to stand up. I put one bare foot in front of the other and measured out the length and breadth of the cell and then lay down again. They are going to hang me up from a hook in the ceiling, perhaps from the one my fan dangles from.

My cell is ten feet by six feet. If I lie across it like this, it is not as comfortable as if I lie lengthways. This way my feet are scrunched up against the wall. But I can't be bothered moving, and besides, Mohammed told me to sleep this way. Mohammed is going to smile his glinty smile as he beats me. There is a dust ball about eighteen inches away. I can't be bothered blowing it. I wonder how long this bottled water will last or whether I will need it all. I will read the label: "From Tigers. The Mesopotion Rivers With A History and Civilization Learned TheHumanty Writing And Reading Since Oldest Era."

I read it again and then moved on to another message on the bottle. "One Ton of Water Passes Through Our Bodies a Year Beware of the Water You Drink."

There was nothing else to read. Already I longed for a book that I could disappear into. There was a Shakespeare sonnet I had sunk into my brain a year ago, and surely, if I really tried, I could dig it up. "From you have I been absent in the spring / When proud pied April, dressed in all his trim / Hath put a spirit of youth in everything / That heavy Saturn laughed and leaped with him. . . ." Ten more lines to go but I couldn't get any further. I'd thought of my girlfriend when I had first learned it, a year or so before, and I thought of her again and couldn't remember this poem I had once recited to her. I am going to fucking die, I thought. What does it matter?

An older guard wearing a gray winter jacket came to look in on me. I had heard him speak some English. His cheeks drooped a little with his years, and there was a slowness in his eyes that made me guess that he would not be the one to torture us. It was the sharp, fast-eyed men like Mohammed who made me worry.

"Excuse me," I said, remaining as meekly as possible on my blanket.

He looked at me. "Yes?"

"Could you please tell us why we are here?"

"But you must know why you are here," he said quietly, with a look of confusion. "What did you do wrong?"

"I don't know. Nothing, we've done nothing wrong," I said. He looked even more amazed at my apparent sincerity. And he seemed very uneasy about discussing my possible crimes, whatever they might be.

"You must have done something to be here. But honestly, I don't know."

"We left some cigarettes with our bags. Would it be possible to get them?"

"I will ask," he said, and moved on out of my narrow view.

It was the first and last time I asked anyone in Abu Ghraib why we were in prison. No one had given us any explanation, but there was only one possible reason. They suspected us of spying. All I could think about were the possible futures that we faced, and I continued the calculations I had begun as we sat in the corridor of the processing wing. Overall, I reckoned, we had a 5 percent chance of getting out and a 95 percent chance of dying.

Nothing was in our favor.

They had let us see their faces. Our countries were all part of a coalition now attacking Iraq, and those military forces were reportedly only fifty miles south of Baghdad and closing fast. We had indeed broken several Iraqi laws and had acted in ways that could lead a hanging judge to hang us. No one, as far as I knew, had any idea that we had been taken or were in the custody of the Iraqi authorities. Even if our families and employers and governments found out where we were, what could they possibly do to get us out?

A man with an unmoving thin face came round the cell block and passed two hot boiled eggs wordlessly through the bars of my door. I hate boiled eggs, but I leapt up from my blankets and took them. Perhaps this was the day's food ration. I had no appetite but told myself that I would need the fuel. So I peeled away part of the shell. And then I gave up and left the eggs on the concrete floor, amid the dust. It was hard to care about the dirt.

Fear came again, unwanted but utterly stubborn. Of all the options that faced me, the one I feared the most was torture. If it began, I knew that they would already have decided my guilt, and therefore the future would only be more torture followed by death. So I would beg them to shoot me if the torture began. And that began a new line of thought, one that at last gave me some comfort: if they declined to kill me at that stage, how could I kill myself?

From the floor I looked up and around the cell and identified some opportunities.

There were five nails hammered into a piece of wood on the opposite wall. They looked like they had been used as clothes hooks. A few other nails stuck out of the wall. All I would need was one. Or I could quietly break the glass in the window and use that. An easier and deeper cut. It would make a mess, slashing my wrists, but hopefully the blankets would soak up enough of the blood so that I would die before a guard noticed.

Overhead was the fan that was firmly attached to that hook in a steel bar in the reinforced concrete that formed the ceiling of the cell. If I ripped a strip off my pajamas and turned it into a noose, I could hang myself. The fan was just the right height—low enough for me to reach up and tie the knot, high enough so that I could dangle. I doubted that I would be allowed to hang long enough before a guard came by though.

Probably the quickest option—and somehow my least favorite—

would be electrocution. I could simply rip out the cable from the wall that led to the fluorescent strip light above my head and hold on. I worried that the voltage would not be sufficient. It could be pain for nothing.

The quiet nail seemed like the best option.

Perhaps all suicidal thoughts are at the very least tinged with cowardice, no matter the circumstances. But killing myself seemed like it would be an attempt to reclaim control over my life, even by ending it. It would be my choice, not the choice of strangers. It was my life, not theirs. I would run at the firing squad, too, if they chose to shoot me. I would try to grab one of their rifles on the way to the wall against which I would be shot. I would take one or more of them with me.

Those fantasies ebbed and I returned to suicide, which remained realistic. Fear rushed back and the strangely comforting narrative of death by my own hand slipped away under a sudden deluge of panic. I lay on my side and sank my teeth into the base of my right thumb.

What have I done? This is all my fault, I thought. I don't do this job to help people, I thought, or to throw light on unseen parts of the world. That's all just bullshit that I tell myself. I do it to satisfy some dishonorable, selfish urge to taste death and danger without suffering the consequences. I should have left Iraq earlier when other journalists were pulling out. Moises would not be here if I had not been so blinkered about staying, and now it's going to get him killed. We had worked in some dangerous spots together, and I knew he had his own bank of experience from which he could draw his own conclusions. I always told him that he should make his own decisions when it came to risky situations, particularly in the days before the war, but we both knew, in the unspoken way we often had with each other, that there was no way in hell that he would have left if I had insisted on staying. Now he was going to die.

I will cause such grief among my family and friends. I have let my newspaper down. They put their faith and trust in me, letting me stay in Iraq to cover the war and all I have done is end up in prison. I have failed at my job in the most emphatic way. And when they realize that we have disappeared and are not just on our way to the Syrian border or hiding out in a safehouse in the city, they will go through a different kind of hell, perhaps no better than my own.

Why didn't we leave? Why do I push those limits? If we ever do get out of here, I'm going to give up journalism. I'm going to open a restaurant, a bar. I'm going to work for a charity. I'm going to hide somewhere and atone somehow. My girlfriend is going to hate me for putting her through this. My family will live with a sadness for the rest of their years. Nothing pained me more than their pain.

And my colleagues from other newspapers will be pulled out because of our disappearance, and they will resent us for that. At best, their lives in Baghdad will be full of increased anxiety and tension.

I'm sorry. I'm sorry I'm doing this to you, I said to them all through the walls of my cell and across the thousands of miles to London and New York. And then I found myself apologizing to God, in whom I did not believe.

Perhaps crying would unload some of the panic, give me a little break from the panic. I turned to lie on my left side, facing away from my cell door. I didn't want the guards to see this. I tensed my stomach and my face, trying to kick-start tears. Nothing happened. Perhaps it's too hard to cry for someone for whom you feel little but contempt, even if it's yourself.

I looked at the hairs and dead insects trapped in the weave of the blanket and fell asleep.

My dreams were about the prison and when I awoke the reality was worse. It was beginning. The torture. I could hear the electricity in the corridor. I could see the white flash bouncing onto the walls of my cells. Only yards from me, someone must be absorbing an enormous voltage into his body. And yet there were no shouts, no voices at all. Perhaps they were just warming up the machine, getting it ready. The electric charge gave off an unmistakable sound. It hummed and crescendoed, filling every corner of the cell block with its growing threat, and then the charge was unleashed in a massive buzzing. That's when the white flashes came.

I lay on the floor and didn't move. I was surprised that they would begin the torture so soon—I guessed it was early afternoon, judging by the bright light in my window—and turned to gaze at the nails sticking out from the wall. Perhaps I should do it now, just score my wrists and fall asleep for the last time.

Again and again, the electricity rose until it burst with fury in that buzzing.

But no screams, no talking.

I don't know how long it took for me to realize that it wasn't torture I was hearing. This was the sound of welding. A man in the corridor was welding metal together. Perhaps it was meant to scare us, but they were not going to use it on us yet.

Actually, there was a very good, practical reason why they would be welding now: For some reason, they didn't have the keys to the doors of the cells. Either these cells had been empty for a long time or they had not been locked recently. Now all they had was padlocks, hooked through the new metal loops the man was welding onto the doors.

By the time he finished his job, another noise had taken over. It was the wind that had been building all day, causing the dust storm that for a while trapped the American and British forces in the desert. I guessed that their advance would be slowed down and cursed the weather because I had begun to fantasize that they would soon be here to rescue us. The cold wind rushed in through the open half of my window and between the bars of my cell door, powdering my body, my hair, and every surface in the cell with red dust.

Molly began to cough in the cell next to mine.

For one of the first times of many to come, I managed to escape for a few minutes into the memory of a film, a novel. In *The English Patient,* Katherine and Almasy are trapped in their car in a desert sandstorm. The Hungarian explorer tells the married Englishwoman of the different kinds of winds as they fall in love. Winds so fierce that they challenge armies in full battle dress to attack them; winds that carry red desert sand to the skies above the south of England until it rains blood on the coastline.

Footsteps sounded in the corridor and came closer.

"What is your name?" asked a man I had never seen before.

"276," I said, worried that I would fall into a trap by giving my real name rather than my prison name.

"Not number, your name," he said.

"Matthew," I said.

"Come, Matthew," he said. Another guard brought the key to the padlock on my door and I stepped out and followed the man down the corridor. It was nighttime and the dust softened the glare of the lights.

Down the corridor, a right turn out of the building into what seemed to be the garden area and straight along a path with walls to my right. I would find out weeks later that with each step I was coming closer to a building that had become the wartime interrogation center of the Mukhabarat, perhaps the place in Iraq that anyone who was not a Mukhabarat officer would least want to be. It was run by men from a particularly powerful organization within the Mukhabarat know as Al-Hakmiya—the judgment. The Hakmiya men were the intelligence service's interrogators. I had deep worries about what lay ahead in the building, but my investigators had already used their first technique of psychological softening up without my even realizing it. They simply let a new prisoner sit alone for a while, allowing the natural acid of fear to strip away any remaining feelings of resistance and deception. It had already worked on me: I wanted to talk, I wanted to see someone who had the authority to decide my future. I wanted to persuade them that this was a mistake.

I followed the man all the way, padding slowly behind him in my flip-flops through the haze and wind. He led me into the single-story building, a cell block with larger cells and even more ornate murals. In the corridor were other prisoners, none of them Westerners. They were all blindfolded. Some of them stood motionless. Others squatted on their haunches facing a wall. All wore the same blue-and-white striped pajamas that I did.

The man led me into an office on the left side of the corridor. It was a large cell turned into an office, the furniture spare; a desk, with two white plastic chairs at each side and another directly in front of the desk but separated from it by a distance of about four yards. This would be my chair.

There were three men in the room, all in uniform.

"Sit down, Matthew," said the man behind the desk. It was Abu Ibrahim. He was smoking an *argileh*, a water pipe, and had changed out of his relaxed civilian wear of the morning.

"Hello, Matthew," said a heavyset man to my right, sitting on a plastic chair in front of the desk. I had seen him when checking in. He gave me a look full of scorn and chuckled as he said my name.

"Hello," said the third man, sitting to Abu Ibrahim's right. He wore glasses and had a red kaffiyeh wrapped around his head. A short man, I could tell. He had a kindly face and immediately I wanted us to be friends.

I sat on the plastic chair in front of the wooden desk with my feet flat on the ground. It was cold.

"Are you being treated OK?" Abu Ibrahim asked.

"Yes, thank you," I said.

"What is that?"

Abu Ibrahim pointed to my right thigh and his eyebrows came together in concern. There was a large tear in the pajamas. I had no idea how it had appeared there. When I had gone to sleep it had been whole. "It's fine," I said. "It's no problem."

"Mister Matthew," said the man with the glasses, "we have some questions for you. It is important that you answer them truthfully."

He was clearly going to be the translator. His English sounded excellent. "Of course," I told him.

First, the basics. Abu Ibrahim asked the questions and wrote down the answers in a file on his desk. What was my name? What was my nationality? When was I born? What was my job? How long had I worked for *Newsday*? Where did I live? Where had I lived in the past?

This was when I told my first lie. "Tell them everything," I had whispered to Moises as we had sat in the corridor of the processing

wing earlier in the day, briefly out of earshot of the guards. He had
nodded. I knew that if he and I started giving them different stories
then we were in trouble. We could not lie. But it was impossible for
me to answer this question truthfully.

"I lived in New York before London," I said.

In fact, I had lived in Jerusalem for four years. But when you're sitting in prison in Iraq facing the Mukhabarat you simply do not own
up to having lived in Israel. Or even to having visited the Jewish state.
My situation was bad enough—a Briton working with a Spaniard for
an American newspaper. The two of us formed our own little axis of
evil. An Israel connection could sink us, if we weren't already sunk.
I sent a silent, beseeching message to *Newsday*—take all mention of my
time in Israel off the newspaper's website. And another to Moises—
just tell them you don't know where I've been living.

The man in the red kaffiyeh began to ask more difficult questions. They knew things already. I wondered whom they had talked
to, how much they knew of our movements.

"Mister Matthew, our information indicates that you were asking
the identity of certain buildings before the bombing began. Which
ones, and why were you asking?"

I had only asked Yousef these questions, I thought.

"Yes, that's right. I knew the Americans were likely to bomb
Baghdad and I wanted to know what these big buildings were."

I listed the buildings I remembered asking Yousef about. "I wanted
to know what that big one that looked like a ziggurat was," I said, "the
one that was bombed so much. It's in the Republican Palace compound and it looks like this." I made the shape with my hands. The
best thing I could do was to be as open as possible with them, I had
decided. Make them see that I had nothing to hide.

The translator paused and then stared at me before asking this
question. My new friend's face had changed and now I felt completely alone in the room.

"Mister Matthew, what were your plans if the war started?"

"Well, we had bought a generator and car batteries for power,
and lots of bottled water, and . . ."

"Mister Matthew, you are being asked a very specific question. What were your plans? Your answer is important."

I didn't know what he wanted to hear. I came up with more information about our logistical planning, and there was now a hint of anger in the translator's stare. Abu Ibrahim took no notes. This was not what they wanted to hear.

"What were your plans?" he asked.

Then something occurred to me.

"We had a room at another hotel, the Al-Dar, five minutes' walk from the Palestine. We had that room in case there was a civil war or chaos and we needed somewhere nearby to hide."

Abu Ibrahim nodded and looked at the translator with a small smile, as the smoke from his pipe floated around him. I had told him something that seemed to confirm what he already knew. And it only added to my feeling that they had interrogated Yousef already. Or perhaps, I wondered, was Yousef one of them? Was he perhaps listening in to this in the corridor? Would he appear at my cell door and tell me how silly I had been? I hated myself for thinking it.

"And what else?" the translator asked.

This was the most awful moment I had yet faced. In a split second, I had to make a calculation about whether to reveal a piece of information that could endanger an entire Iraqi family as well as Moises and me. A family that had shown us only kindness and courage. Yousef's family. And yet if I lied and they had already found out from Yousef what our plans were, what favors he had done us, then we would be in even worse shape, and so would he. It was a calculated risk, ringed with cowardice. And it had the bitter taste of betrayal.

"We had agreed with our driver that if things got really out of hand we could hide at his house," I said.

Abu Ibrahim nodded again, showing no surprise. I think he knew already. His face always seemed to suggest that nothing I could say could possibly surprise him. He sucked on his pipe with one hand and scribbled notes with the other. He gazed at me across his desk, his eyes barely blinking.

"What is your driver's name?"

"Yousef."

"Was this your idea or his idea?"

"Our idea," I said. "But we had actually decided against it by the time we were in the Palestine because the situation had changed. We were not going to stay there."

The translator looked at me again.

"Mister Matthew," he said, "did you leave any of your luggage at Yousef's house?"

I had been dreading this one but to deny it now would, I believed, have made it worse.

"Yes," I said, "a small satellite phone."

"Did you teach him how to use it?"

"No," I said, speaking the truth.

"Who translated for you when you were working?"

"Yousef," I said.

"Why did you not get a minder from the ministry?"

I explained the whole story about our visas and why we had not gone to the Ministry of Information. At the end, the three men conferred and then paused in silence for a bit.

"Mister Matthew," said the translator, echoing Abu Ibrahim's question, "would you agree that you violated the rules of the ministry?"

They looked at me, and I had less than a second to try to calculate whether an acknowledgment of my indiscretions would be taken as a sign of good faith or a confession to a capital offense.

"Yes," I said, and Abu Ibrahim smiled and nodded. "But we did it for a good reason. We felt a strong moral duty to be in Baghdad to cover the war from here, from inside Iraq. We pushed the limits and broke some rules. And I am very sorry that we did. But we did it so that our newspaper could offer its hundreds of thousands of readers an accurate perspective of the war and of the Iraqi people. That's all we came here to do, and that's all I want to do now. Please let us go back to the Palestine Hotel and let us continue our work."

The interrogation was winding down, I could tell. Abu Ibrahim seemed satisfied and relaxed. We would talk more tomorrow, the translator said. I should be prepared to come up with more information.

"Matthew, how do you see the war?" Abu Ibrahim asked me, almost as an aside.

"It is a stupid war," I said, seeing an opening. "Bush and Blair are crazy. This country has not attacked the United States or Britain, so I don't understand why Bush has attacked. But they do not understand that the Iraqi people will fight them. The last story I was writing was about how the war seemed to be changing, about how things were going badly for the Americans and how the Iraqi people are united."

"Of course we are," Abu Ibrahim said, smiling in a subtly amused way. "We will all fight. I will fight."

"I want to be here to record that," I said.

"You can come with me to the front line, then," he said, laughing.

"Yes, yes, I would love that. I would come even though the Americans would shoot me too probably. You will take me to the front?"

He laughed, avoided answering, and I laughed too.

"Is there anything you need?" asked Abu Ibrahim in his gentlest voice.

"Could I have a cigarette, please?"

The translator handed me an unopened pack of Viceroy cigarettes, and when I peeled open the pack and asked for a light he gave me his lighter too, urging me to keep it. He was my friend again.

"Could I call my friends to let them know I'm okay?"

The translator turned to Abu Ibrahim, who lost his smile in a second.

"No," he said.

There was no ashtray. So I got up from my chair and, with the translator's permission, stubbed my cigarette out on the concrete floor beyond the patch of carpet we were all sitting on. The interrogation was over. I was still alive. They hadn't hurt me. But I felt no separation from my fear.

A different man led me out of the building, holding my right forefinger in his hand and pulling me through the night. I glanced at Moises and Johan as I passed their cells, their pale faces gazing at me with silent, unanswerable questions.

There was a piece of boiled chicken in broth cooling in a blue plastic bowl on the floor of my cell when I returned. I heard Moises— they knew him as Musa, the Arab version of his name—being taken for interrogation. I peeled bits of flesh from the chicken and ate as much as I could before lying down on my blanket.

They kept the fluorescent light above my head on all the time, but eventually I fell asleep under its humming white glow. Through the murk of unconsciousness, I heard what sounded like a sail or a huge tarpaulin suddenly filling out with the wind and snapping tight. Just outside our block, it happened again, and again, a jolting, massive noise. And then from far away came the gentle whistle of jet engines. In Baghdad it had been hard to hear the planes as they came in from the desert, their bombs usually appearing out of nowhere, but out here they sounded almost overhead.

After the first bomb fell, shaking the concrete that I was lying on, I realized that the sharp, billowing sound I had heard outside was an antiaircraft gun, firing its pointless rounds into the sky and turning Abu Ghraib into a target that it would surely not have otherwise been. Why would the Americans and British bomb a prison known to hold political prisoners, the enemies of Saddam? Now they had a good reason to do so: to defend themselves from the gun battery.

I was delighted. Bomb us, bomb us, I yearned to tell the pilots. Knock down the walls, cause panic, give us a chance of breaking out. I'd rather die like that than at the hands of these men. Come on. Blast this place to hell.

More bombs fell, shaking every cinder block, every bar. They were closer than anything I had experienced in Baghdad. And as they fell I decided that they were not, after all, such a good idea. My escape fantasy faded. The bombs would just kill us, and if they didn't happen to wipe out our part of the prison, who might vengeful and terrified guards be more likely to take it out on than five suspected Western spies?

The bombing seemed to carry on all night. I drifted in and out of sleep as the raids came and went.

In the morning, I found peace for the first time.

Outside, through the holes in my concrete latticed window, the sky was orange. The sunlight that could get through the sandstorm was filtered by the red dust. I tried to eat some of the tasteless rolls that a guard had handed me through the bars, but I needed water to get the few mouthfuls down. My stomach did not want food.

So I lay down on my back, searching as ever for a way to lie with a little physical comfort. My hip bones were already bruised from lying on my sides. Face down, while best for sleeping, wasn't the cheeriest way to spend the daylight hours. And it hurt my neck. But the problem with lying on my back was the pressure it put on my coccyx, the weight of my lower back and thighs bearing it down into the concrete. Then I found a new way. I slid my hands under my buttocks, slightly raising my pelvis and taking the pressure off my tailbone. I knew that sooner or later my hands would go numb, but for a while it felt good. Somehow it calmed my mind, too, to be lying in such a passive, vulnerable way.

"I have no control over this situation," I told myself. "I have no power. There is nothing I can do. If they take me to kill me, I will walk easily and stand there and accept it. I have lived thirty-three years, and I've been in love, I've had great friends, and I have loved my work. Everyone dies at some stage. If it happens now to me, that's okay. It's okay."

And I thought of people who had gone to unjust deaths with calm and dignity, and in spite of my atheism the strongest images— I felt I could almost see them levitating in front of me—were of Jesus and Joan of Arc in their last moments. It is possible to die like that, I told myself. If they can do it, I can.

Five minutes later, the fear came back like a torrent. But over the next days I would increasingly find myself capable of working back to that state of acceptance, understanding that my own powerlessness rendered worrying a pointless way of spending the time. I did not want to forget who I was. I did not want to finish my life in a moment of pathetic groveling and crying.

In weaker moments, there was a story that came to me. Luckily, none of the others in our group of five knew it until I told them when we were safely in Jordan.

In 1989, Farzad Bazoft, a British freelance journalist of Iranian descent, came to Iraq for London's *Observer* newspaper. One day he drove out to a facility where Iraq was widely believed to be developing its nuclear weapons program. Bazoft scooped up some soil from outside the complex and put it in his pocket. His plan was to take it back to Britain to be analyzed for traces of radioactivity; and if it tested positive, he would have his scoop. Instead, he was arrested and tried for spying. He was held at Abu Ghraib. The court sentenced him to death by hanging.

About two days before we were arrested, a reporter friend had told a group of us some of the details about Bazoft's case.

The indications were that the court—at the direction of Hussein, who was under growing international pressure to let the matter slip— would pardon Bazoft when he appealed. It didn't. That left the British consul with an awful duty. He drove to Abu Ghraib and went to see Bazoft, who was in a hopeful mood. "I'm sorry to tell you," the diplomat told the journalist, "that they have turned down your appeal. And they will carry out the sentence in twenty minutes."

As he drove back from the prison to the embassy, the ambassador noticed a vehicle following him. At the embassy the vehicle stopped and some men got out, dumping a large sack on the street. It was Bazoft's body.

This happened when Iraq and Britain had rather friendly relations. An international campaign had failed to save the man's life. Furthermore, Bazoft was indeed innocent. (After the fall of the regime, the *Observer*'s Ed Vulliamy tracked down the former Mukhabarat agent who arrested and interrogated Bazoft. The man, not realizing he was speaking with a journalist, acknowledged that he knew all along that Bazoft was innocent.)

I started to tell myself other stories, as slowly as possible, so that

they would take up as much time as possible. First I traced my love
life from the first time I took a girl to the movies in Edinburgh until
the last email I had sent my girlfriend from the Palestine Hotel. It
was hard to keep the story on track, with fear frothing into the flow
from unseen tributaries, but eventually I got to the end. And then I
began my life again in different versions—work, family, friends,
vacations. I spun the stories out for hours.

Apart from interrogations, the only other times we were allowed out
of our cells was when we went to the bathroom. Walking back from
the bathroom, always accompanied by the guard who had taken me
there even though it was only a few yards from my cell, I could see
Philip and Molly. Philip always seemed to be asleep on his blanket,
but Molly's face was often close to the bars. She would stand up and
look at me as I walked past. Smiling would have been ridiculous but
it was a look of comfort and solidarity.

Sometime that second day we started tapping on the wall that
stood between us. Initially, it was two taps, quiet enough so that the
guards did not hear us. Then it was three. Three taps seemed more
unmistakably an intentional communication than two taps.

It was just a sound but it meant a half dozen different things to
me, and, as I found out later, to Molly.

"Hey."

"You there?"

"You okay?"

"It'll be all right."

"Glad you're back from interrogation."

"Be strong."

And the response—tap, tap, tap—always meant "yes" and never
"no."

I heard that tapping again when the footsteps came down the
corridor that second night. This time Abu Ibrahim himself came to
get me. I didn't know what to make of that. He asked me how I was.
"Cold," I said. The temperature had dropped in the storm. The two
blankets did not come close to keeping me warm.

"I will get you a third blanket," he said, without hesitation. That meant I'd be coming back from this trip, I immediately thought, and then a second later I realized that a little lie like that would be effortless for Abu Ibrahim. "Come with me."

With that easy stroll, he ambled through the dusty night down a different path to a different cell block, and I followed him. He was so confident, so relaxed. He had told me the night before that he was utterly unafraid of the American and British forces, and that he would fight them without hesitation, and I believed him. Now, he walked with his back to me, his hands in his pockets. I could have picked up a stone and smashed it into his head. But he knew that I wouldn't.

We entered the building, past two murals of Saddam—in one he held a giggling little girl on his lap—and down a corridor.

"Wait here, Matthew," he said, disappearing for a few moments into another cell, this one with a solid steel door. He came back out.

"Come."

Inside were about twelve men, all in uniform. Behind the desk at the end of the room was a man who was obviously senior to them all, including Abu Ibrahim. When he spoke, they fell silent. A portrait of Saddam seemed to hover just above his head. There was a computer on his desk. As I sat down on a couch I smiled and nodded. He slightly inclined his head toward me and did not smile back. Abu Ibrahim sat down opposite me, next to the translator, who was the only other man I recognized in the room.

I immediately asked for a cigarette. I had smoked the whole pack the translator had given me the night before and yearned for another. Instead, the men looked surprised at my audacity. One of the two sitting on the couch next to me grudgingly offered me one, and I lit it and smoked it immediately. This did not look like it was going to be as friendly as the first interrogation. If anyone smiled, it was because someone had made a joke in Arabic while motioning to me.

"Mister Matthew, we have continued our investigation," said the translator, who was holding some papers. On the coffee table in front of him were some of my possessions, including my Palm Pilot. "We have found that in our discussion last night you have not been open with us, and you have been dishonest with us."

He paused and let it sink in. I leaned forward in my pajamas and put my elbows on my knees. "I promise you," I said, "I am being absolutely open and honest. I have nothing to hide."

"Tonight you must be more honest with us. Your future depends on it. Do you understand? You must now tell us more."

"What do you want to know?" I asked, a little desperation escaping into my voice.

"You must tell us more information."

They want me to hang myself, I thought. They're not asking me specific questions. They're simply scaring me into confessing my wrongdoings.

"Okay, I thought about two things overnight that I forgot to mention," I said. "There is a satellite phone hidden in our flak jacket. And I also remembered that we left a digital camera with Yousef."

That seemed like a good start. (It was also not true. We had not left a camera with Yousef. To this day I do not know where I came up with that false memory.) They looked like they knew all this already and just wanted to test me, to see how open I was really being. They seemed ready to hear anything, true or false. I wonder now how much they really did know.

"What else?"

"Do you want to know what other stories I did? I'm sure I didn't tell you all the stories I did last night."

And so I listed every single story I could think of that I had written in Iraq, counting them on my fingers. There was the one about the Al-Karkh soccer team when they played the Air Defense team, I said. There was one about how Iraqis were buying guns to protect themselves. There was one about a visit to a Sufi temple.

"Which *takyia* was it?" the translator asked.

"I can't remember its name but it began with a K. Kad . . . Kal . . . I don't remember."

"Takyia Kasnazan?"

"Yes, that was it," I said.

"Why did you go to the *takyia*?"

"I wanted to see the ceremony, where they all move their heads about and spear themselves with metal rods and cut their tongues, and I wanted to see how different sects of Islam can coexist in Iraq so easily," I said, deliberately playing to the regime's insistence that there was no religious discord in Iraq. "They were very kind. They gave us dinner and we watched the ceremony. They were praying for peace."

"Who did you meet there?"

"I can't remember his name, but we met one of the leaders," I said. "He had a big beard. And some others who joined us at dinner."

The translator wanted to know more. Who else did I meet? Did I go back to the *takyia*? Where in Baghdad was it?

"I can't remember," I said, unable to work out why on earth they cared so much about a story that was as apolitical as any I had done. Eventually they moved on and asked me who else I knew in Baghdad. I searched my memory and came up with a few other names of people I had written about and met.

"What about Intesar?" the translator asked.

"What's that?" I asked, not recognizing the word.

"Intesar, at the Amariya shelter."

"Oh, yes, her. We went to the shelter and she showed us around. She was very kind and helpful. A very lovely woman." An informer, I thought immediately.

"How many times did you meet her?"

"Just that one time," I said. The translator looked at me with doubt in his face but didn't press the point.

"Mister Matthew," the translator said, once we had moved on a little. "Why did you write in your essay that Iraq is a 'devil regime?' "

This made my heart sink. Now they were fabricating accusations. Once they started that, could there be a way back to reality?

"I'm sorry but I didn't write that," I said.

Abu Ibrahim interrupted. "It is a very accurate translation of your essay," he said.

"You wrote, 'The American occupation of Iraq will be like the British occupation of the nineteenth century. As soon as there is a war in Iraq, there will be a revolution against the devil regime.' "

I looked at the translator and said, slowly: "I did not write that. I do not think this is a devil regime. I may believe and may have at times written that there is not as much freedom in this country as in other countries, but I did not call it a devil regime. Could I see the original?"

One of the men sitting on the same couch that I was perching on promised to bring it to tomorrow's interrogation.

There was a pause. The translator opened up my Palm III.

"You seem to have many relations with people in Israel," he said. "What is your relation with Amir Rappaport of *Yedioth Aharanoth*?"

One of my greatest fears had suddenly come true. In his hands the translator had proof that I must have been to Israel and had hundreds of contacts there. As it happens, I have never even spoken with Amir Rappaport, an Israeli journalist with *Yedioth*, Israel's most popular newspaper. I just happened to have his number. But that seemed irrelevant, so I took the only tack I thought was now reasonable. I went slightly on the offensive.

"Listen, I have been to Israel many, many times," I said, trying to look as relaxed as possible. "Many times, and I have no apologies for it. I cover the Intifada, and I have hundreds of Palestinian names in there and hundreds of Israeli names. I'm a journalist. It's a very big story, the Intifada, and a very important one."

The translator fiddled around with my Palm. He asked me about a name I had never heard, an Arab name.

"Can I see?" I said and stood up to look at the entry. I noticed that it was under "Mohamad's Lebanon Phones." This looked like a lucky break to me.

"That's actually a note from my colleague, *Newsday*'s Mohamad Bazzi, my friend," I said.

This intrigued them. I had an Arab colleague.

"Where's he from?"

"He was born in Beirut and is Lebanese-American," I said. There was a murmur around the room as the translator explained to the gathering what I had said.

"You also have the number for Ahmed Chalabi," the translator said. Chalabi was a leading Iraqi opposition leader who was based in London. I had interviewed him there four years earlier. I explained this to the interrogators.

"And you have numbers for the PUK and the KDP," he said, referring to the antiregime Kurdish groups that held power in the autonomous northern region of Iraq.

"I went there when I first visited Iraq in 2001," I said. "I spoke to them. That was in the days when you could drive from Baghdad to the north without any problems."

"You drove from Baghdad?"

"Yes."

"We have information that you entered from Iran," said the man sitting next to me. This was another fabrication and I felt desperate again.

"No, that's not true. I can prove it. I went with a minder from the Ministry of Information whose name is Saad and a Kurdish driver from the ministry, Goran. You can check with them."

Abu Ibrahim made a note.

"Mister Matthew, that is all for now," the translator said. "We will meet again tomorrow morning. And I want you to think very hard between now and then of the other people you know in Iraq. I want you to tell us their names. And any other information that you think we should know."

I translated that as: "In the morning, you will have your last chance to tell us the names of your fellow spies in the ring that you are clearly a part of. If you do not tell us, the consequences will be grave."

I did not want to leave things this way. The interrogation had gone badly. They thought I was close with Israel and the Iraqi opposition. They thought I had written that the government was a "devil regime." They had some inexplicable interest in our visit to the *takyia*. They thought I was lying. I wanted to stay, to explain myself more, to persuade them to let me go. Tomorrow could see the beginning of the pain, I thought, and I wanted to fend it off.

"I have nothing to hide, nothing," I told the translator. "I'll tell you anything you want to know."

A man led me into the corridor and along to the large room with the murals of Saddam Hussein. About six men gathered round me, making jokes.

"How old are you?" one asked.

"Thirty-three," I said. There was a murmur.

"Beautiful," he said, and I gazed at the ground and thought of the condom packet under the desk.

At first it sounded as if the guards, who played pool throughout the night in a room at the end of the cell block, were having a play fight or, at worst, an argument over what the house rules might be at Abu Ghraib.

The clicking of the pool balls had stopped. Shoes that usually padded or snapped down the concrete hallway between the two rows of cells were rushing this time. Several pairs of shoes or boots. There was shouting too.

A body thudded to the ground and now one of the shouting voices was coming from the level where I lay, on the cold floor of my cell. That voice was different from the others. It wasn't that it was quieter, because the man was calling out almost as loudly as the others in this group. But it came from a throat contracted by fear. It seemed about two or three yards from me.

I recognized one of the other voices. It belonged to a guard who had broad shoulders and wore wire-rim glasses. He walked like an unneutered tabby cat, in small, wide steps with his feet pointing out slightly. When we checked into the prison, he had searched the pockets of my black fleece, pulling a drawstring tight around my waist for no apparent reason. He had stood beside me as I stripped to my boxer shorts and put on my blue-and-white striped prison pajamas. In our new universe full of dark stars, I intuitively picked him out as perhaps one of the blackest, and ever since I had avoided eye contact with him whenever he walked past my cell door.

He had a loud voice normally, angrily barking commands to the Iraqi prisoners who occupied the cells opposite ours. His was a nonchalant aggression. Now his voice was unrestrained, furious. And it came in a new rhythm, alternating with another sound.

In the early 1990s, I once saw two men rush out of a warehouse building on a quiet street in downtown Manhattan with baseball bats to beat up a man who looked like a drug addict. The man had been clumsily, hazily trying to break into a car. The sound of the bats against his gangly body has always stayed with me. That was the sort of sound I was hearing now, alternating with the shouts of the heavy-set guard.

The prisoner was on the ground and he was being beaten with something that wasn't a fist or a boot. A shout and then that slightly resonant sound of flesh and bone giving way to something very hard that was moving fast. And then another shout from the guard, another blow. It went on.

Voices mingled, but it sounded like the other guards were perhaps trying to persuade the big guard to ease up on the prisoner a little. But perhaps they were egging him on, because the beating did not stop, nor did the yelps coming from the tightened throat of the man on the ground.

The fluorescent strip above my head made me plainly visible to the men in the corridor, and I did not want to be seen watching. As soon as I had sensed the violence beginning, I turned onto my left side and lay motionless, staring at the painted marine blue strip that ran around the base of the walls.

Journalists are meant to bear witness: that's rather the point of our job. We watch and record and tell other people what we have seen, perhaps in the hope that an account, a witnessing, could eke away at badness. But I turned away and chose not to see anything.

Eventually the beating stopped and the man was dumped into his cell. The big guard seemed to have exhausted his fury. The block echoed as it always did when the iron bars of the prisoner's cell door was closed and the click of its padlock confirmed that he would not be leaving his room that night.

With each breath he made a sort of crying sound. Sometimes he broke that rhythm to exhale his pain with more force, and the otherwise silent block filled up with what I wondered might be the man's last gasps.

A guard ambled back and spoke to him, asking him a question. The man just continued to whine in agony and the guard walked away.

After a while, two guards came back. There were more questions, and this time the prisoner responded. The cell door opened and there was more talking, then the door was locked again and the two men walked away.

For a long time, the prisoner's whimpers filled the cells. Eventually silence came back to the block.

In the morning, I could see through the bars that the prisoner was alive. Moises told me later that he had seen blood on the floor.

Sometime over the next two days I betrayed the prisoner. I came to see the big guard as a source of some comfort. He smoked and I heard Molly successfully wheedle a cigarette from him.

"Beautiful?" he asked, out of my sight. I assumed he was asking Molly what she thought of his looks.

When he walked past I asked for a cigarette also, and the man held out a pack of extra-long, superthin Pine cigarettes that should really have been dangling from the fingers of a bejeweled beauty in an early Bond film. These were the "beautiful" things.

I thanked him with all the warmth I could generate. In prison, a cigarette was a companion, a comfort, a distraction, an unspeakable luxury.

"No problem," the man said in a gentle voice, smiling kindly.

Abu Ghraib did things like that—making me turn away from beating and then form a tiny alliance with the beater. In the second-by-second struggle to survive, I could unhesitatingly betray the very essence of human solidarity, and a deposit of guilt could be made on my soul.

10

The Hakmiya

MAY 1996

Travelling to the north of Iraq during Saddam's time, to liberated Kurdistan, was deceptively comforting. I drove up there from Baghdad in May 2001 with my friend Sandro Contenta from the *Toronto Star* when relations between Baghdad and the Kurdish leaders still permitted easy access to the north from the rest of Iraq. Among the rolling hills and devastated villages, we could talk to Iraqis and they could tell us of their hatred for Saddam. It was an enormous relief to be able to chat openly with Iraqis, and have them speak their mind. I suspect that Saad Jassim slipped into a similar comfort zone during his fatal trip there.

One day, Sandro and I asked our driver to take a detour off the main road so that we could look around one of the several palaces that Saddam had once used as a vacation spot. The driver's name was Goran and he was Kurdish, but he was also an employee of the Ministry of Information. Another colleague had told me about him, reminding me that in spite of his ethnicity, Goran was one of the ministry's "house Kurds." He would inevitably submit a report to the ministry upon our return about where we had been, whom we had spoken to, what we had asked. But for a short while, among the relaxing greenery and freedom of Kurdistan, I forgot.

Sandro and I were fascinated by the ruins of the palace. It stood above a small village and a manmade pond that the president had used for boating or fishing. After the Iraqi government forces had retreated in 1991, the Kurds laid waste to Saddam's country homes, leaving little but the outside walls remaining. We clambered over the masonry into the building, feeling closer than we ever possibly could in the rest of Iraq to being in the presence of Saddam himself. I had asked for an interview with Saddam and the then head of the press center smiled at me and explained that "the president sends his apologies." This is where he must have slept, we said, peering into a rubble-strewn bedroom. It was strangely thrilling. We moved on to the largest room. This is where he must have eaten, we said. The walls of this room were lined with molded plaster, colored in the pastels typical to Moroccan interior design.

This is so cool, I thought, and I bent down and picked up a piece of the plaster. I'm going to take home a chunk of one of Saddam's palaces. As we walked back to the car, I began to have doubts. Isn't this the kind of thing that got Bazoft into trouble? I asked myself. Goran opened the trunk so that I could put my souvenir into my bag. He said nothing but looked troubled.

"You know what, I don't really want this," I said, and chucked it on the ground. Goran looked relieved. It wouldn't have to go in his report. I wouldn't have to hide it. My piece of plaster was utterly harmless, but it was a souvenir of one of the president's defeats. It was his property. And it could get me into trouble. Kurdistan, as it had Saad several years earlier, had lured me into forgetting that Saddam could still reach this far.

"To hell with you, Saad," said the man Saad never saw because he was always wearing a blindfold when the man tortured him. "We're getting nowhere."

The Hakmiya officer picked up the phone in the interrogation room and spoke to the guards, telling them to take Saad away and then "get rid of him." He'd had enough. All the torture, the questions, the weeks of solitary confinement had apparently not produced the answers that he needed. What really scared Saad was how relaxed the man suddenly sounded and how pleasant the guard was who came to fetch him.

With his hands bound, as ever, he was led along the corridor to the elevator. Saad could tell that it was going all the way to the basement. He'd been on this journey before and he knew what was down there. It was the main torture room, the place with the ingenious instruments of pain. The elevator stopped with a gentle tug, the doors slid open, and they stepped out and along the familiar route to the room that Saad calls "the worst place on earth."

"This guy's going to take care of you," the soft-voiced guard told Saad, handing him over to another man in the torture room.

There were other voices in the room, as usual. But this time they talked among themselves about shooting their victim instead of hauling him up from a pulley and beating him for hours. One of the men guided the sightless Saad toward a wall.

"Hey, move aside so you won't get hurt," a voice said.

"Move away from him so you won't get blood on your clothes," another one warned. Neither of the men were talking to Saad.

The leading voice told Saad that he was going to ask him a question. "Why don't you tell the truth? This is your last chance."

"I'll sign anything you want, anything," Saad said.

"Okay, there's no use for this guy. Prepare yourself."

Saad heard the sound of a gun being cocked. For some reason, his fear had left him. He felt calm, ready to die. He had had a lot of time to think in the Mukhabarat's custody and he had felt and thought things that he would never have imagined. If this was to be his fate, then so be it.

He heard the gunshot and at the same moment felt a searing pain under his left nipple. But the round was a blank and the small circle of fire pushing into his chest was the tip of a lit cigarette. The guards led him back to his cell. He still has the scar.

They used various methods of torture on Saad. During his first three days in the Hakmiya building, where he had been taken in a minibus from the Mukhabarat building in Mosul, his new interrogator would ask him questions, and when he did not receive the answer he wanted to hear, Saad would feel the lash of a cable across his back. Sometimes the man would attach two wires to different parts of Saad's body—his ears, his lips, his tongue, his penis—and then Saad would hear the whirring of a hand-driven generator, the old-fashioned military sort. The interrogator would wind it up and then press the button. All Saad ever remembered was his initial scream, and then he would find himself lying on the floor some time later.

While he did face being hauled up and beaten in the torture room in the basement, he was spared some of the other implements they kept down there. They never forced him into a coffin and then nailed the lid shut and went away for hours. They never strapped him into the hydraulic chair with the hole cut out in the seat and the glass bottle positioned under the prisoner's anus. One man Saad knows, a Syrian, had bleeding spells for two years after his time in the chair.

But most agonizing was when they did nothing to you. And the longer nothing happened, every minute that Saad spent in his cell, his own thoughts tore into him more deeply than cables and electrodes ever could.

"Torturing is better than waiting," Saad told me. "This might sound strange. But the brain tortures itself. If you sit in the room, thinking what they want from you—especially when you don't know what they're going to do to you—that's torture itself. True, the body hurts, you start screaming, it's painful. But it's nothing like the brain. Nothing like the brain. I tell you that much."

After the war, in early July, I found one of the Mukhabarat's top career investigators living quietly, unemployed now, in his rented house in a predominantly Sunni neighborhood of Baghdad. A Shia, he had nevertheless climbed high in the Mukhabarat, which he had joined as a young man twenty-seven years earlier. In his first job he would clock

in from eight in the morning to two in the afternoon as a counteres-
pionage agent. He loved it so much that he would often stay into the
evening, reading and assessing the reports of field officers. Those were
the great days in the Mukhabarat, when all the new recruits were
highly educated and idealistic, he told me, smiling gently in the glow
of nostalgia. It was more than a second family, he said. He certainly
wasn't hired for his brawn; he's a short man, no more than five feet
three, with a graying moustache and a bit of a paunch.

Resolutely convinced that I worked for the CIA, MI6, or the
Mossad—he tested out his Hebrew on me after lunch one day—he
spoke as if to a fellow intelligence officer, just like a retired KGB agent
sharing laughs over a beer with his CIA counterpart in a movie. He
joked that I would have been lucky to have him as my interrogator in
Abu Ghraib. I insisted over and over that I was indeed a journalist,
but he would simply reply, with a certain degree of internal logic, that
seeing as all Iraqi journalists sent overseas had worked as spies for the
Saddam regime, then surely all journalists who came to Iraq must be
spies. To him, journalists and spies were basically the same thing. Even
the word *mukhabarat* reflects this blurring. It comes from *khabar*,
which means news, information, intelligence, report, rumor, message.
The prefix *mu* refers to the people who act in relation to the noun—
in this case, the people who seek news, information, or intelligence.
Within the contours of the word *Mukhabarat*, it's a fine line, then, between being an intelligence-gathering agent and a news-gathering reporter.

I had to promise him anonymity: he had a senior enough position
among the 10,000-strong staff of the Mukhabarat to be wanted by
the American forces. By the time the war started, he was head of
one of its most important investigative departments. The Hakmiya
building was one of his old haunts.

Toward the end of our second long chat, I asked Abu Thar, as I
shall call him, about torture.

"In my whole life as a Mukhabarat officer I never witnessed a case
when someone was forced to say anything against his will," he began,
with the absolute composure and slow, measured way of speaking I

had noted in Abu Ibrahim. "We have three approaches to getting someone to confess. The first is to make friends with him. I had so many friends, and I cried when they were executed. The other is to have them in a psychological war. We would tell him that his son had an accident or something, and when he felt that he was losing members of his family, he would collapse and start talking. Others with no good family relations would only fall for torture. Other guys said, 'I will confess anything, just don't lay a hand on me.'"

Once the detainee had signed his confession, he would go to the Hakmiya judge, Abu Thar explained. And the judge would ask the accused whether the confession was true and whether it had been signed under any physical duress. If the accused said that he had been tortured, the judge would send the case back for further investigation.

This seemed utterly logical and fair to Abu Thar. He was so much part of the Mukhabarat machine, so infused with the self-righteousness that I had found in every intelligence officer I had met, that he could not possibly see that a prisoner who had just been tortured into making a false confession might be so terrified of more torture that he would tell the judge that no, everything had been just hunky-dory and that he was guilty as charged.

I listed all the methods of torture that Saad and others had told me about, and Abu Thar nodded slightly at each one. These were "short-term methods, silly methods." But Abu Thar was refreshing in his willingness to admit to having used torture.

"As soon as I feel that the criminal is guilty and has no bond with his country, and there is strong evidence against him and he would not confess in the right way and had done a very, very bad thing against his country and against his people, we would use these means against him. All over the world treating such people in this way is a necessity. But 95 percent of my investigations were not about torturing and hitting people. Investigation is like a wrestling match between investigator and the guilty man. The successful investigator would not use methods of force or torture to achieve his aim."

What about the 5 percent? I asked. What was passing through your mind as you tortured someone?

"I would use this method but I would feel pain inside for the guilty man. But this was the only means I was left with. All over the world it depends on the type of guilty person. Some would be convinced if you slapped them in the face. Some if you just insulted them. Some of them would not confess unless you hit him with a rod or something like that. So it depends on the type of the guilty person. And how he responds to investigation. These methods are used all around the world."

Abu Thar wanted to tell me a story to show how inventive the top investigators in Iraq could be. One evening in the 1970s, the then head of General Security, Nadum Gazar, was having a drink in the small garden next to his office. He liked to go out there at night and cool down with an icy beer or two. As he sat there in the warm night, one of his investigators came and told him that the head of the Iraqi Communist Party, being held on charges of subversion, simply would not confess. They had tried everything and the guy was still holding out.

"Okay, bring me twenty bottles of beer and bring the guy to me," Gazar said.

When the communist leader arrived, Gazar asked him to take a seat.

"I thank you for your principles in not wanting to confess," he told the man. "It's your right. Now have a drink."

"Oh, come on, sir, how can I drink with you?" said the man, whose name has been lost to posterity.

"Let's consider ourselves friends," Gazar said.

The man started to drink and after a while had downed seven bottles. Finally, he said he had to go to the bathroom.

"You can't go unless you confess," said the relaxed security boss.

Gazar then ordered his officers to tie thread so tightly around the communist's penis that he could not urinate. And then he ordered the man to keep drinking. Another seven bottles went down his throat and with every gulp and every second, his pain increased. Eventually he broke down and confessed.

Abu Thar laughed as he told the story. "These methods really depend on the mind of the investigator," he said in admiration for Gazar's ingenuity.

Again and again as we spoke, he insisted, echoing the words of other intelligence agents, that Mukhabarat officers were not like the thugs who worked in Special Security and ran the ministries and fully infiltrated the Mukhabarat in the 1990s: the uneducated peasant louts from Tikrit, the distant relatives of Saddam who had no training and no restraint. They gave the Mukhabarat a bad name, Abu Thar told me. They dragged it down.

"So many people had bad ideas about the Mukhabarat. They think it is an instrument of the government, a brutal instrument or an unjust instrument. Yes, we used to follow the government's main line, but Mukhabarat people were mostly educated and lived abroad, so we knew how to deal with human beings and we could distinguish between good and bad. We had to follow the main line, but we had our own way. Not like those people coming from Tikrit who never mixed with other people."

When Saad was brought to the Hakmiya, the officers there gave him a number, 681.

"Six is your name, eight is your father's name and one is your grandfather's name," an officer told him, referring to the way Iraqi men are named.

"What is your name?" the officer asked.

"Saad Hamid Jassim."

"No, you're wrong. What's your name?"

"681," Saad said.

"That's right. Never mention your name. You are a number now."

The Hakmiya building stood opposite the passport office on Fifty-second Street in downtown Baghdad. Saad, like most Baghdadis, never knew what the unobtrusive, shiplike building was even though he had been to the passport office at least ten times. It was dust-colored, like most buildings in the city, and while the Arabic, Baathist star on the front gate suggested that this was a government office, there were no barred windows to suggest that it was the Mukhabarat's main center for detention and torture.

Saad's interrogator, who had been handed the make or break career assignment of procuring a damning confession from this American spy, was keen to see him immediately. It was only after two hours of countless questions and blows that Saad was led to his new home.

"Send him up," the interrogator told the guard, and Saad made his first trip to the second floor in the elevator. Like the exterior of the building, there was nothing about the elevator to suggest that its job was to ferry men back and forth from the physical torture of interrogation to the psychological torture of the cells. Its walls were of fake-wood Formica and a sign, in English, warned that "Children below school age must not use this lift unless accompanied by an adult."

The guard took off Saad's blindfold when he was in the cell. Then he closed the door, a solid metal slab with only a small flap in it to allow the guards to look inside or pass food through. As he adjusted to seeing things again, Saad felt like he had landed in a new sort of hell. Cell number 8 was red.

"Red walls, red door, red light, red ceiling, red floor, red plate, red cup. Red. It was completely red."

The red cell was about six feet wide and fifteen feet long. At the far end, partially hidden by a tiled wall, were a toilet and two faucets, one hot and one cold. There was no window. The only light came from the red bulb, protected by a square metal grille.

That night, Saad's brain began torturing itself. "I didn't know what to think. One thing for sure, I knew they were going to hang me. I knew that part. It's an indescribable feeling. I was singing one hour, crying the next. Praying. Thinking how to get myself out of there, not escaping really, thinking how to outsmart them, hoping that when they send me to the court I could talk to the judge and tell him that all this interrogation was bullshit and I would tell him my true story, hoping that, you know, something will come up and stop all this interrogation, all this horror."

Nothing stopped it.

"They open the door in the morning, call me for interrogation. I was getting up, terrified, walking with this guard, getting in the elevator, all the way to the interrogation room, sitting down. The interrogation started, the guy shooting questions, answering him, cables on my back, getting me out of the room, taking me to the big torturing room with all this big equipment in there. That's painful, but you know what's happening. The good thing is when they say, 'Take him back to his cell.' The rest of the day is a vacation. You just hope that that night doesn't end. But when the next day started, it's back to the thinking and wondering, and that's the real torture. The thing about them, the Mukhabarat people, they know how to fuck up your mind. No matter how smart you are, they have experience. They know how to deal with each case."

At the end of the third interrogation, Saad's Hakmiya officer told him: "Go back, think about the truth. I'm going to call you tomorrow and I'm expecting the truth."

Saad had already repeatedly confessed to spying. He had given details that weren't true but matched the fabrications he had begun in Mosul as accurately as he could remember them.

"He left me thinking, 'What does this guy want exactly? This is hanging itself. I just wrapped the rope around my neck. What else does he want?' This guy was asking for more. I didn't know what to tell him."

Saad was moved to cell number 49. It too was red. There the real torture started. The morning came and no guard came to collect Saad for the promised interrogation. It was the same the next day, and the next. No one came for four weeks. He almost missed being tortured. At least then he could have contact with other human beings. Saad was left alone to discover that he was his own most ruthless torturer.

He told me all this in early July in one of our many talks. Sticking to the facts, he had walked me through his interrogation process. And so I asked him what was going through his head during that time. He paused, as he often does when talking about his time in captivity, and as usual I remained silent and waited. But this time nothing came out.

I thought of an urge, or rather a calculation, that had visited me frequently in prison.

"Did you ever think of killing yourself?" I asked him. This elongated his silence, and then he finally spoke, talking about something he had not planned to tell me.

"I was lying down and I saw this light in the ceiling and it was covered with a metal box. I pulled out the lightbulb. There was a screw in the box. Somehow, I can't remember how, I took that screw off—maybe with a spoon or something. I took the bulb. I went behind—there is a little wall in the middle of the room that separates the toilet seat from the room. I sat behind that wall, I broke the lightbulb and pulled a piece of glass and I started cutting my wrist. Blood starts coming out. I was really crying. I was seeing the blood coming out and I remember my wife and my son. It was like I was facing death. I asked God to take care of my son."

Saad bled for an hour, and then his cuts closed and the blood stopped. He put his wrist under the tap again and still the blood wouldn't come.

"I was disappointed and happy at the same time. I was afraid that they will discover what I did and beat me again, punish me somehow for pulling that screw off and pulling that lightbulb. And I was happy because I didn't die. Something inside of me told me that there's still a chance you may get out of this. But believe me, in that cell there is no room for happiness and there is no room for hope. But somehow, I think because I stopped bleeding, I went back to my blanket and sat there. I took off my boxer shorts, wrapped my wrist, just sat there thinking of nothing, of what I just did. But at night the feeling came back to me, that I wanted to commit suicide again. So the next day I did it again. I slashed my wrists a second time. And then I started bleeding for more than two hours. I really wanted this thing to work, so I kept my arm under the water so the blood won't clot. So I kept bleeding for two hours. But the funny thing is, it hurts when I cut myself so I didn't cut myself deep. I had cut enough just to see the blood coming. The guards didn't notice because they leave you, apart from bringing food. The window on that door is [very small]. It's dark in there. When you're standing outside you have to get real close to the window to see what's going on inside. And they don't want to do that because it stinks in there. When they talk to you, they maintain a distance between them and the door."

With his wrist under the running water, Saad had more success—initially. He became weaker and weaker, eventually fainting on the floor of the cell. When he woke up it was all he could do to crawl over to his blanket. Sleep came again for a few hours.

"I opened my eyes and it was dark already. When I opened my eyes I heard the guy who brings dinner at the door. So I took my plate and handed it to the guy. He put some food in it and I took the plate, holding it with both hands and it was so heavy. One scoop of food and it felt so heavy because I had no strength at all. I put the plate on the floor and fell asleep again. I woke up the next day, wrapped my wrist and decided to forget about the suicide thing. I figured two attempts didn't work—it's not my destiny."

Resolving to leave his fate in the hands of others did not bring Saad peace. The weeks went past. After a month without his door opening once, the guard came and brought him for another interrogation. It was a relief to be out of cell number 49 once more, even if it was for more torture. After the session, it was back to the red isolation.

"You can't talk to nobody. I really wanted to see people, to talk to people. Being in that cell all alone, I was glad to see a cockroach. I was glad to see an ant passing by. This isolation thing brings thoughts to you that in your whole life you'd never think you'd be thinking. It makes you think you took your whole entire life for granted. Thinking about your dad, your mom, your baby brother, how you beat him up, how you shout at your mama. I was saying to myself, I wish I could get out of here and make it up to them. Sometimes I think I just wanted to say these things so I could get out. It was one way of tricking God."

When you have no one to talk to and no power over your future,

God tends to become the only available conversationalist. He was for me when I was in Abu Ghraib, and I didn't even believe in him. Saad believed, but he wanted proof.

"I was sitting, really giving up on everything. How can I get a miracle from God? I was talking to God like he's a friend of mine, someone who must answer me. 'If you really exist and if you are really a miracle man, show me a sign. Or something to prove that you are God and you are going to help me to get out of this.' "

All day long he prayed and insisted and challenged and nothing happened. And then, without warning, one of the guards opened the door to his cell. It was the first time in weeks that the door had creaked on its hinges. Its very opening was a huge event for Saad, even though it terrified him.

"Come out, stand right here behind the door," the guard said. "These guys, their toilet is busted and need to use your toilet. Stand right here."

One by one, three prisoners walked silently into Saad's cell, used the Western-style toilet and washed their hands. Without a word, they came back out and stood in the corridor. When they were all finished, the guard locked them in their cell and then put Saad back inside. The solid iron door slammed shut and Saad heard the lock turn. He was back in hell.

He glanced at the wall next to the toilet. And there, in white letters, was a message written by one of the visiting prisoners with Saad's bar of soap. "Be patient. God helps those who are patient."

Saad fell to the floor and began sobbing. "I knew then that this is the answer from God. Believe me, it was a major thing for me. It's like hope is back again to me, God exists, God has miracles. And I knew then that I'm going to get out of there alive. I knew there is hope for me."

The next time a guard opened Saad's door his time in solitary was over. He walked with the guard to cell 47 and when he stepped inside the much larger but equally red cell, he saw ten or twelve faces. And they were allowed to talk. After weeks alone, but for his time with his torturers, Saad couldn't stop the words from pouring out. Not only was he among others again, but he was with people who had been through it all before. Relax now, they told him. The worst is over. They would never let you out of solitary if they felt they had more to get out of you. It's almost over, one way or another.

Able to talk to others, he found new perspectives on things. It was the mid-1990's and Iraq was under pressure from the United States and the United Nations; to hang an American citizen would have been asking for trouble that the regime really didn't need, Saad and his cellmates reasoned. His conviction that he would be hanged faded away into a confidence that he would be spared. The American government would apply pressure and get him released as part of some kind of deal, he was sure.

Saad's fifth and final interrogation session convinced him that the next time he stepped out of the cell, it would be to go to court, where he would tell the judge that he was innocent, that he had given a false confession under torture. He knew from hearsay that if the judge rejected the confession he would be more likely to send Saad back for more interrogation than to release him, but it was a hope worth clutching at.

Four months after his arrival at the Hakmiya, Saad faced his final interrogation. It was brief and hurried. They asked him the same questions and let him go back to his cell. Two days later they came and took his photograph and his fingerprints. "My friends told me, 'This is it, it's over.' I knew the next time they call me it's going to be court. I waited for two or three weeks and then they called my number."

Blindfolded, number 681 was led on the familiar journey to the elevator and down to the basement. But this time they took a new route and the fifty or so prisoners whose court date had arrived were taken out of the building and put on a bus. Saad peeked out from under his blindfold at the outside world for the first time in months, the beaten-up orange-and-white taxis of Baghdad trundling past. One of the prisoners in cell 47 had cut out a square centimeter from the blocked-up window, and the dozen men in the room had sometimes taken turns gazing out onto the officers' parking lot. But now, to see the streets and cars and people gave Saad a connection with humanity that was, for a moment, euphoric.

The bus pulled up at the General Security headquarters. When Saad's blindfold was taken off, he was standing in the dock of a broad courtroom with wood-paneled walls. He was still in his pajamas and he was barefoot. Next to him was his interrogator. Although Saad had never seen the man's face he knew as soon as he heard him speak that this was not the same man who had tortured him and questioned him. He had a different voice.

Sitting behind a raised dais was the judge, Ajil al-Ajili, a cousin of Saddam. Two men sat on either side of the judge.

When Al-Ajili asked if Saad was guilty, 681 took his chance. "I am innocent," he said, and began to tell the true story of his journey to the north.

Al-Ajili turned to the interrogator.

"You claim that he spied on the Al-Rashid military base. Do you think he really did?"

"Judge, Saad said so," the man said.

"Have you been in the Al-Rashid military base?" Al-Ajili asked Saad.

"No, Judge, I've never been there."

"What do you think—you think the satellites do not see everything in the Al-Rashid military base?" the judge asked the investigator scornfully.

Saad felt hope rising. This guy was on his side. He was already ridiculing the interrogator, who was struggling for an answer.

"Sir, he said so," was all the man could say.

Saad told the judge that he could not have possibly visited the base, because in those days he was spending all his time at a multitude of different directorates and ministries applying for licenses and permissions to operate and expand his father's farm. He had the paperwork to prove it. Al-Ajili glared at the interrogator, who, because he had obviously been poorly briefed by the real interrogator, was at a loss for words and convincing details. Saad sensed that the judge wanted to help him—or harm the Mukhabarat. Perhaps he had personal reasons. Many senior officials in the regime bore grudges against other organs of the government.

It was a short hearing, ten or fifteen minutes. At the end, Al-Ajili slid a piece of paper out of his file. The verdict and sentence had already been written down. He began to read.

"Saad Hamid Jassim, you came to Iraq and committed this felony. We have sentenced you to twenty years in jail."

Saad stood there and thought, "Guys, at least send me outside, make me wait for an hour. Pretend."

Al-Ajili handed the verdict to a guard, and the guard led Saad out of the court and onto a bus back to the Hakmiya building. Two weeks later another bus took him west toward Abu Ghraib.

1 1

Great Escape

Whoever goes in is lost. Whoever comes out is reborn.
IRAQI SAYING ABOUT ABU GHRAIB PRISON

MARCH 2003

They didn't come for me in the morning, as they had promised. Footsteps came and went but they never did stop outside my cell, presaging the calling of my name. It was always just the guards, gazing in to see that we were still there or stopping to give us our breakfast of bread, processed cheese, and tea. Or our lunch of rice and potatoes or tomatoes or beans in the same plastic bowl that we ate all our meals from. At times I thought that the metal spoon they had given me could be sharpened into a weapon.

The morning wore on and I spent much of it oscillating between the passiveness of accepting death and my other way of removing myself from the cell—fantasy.

I have seen *The Great Escape* at least a dozen times. My father had force-fed it to me, along with *The Magnificent Seven,* when I was a kid.

Steve McQueen came to me now, sitting alone in "ze cooler" in the prisoner-of-war camp, after yet another escape attempt, throwing his baseball against the wall and catching it in his mitt. I yearned for a baseball. And for his cool as he worked out the blind spots on the camp fence during the day so that he could slip underneath the wire at night.

I would get out of this prison, I told myself. I'm going to dig. I'm going to scratch away at the mortar and make a hole in the wall. There were a surprisingly large number of potential digging implements in my cell: nails, bits of metal that I could twist off a shelf that looked like it had once supported a television. But with the light always on in my cell, I couldn't hope to dig out during the night without being noticed. So my only chance was that an American bomb would crash into the prison and kill my jailers. It would then be a race against time and starvation as I chipped away the mortar between the cinderblocks. Once out, I would rush around to the front of the building and free my friends and the Iraqi prisoners. We would grab Kalashnikovs and fan out, mowing down anyone who got in between us and the advancing American forces, our saviors. Who, I reckoned, would probably shoot us as we approached them in jubilation.

The various permutations of my escape fantasies were endless and nearly always violent and murderous.

One night, I was just about to fall asleep when I heard the sound I had so wanted to make. Someone was actually digging. I was sure it was Molly, and I cursed her and almost broke the "no speak" rules and told her to stop it, stop digging. You're going to get us all killed, I wanted to hiss at her down the corridor. But I just sat there and begged her silently to stop, and eventually she did. I would find out later that the noise had been coming from the other side of my cell, from Johan. He was chipping away at the mortar. The guards couldn't hear him, he assured me. But it sounded amplified and obvious to me in the next cell and I'm grateful for whatever made him give up.

There was no escape. Beyond my cell was a field of green plants. About forty yards away was the perimeter wall. It was at least twenty feet high and was topped with curls of barbed wire. A guard tower stood to the left. Let's say I somehow busted out, crawled undetected through the tall plants and then developed an aptitude for freestyle alpine climbing; there I would be—a Westerner wearing blue-and-white-striped pajamas in the heartland of Hussein's Iraq about fifty miles in some undetermined direction from the American military.

But those fantasies were nourishing. They gave me a tiny grain of hope and, more importantly, steered my thoughts away from the fear and provided a stubborn flicker of power.

On that third morning, when no guards came, I had an unexpected visitor. A ginger cat had leapt up to the vent in the lower half of my window and stood there gazing at me. "Hello," I said, and the cat stared back. He was from the outside world and I longed to be him. An hour or two later, the kind-faced English-speaking guard whom I had asked why we were being held showed up at my cell door. He held out a cigarette and I jumped up from my blanket. "This from me," he said, looking nervously down the corridor. "If anyone come, keep." He was breaking the rules for me, and I smiled, trying in vain to show the depth of my gratitude. I sat down and kept the cigarette out of sight for several minutes before lighting it.

Two forms of life had come with their different acts of beneficence. The cat's kindness was of my own imagining, but it was hard not to take these visitations as a sign. I had, contrary to my passionate atheistic beliefs, been talking to God ever since I had been arrested. Most of my words were contrite. Forgive me, I asked. If I am to die, I just want to be forgiven for all the wrongs I have done in my life. But there was also an undeniable element of pleading for mercy in my prayers. It would take a miracle, I said to God, to get us out of here, and only you can do it. If we get out, I will know who to thank. I will maintain my faith for the rest of my life.

After lunch the English-speaking guard returned and opened my cell door. This time he had a less endearing mission. He led me to the end of the corridor and before we walked outside, across the gardens, he told me to stop and turn round. He had a torn strip of pajama and he was going to blindfold me.

"What's this for?" I asked in the weakest of voices.

"Don't worry. It is like Miss Molly."

Molly had been taken from her cell before me and had made it back alive, walking past my cell with a sideways glance at me.

"But why do I have to wear this?" I asked him.

"It's okay, just some more questions" he said, his voice full of sympathy, which only reinforced my terror.

I followed him across the sunny gardens, and in fact the blindfold was pointless. He had tied it a little too high and I could see everything by tipping my head back a little.

"Take it off," said Abu Ibrahim, who was waiting for me outside the building in which I had been interrogated on the first night.

Suddenly we were at a summer garden party. There was a white plastic garden table surrounded by white plastic chairs, and the sun was out now that the dust had settled and the wind was gone. Everyone seemed to be in ever such a good mood.

"Mister Matthew," said the translator, "please sit down. I am going to ask you some more questions, like the ones we have asked you, and we are going to write a statement, and then would you please sign it?"

"Will it be in Arabic?" I asked, enjoying direct sunlight for the first time in days. Being outside in the spring weather was like tasting life again. I wanted this encounter, wherever it was leading, to last a long time.

"Yes," he said.

"I can't really sign it," I said, as politely as I could given that I was directly defying my captors for the first time. "I don't read Arabic and I wouldn't know what I would be signing. Could I sign an English version?"

He looked at me as if I were just causing him extra work. I found that enormously comforting, the first solid sign of hope in three days. If this was a charade that would ultimately lead up to torture and execution, it was beginning to be a good one. Why would they be bothering with a statement and a translation? The men around the table seemed relaxed, as if the decision about our future and their roles in it had been taken from their hands. Abu Ibrahim brought out his water pipe, and I smoked more of the translator's terrible cigarettes.

More of the same questions produced the same answers, but this time a scribe wrote them down as I squinted in the sunlight. He wrote nearly three pages and at some stage on the second page was included the sentence, "I am not working for the CIA or the Pentagon and I have not been sent on any missions by those sides." This was the first time the topic of spying had been directly raised. And now it seemed dismissed. It was tempting to see it as a relief, as the beginning of the end, but I trusted nothing in these men.

"Now you will write out a summary in English," the translator told me, and I wrote in an illegible scrawl—partly on purpose, partly because I was shaking and weak—while he dictated. It seemed like harmless and truthful stuff to me, so I agreed to sign the document. I also wrote "I have signed the English version" at the foot of the Arabic statement.

"Mister Matthew," said the translator, standing up, "come with me."

I followed him into the building, scared for yet another time. More prisoners squatted in the hallway, blindfolded and silent.

"You will now receive the judgment," he said.

We entered a dark room, another of the converted cells. There was only one person there, an older man in a beige suit seated behind a desk. We sat in front of him.

He asked some more of the same questions, only a few. And then he said the momentous words: "This is the judgment of the intelligence service."

And I waited. And nothing happened. I have no idea even now what was going on, but there was no verdict, no judgment, no decision. I can't even remember what he actually said, but it amounted to nothing.

"Does this mean we can go?" I asked him, trying to form something solid out of the vagueness.

"*Inshallah,*" the man behind the desk said, smiling. Which means, God willing. Which sometimes means yes and sometimes means absolutely nothing.

But he did say this: "If we let you go back to London, do you promise to tell the truth about Iraq?"

"I promise," I said. "This is a stupid war and people need to know the truth. I came here to cover the bombing of your people, and that is what I will tell them in London."

"Have you been well treated?"

"Yes, everyone has been incredibly kind to me. I am very grateful. But I know that it is typical of Iraqi hospitality."

Then the judge dismissed us and I left the cell as befuddled as I had entered.

"We are giving you a very big chance to tell a story about this place," said the translator conspiratorially as we walked out of the building. He was smiling. I trusted nothing.

"I don't want to write about it," I said. "Do you mean we can go?"

"In one or maybe two days," he said.

Back in the sunshine I was told to sit in a white plastic chair about fifteen yards from the table. Another of the intelligence men sat next to me, and I bummed a cigarette off him and tipped my head back to soak up the sun and perhaps show a white, Western face to any American or British spy planes cruising silently overhead.

"The problems are nearly cleared up," the man said in a friendly way. "Maybe tomorrow you go. All of you, in a group."

"The whole group?" I asked. This was almost becoming a chorus of good news.

"We hope."

And there, all of a sudden, were Moises, Johan, and Philip being led down the path and to the table. Moises went through the same routine with the statement.

"Musa, if you could take any photographs of this place, what would you photograph?" the translator asked.

Knowing Moises, knowing that he would leap at the chance to take a picture under almost any circumstances, I did the single most annoying thing that a reporter can ever do to a photographer.

"No pictures," I called over. "We don't need to take any pictures."

And I heard Moises agree. "I think I'd just like to forget all this," he said. "But if I could take some pictures, I'd shoot the paintings on the walls. They're very nice."

This was what I call the right answer. Innocent, unthreatening, cooperative.

"The prisoners do all the paintings themselves," the translator said.

"They're very nice," Moises said, smiling with polite interest.

Abu Ibrahim strolled over to where I sat. In bad English, he said something about my writing a story about the prison. Again, I smiled and said I didn't want to write anything. "Can we go?" I asked him.

"Yes," he said.

"When?"

"Today," he said, smiling. I touched his forearm—the first time I ever touched him—and he ambled away.

Back in the cells I called for the guard. I needed to go to the bathroom. I called several times but he clearly couldn't hear me.

"Matt," Moises said, his voice traveling throughout the block.

"Yeah."

"What did they tell you?"

"Maybe tomorrow."

"Yeah?"

We ended it there. We were terrified the guards would hear us speaking, and equally scared the Iraqi prisoners opposite would tell the guards in order to gain their favor.

The bombing was bad that night. It happened every night, with American or British planes screeching across the sky before the bombs they dropped shook the walls of my cell. But this was different.

The antiaircraft gun sounded like it was sitting outside my window. Actually, there were two. The first seemed like a regular-sized battery. It was like a big machine gun, erupting in a series of incredibly loud bangs. That stuff was pretty useless against coalition jets, I knew. This new gun, however, was something else. It fired single shells or missiles. Its booming was terrifying, more frightening than any of the bombs dropped. The concrete under my blanket trembled.

The gunner was playing a cat-and-mouse game with at least one jet in the skies above. Probably hiding in the darkness, the gun would remain silent as the jet swooped lower, the noise of its engines rising to a scream in my ears. It seemed to be diving right toward the prison.

And then, boom, the Iraqi gun, or missile launcher, would hurl out its projectiles, one at a time, hoping to blast the coalition plane out of the night. The jet would climb and presumably circle before coming back for more.

Give up, I wanted to shout at the Iraqi gunner. You're only going to get us all killed. Sooner or later the pilot is going to spot you, and a few seconds later we will all be incinerated. Weeks later Saad would tell me that I wasn't the only person in the prison to feel that way. The Mukhabarat men had gone out and found the gunner and begged him until he gave up.

Day four dawned and again nothing happened. No one came to release us or interrogate us. I felt awful for giving Moises and the others false hope. They hadn't been told about our possible release. Yesterday's garden party had been a charade. I had told myself over and over never to believe a word that my captors told me. But I had failed, and the day before a deceitful hope had elbowed its way into my thoughts. I knew that hope would just make the descent into despair steeper.

"This is a difficult time for you," said the kindly guard who had blindfolded me the day before. He stood looking at me through the bars.

"Yes," I said. "But what can you do?"

"Yes, it is difficult for us all."

"Do you have children?" I asked.

"Of course. Five."

"They must be scared of the bombs."

"They are so afraid," he said, "so afraid."

"I'm sorry," I said.

"This war is bad for everyone. Why? Why? It's stupid."

He shuffled off and the day trickled along.

Around this time I began to reassess the decisions I had made and my plans for the future if I ever got out. Of course, if I had known that we would be thrown into prison, I would have chosen to leave Iraq before the war began. But lying on my blanket, staring at the wall, I found a renewed confidence in my decision-making process, and I knew that I would not do anything differently if I was given the same choices again. I push the limits sometimes, I acknowledged to myself, but I do it in a calculated way and I do it for good reasons. If I ever get out of here, I said to myself, I'm going to work harder. And I'm never going to forget what it's like to be put in prison for no good reason.

I think that for the first time in my career as a reporter I felt sympathy give way to empathy. It's pretty easy to see the misery of refugees from Kosovo, Afghanistan, or Palestine, for example, but it's another thing to have experienced what they have experienced. I've never had a parent blown up on a bus. I've never had a sister killed because she was from the wrong religion or ethnic group. But I realized that I was now experiencing powerlessness, the prospect of violent death, and the deprivation of freedom. And I decided that should I get out of this place alive, I would not forget those feelings when I went back to work.

On day five, another guard took me to see Abu Ibrahim and another intelligence officer in the garden area. This time they asked me only two questions: What was the combination on my locked suitcase, and how did I send my stories to New York?

These questions amazed me. I had told them several times that I used my computer and satellite phones to email my stories to *Newsday*. No, I told them, I did not use a fax. I was beginning to realize that even though their groundwork intelligence gathering was sophisticated, their technological know-how was stuck in the age of the fax machine. Most astonishing was that none of our computers were ever opened and turned on at any stage. The last file in Microsoft Word that I had accessed, the story I was writing when the intelligence men came to my room, was not opened between that moment and the time I reached Jordan. And the computer showed me that that was the last file opened. They had simply overlooked—or felt intimidated by—the single most important sources of information on all of us.

As for the suitcase, they had waited four days to ask me for the combination. So little of it made sense to me. There was no talk of release this time. Abu Ibrahim's lightness had gone.

When I came back to my cell an Iraqi prisoner was inside, pushing around dirty water with a mop. He had placed my blankets, bottles of water, plastic cup and bowl and spoon on the shelf. I stood in the corridor and waited for him to finish. We didn't say a word to each other when he left my cell, its floor covered in a sheen of water. I was scared of the Iraqi prisoners, and I imagine they were scared of me. Communicating may have been a human impulse, but how could we trust each other not to report the initial contact to the guards? Once or twice I nodded to the large, bearded man across the corridor as we both stood at our doors. He nodded back. Then we turned our eyes away.

At night, when there was nothing to see but the walls of my cell, I would understand how a prisoner's understanding of the world about him is often almost purely aural. The shuffling or clicking of a guard's shoes told me that I was about to be looked at. Screams in the distance—coming from the interrogation rooms of Section Three— told me that it was someone's turn for questioning that night. Pool balls clicking meant that the guards were awake and nearby. Martial music echoing from a radio told me that Saddam was still holding firmly on to power. Truck engines reminded me of how physically close to relative freedom I was. Gunshots made me wonder if I had just heard the last sound that another prisoner would ever hear. And the worst sound, the sudden and vicious howling and growling of a pack of hungry dogs, made me close my eyes and pray that when it was my turn I would face a noose or a bullet.

Day six came and went and despair had thoroughly coated my

hopes, like the red dust that had left its film over my body a few days before. They had been playing us. They had thrown away the keys. Each day that passed made our release seem less and less likely. The Americans must be approaching by now, I thought. The storm is long over, and they will be powering their way north. Abu Ghraib is on the outskirts of the city, and it will be one of the places they get to first. I can't imagine these men will just let us go as they fight for their lives against the soldiers from our countries.

I smelled hellish and still refused to wash. I will not let this place become my normality, I told myself.

The stories I told myself now were no longer about my past life. They were about the future, about what life would be like if we were ever released. I guessed, correctly, that *Newsday* would be putting everything into getting us out, that prominent political and religious leaders like Jesse Jackson and Jimmy Carter would be on the case. I yearned to see Jackson stroll through the corridor to announce our release as he had helped spring Saddam's Western hostages shortly before the first Gulf war began, as he had secured the release of three American soldiers captured by the Yugoslav army during the Kosovo war. That event had knocked what I considered one of my best stories off the cover of *Newsday,* and I had used uncharitable words about Jackson at the time. All would be more than forgiven, Reverend, I said silently, if you'll just come and get me out of here. But no one came. (In fact, he was preparing to come. My sister spoke to him twice while we were in prison.)

As ever, I calculated. If they were going to release us, I thought, perhaps they want to give us a punitive week in prison first. That would make day seven—or perhaps day eight—the end.

Morning came on Monday, March 31, and as ever, so did breakfast: the usual glob of processed cheese, five rolls, and a mug of tea. My body was weakening and thinning, but I forced myself to walk up and down the cell for a while. I sat down. Then I heard the voice of a guard who always wore a well-fitting pressed blue shirt.

"Today you go home," he said.

"Really?" It was Moises's voice.

"Yes, you go. But Matthew, he a problem."

I jumped to my feet and pressed my face to the bars of my door to listen.

"Matthew a problem?" Moises asked.

"Yes, small problem."

There were parts of the conversation I had missed, parts I couldn't catch. Then I heard the guard's footsteps receding down the corridor.

"What did he say?" I mumbled to Moises.

"He said we're getting out," he said.

"Did he say there was a problem with me?"

"Nah, he said we're getting out."

I knew Moises was lying to make me feel better. I knew what I had heard. I was to be the sacrificial lamb, I thought, and felt the cold bars against my forehead.

The footsteps came back. Two pairs.

"You go," a voice said. And suddenly the guards were unlocking the padlocks to all five cells. "You go home."

We assembled at the end of the corridor. There were perhaps three guards there and one of them held several black plastic blindfolds. These were not the flimsy ripped strips of pajama that the kindly guard had tied around my eyes.

"This isn't good," Johan said, speaking the first words to me since I had asked him on the second day if he was all right.

"No," I said. We had all seen just about everything there was to see in our compound, so why would they suddenly want us blindfolded?

We were led out of the building into the sunshine and along the same path we had taken when we were first brought to our cells. I could see the path under the bottom of the blindfold. We were going in the right direction. But who knew? Perhaps the execution room was also along this path. I trusted nothing and no one.

And then we were back in the block where we had checked in. And now we were checking out.

Abu Ibrahim was there, all smiles. "Do you have everything, Matthew?" he asked as I grabbed at my bags and clothes.

"Yes, everything," I said, not caring what I left behind as long as I had my passport. I did not even care much about our money, but they meticulously made sure to give back every dollar and dinar we had arrived with.

We threw our pajamas off. I was shaking. I put on my Levi jeans again, my long-sleeved T-shirt with its an unfortunate legend across the front—We Keep America Warm—my fleece, my boots. Moises and I cobbled together a toothbrush and toothpaste and scrubbed our teeth for the first time in a week. He produced some face soap and we covered our faces in it at the cell-block sink, splashing water everywhere in desperate urgency. We grabbed at our packs of Marlboro Lights and sucked them in, one after another.

And when it was time to leave we tried to get out of there without hauling along the microwaves and the car batteries. "No, no, you must take everything," Abu Ibrahim said.

"Look, you motherfuckers, just keep the fucking microwaves," I screamed inside. Instead, we carried them out of the prison, with our equally unwanted and heavy generator and car batteries and boxes of booze and food.

There was one other thing that I did want to take with me. I wanted my pajamas. I asked the guards and Abu Ibrahim, and they laughed. One of them came out with a new pair, clean and pressed. But I insisted on taking my own torn, filthy pajamas and stuffing them into a bag.

A tall, balding man arrived and took our passports.

"I am from the Residence Directorate. We will go to Baghdad to get exit visas," he said. "You can never come back to Iraq again. If you come back, you will be put in prison."

We carried all of our gear out to a large white van that had no windows, only a sliding door. Once all our bags were inside, we climbed in and they closed the door. And then nothing. We were silent inside and I'm sure the others feared what I feared—a hail of bullets slicing through the walls of the van. But then it took off. I felt no relief, only suspicion.

Two minutes later the van stopped. Eventually the door opened.

We were still in Abu Ghraib. The plan had changed. Our passports disappeared with the balding official and we were told to unload our bags. Two or three hours later, someone said, we would drive to Jordan.

Jets screamed overhead on daytime bombing raids that made every vehicle a possible target.

"He's never going to get there on that road," Molly said, looking at the planes cutting through the sky as the residence official set off for Baghdad.

We entered an entirely different wing of the prison. The guards here all wore khaki uniforms and, unlike in our last lodgings, these men helped to carry some of our bags. We walked into a world of massive holding cells, dark passageways, and chatter. This wing was home to hundreds of prisoners, men arrested as soon as the October amnesty had passed. On the left side were enormous rooms full of men, many of them pressing their faces through the doors and windows, their hands reaching out or wrapped around the bars. Inside they milled around, wearing their own clothes. Guards stood in the wide corridor, patrolling up and down or sitting around desks. The whole wing seemed to be painted dark blue, and it was a terrible mess. Sections were wrecked, and I was sure that was a result of the destructive anarchy unleashed during the October amnesty. Whole branches of cells off the main corridor to the right seemed trashed, with rubble and twisted metal piled up and ignored. These parts seemed written off.

It was a long walk to our cell. The guards led us to the single most distant cell in the final block on the right. In the back of the cell was a four-foot-high wall that hid a toilet. At least we had been upgraded to an en suite cell.

Molly stayed to watch the gear. Moises, Philip, and I returned to the van, where Johan had waited to keep an eye on our remaining bags, boxes, and assorted electronic equipment. It took two or three more trips. On the final one I thought I would collapse. I had lugged this stuff all over Abu Ghraib all day long, it seemed, and now I had to deliver a Daewoo microwave oven to the depths of the Middle East's most notorious prison. As I picked it up, I noticed one of the guards skipping over to a car, opening the trunk, and taking out a can of gas.

"Matt, that guy has a can of gas," Moises said to me as we began our final lap back to the cell. Such was my now institutionalized inclination to fear and distrust that I knew what Moises was thinking and I shared it fully. They were going to lock us and all our stuff— every evidential trace that we had ever been to Abu Ghraib—in the most distant of cells in this already ruined prison, and then they were going to pour gasoline in through the bars. A cigarette butt thrown in through the bars would do the trick and we would be gone.

I staggered down the passageway, with the microwave now perched on my right shoulder, turning round every thirty seconds to look at the guard with the can of gas. In all the moments of our incarceration, I don't think I had been more terrified. I was convinced that we were minutes away from immolation.

Two-thirds of the way down the corridor the guard dropped off the can of gas at a side door.

The prisoners gazed at me and my microwave oven as I walked past them.

"Two or three hours," the one English-speaking guard said.

We were together. We could touch each other and talk. We could talk. As it happens, Moises, Johan, and Philip are not big talkers. So Molly and I did the job for them.

"Philip, pull up a microwave," I said, as we formed a circle.

I pulled out a bottle of scotch and we began to drink it furtively, keeping it out of sight of any guards who might walk past.

We faced a huge temptation. Should we try to use our sat phone? If caught, we could be in huge trouble. But our window faced the right direction, south, and we might be able to get a signal through the latticed concrete. Moises and I quietly, intermittently, debated it and then let it fall. We drank instead.

Johan told me days later that he thought that that evening and night we spent in that cell together was crucial to our well-being. I think he was right. Even though we still thought we could be killed at any minute, just being together was a luxury we had only dreamed of. It worked as a sort of decompression period.

We laughed at each other. I told my three favorite sheep jokes. Molly pulled out a book written by a friend of hers, and Moises read aloud a chapter that was, rather amazingly, a true story about a photographer friend of ours. The author and photographer were lovers, and the story was about how the photographer had sent her a thousand red roses. Molly read another part of the book and we began to slope off to the side of the cell that we had designated for sleeping.

No one came in the morning, by now a familiar disappointment. We were up at eight, desperate for the balding man to return. Moises successfully begged for a pot of tea, and we poured it into two mugs he had bought a few days before we were arrested. When you lifted these mugs a chime would begin from somewhere inside the ceramic. Jingle bells, jingle bells, it bleeped and we could not stop laughing or wanting to smash them.

At 11:00 A.M., the guards came. It really was time to go. And at last, we persuaded them to let us leave our microwaves behind. And the car batteries and the food and the booze. They were delighted at the bounty.

I left my microwave in Abu Ghraib, I sang to myself silently to a country-and-western tune as we left the prison. During the war in Kosovo I had penned a similar ditty entitled "I Left My Pants with the KLA." It felt good to laugh to myself.

Two Chevy Suburbans were waiting for us. These were the vehicles that worked as taxis between Baghdad and Amman.

I sat in the front on the way to the border and the noise of the vehicle lulled me. I had lost the inclination to talk and heard the others talking in the back only as a mumbling sound. We headed west and I opened a book. I didn't feel like talking.

At the border we tried to hurry things up by telling the Customs officials, perhaps the single most venal people in the entire corrupt Iraqi government, that we had been in prison for eight days and had had all our gear searched several times, so we didn't need it searched again.

"That was prison," the English-speaking official said. "This is here."

They searched everything and found thousands of dollars in Moises's belt pouch. And thousands more in mine. Sixteen thousand, to be precise.

"Do you have a declaration form for this money?" he asked.

"I've been to Iraq three times," I said, "and not once has Customs asked me to declare my money."

I knew that in the days leading up to the war these officials had fleeced Western news organizations for tens of thousands of dollars on the same pretext. It was hopeless. After a charade of decision making, they let us keep $2,000. The other $14,000 would be kept in the bank, the official said. We could come back and get it any time we wanted.

"I don't think you understand," I said, as calmly as I could. "We have been told that we can't come back to Iraq. We've just been in prison for eight days, you know."

"Then you can give your receipt to a friend and he can pick up the money."

There was no point in arguing.

We went with another official to a bank clerk's room. He filled out a receipt, which we had stamped by another man in another room. He counted every bill. The clerk, all sinew and anxiety, led us to yet another room where there was a collection of safe deposit boxes. And then, as if I were a rich man making a deposit of my family jewels in a 1960s movie, I was instructed to place the massive wads of cash into safe deposit box number 27838. The wiry clerk turned to me and handed me the key.

I have it still and I plan to keep it on my key chain for the rest of my life. A few days later Iraq descended into chaos as the regime fell. The employees at the border ransacked the safe deposit boxes and safes and looted every last penny they could find before they disappeared.

It was night when we crossed into Jordan.

12

Vanishing

Word spread to the prisoners in Section Four that the American troops had arrived. The invaders had set up a checkpoint near the prison as they pushed toward the center of Iraq's capital. For three days, starting in the first days of April, the guards would lock Saad and the other forty-four men inside Section Four all day and then disappear. The prisoners heard the rat-a-tat-tat cracking of automatic rifles and ragged thuds of artillery nearby. When the guards returned in the late afternoon, they were drained and on edge.

"The Americans are already in Baghdad," Saad told me. "These guys are very nervous. They know they're losing, and they're very nervous about it. Especially around me and Mohammed Fakhri. We are trying to avoid them as much as we could because we are American. They would say in a joking way, 'Well, we should kill Saad and Mohammed.' One officer would say, 'Saad is my share.' And another would say, 'I guess I'll take Mohammed.' We had to laugh because we don't know what's going to happen. It was said in a joking way, but you never know the way they're thinking."

On the fourth day the American tanks powered through the abandoned market next to the prison and arrived at its side gate, reserved usually for visitors. It was about three in the afternoon when an officer named Khaled rushed in to Section Four. "Grab one blanket and one pillow," he shouted. "And hurry up."

Saad was wearing a gray T-shirt and brown polyester tracksuit pants. They were hot and sweaty, bad for a day like this. His other pants were in the laundry. He slipped on his plastic flip-flops and headed for the door.

Four Mercedes buses were waiting for the prisoners, one brown, one blue, two beige. The forty-five regular prisoners boarded one bus. The roughly three hundred Hakmiya prisoners, all in their pajamas, were herded out of the other sections and onto the other three buses. The drivers started the engines and the buses began the drive through the desolate prison grounds toward the main gate. And there at the side gate, only a couple of hundred yards away, was an American tank. Its gun barrel surveyed the compound. The tank was the color of the desert.

As his bus made its way to the main gate, Saad could not believe that he had come so close to being liberated. "You see freedom just right before your eyes, and it's vanishing away. They told us, they were swearing to God, that they are trying to protect us because the Iraqis are planning to attack the Americans and we are going to get caught in the crossfire and they were afraid for our lives. We believed them at first. But when we saw the tanks we knew they were lying."

I was in London at this time. Ravenous for some beauty, I decided to go to the National Gallery in Trafalgar Square to see an exhibition of Titian, one of my favorite painters. I passed through the neoclassical galleries among the crowds holding audio guides to their ears, but it was hard to focus on the Venetian master's playful scenes of eroticism, myth, and religious devotion. In my mind's eye, I was seeing scenes of violence and destruction. Baghdad was falling. I was hungrier for Iraq than I was for Titian. And besides, I was feeling much better now. The dreams and crying had stopped, I told myself. So I called my foreign editor, Dele Olojede, and told him that I had already booked a flight back to Amman. I would visit the Hampstead psychologist once more and then head for Heathrow. After twenty minutes I walked out of the gallery into the pigeons and the red double-deckers. My phone rang. It was Dele. You cannot go back yet, he said. It is not a good idea. For once, I didn't argue. And ten minutes later I knew he was right. As I was waiting for the underground train for Hampstead to come, I had to turn to the tiled wall to prevent other people from seeing my face crumple. The next day I took a train to Scotland to see my father and to hide in our country house, which overlooks the islands of the inner Hebrides.

In *Newsday*'s offices on Long Island, a few days later, I spoke to Yousef. He was in his garden, using Phil Sherwell's satellite phone. Phil had returned quickly to Baghdad after April 9, the day the regime collapsed.

I have never been happier to hear someone's voice. The Mukhabarat had interrogated him once, Yousef said, after our arrest. He had given the intelligence men the bag with the Thuraya. They had let him go without hurting him. His family was safe. I apologized for getting him into such deep trouble, and he laughed at me, reassuring me with a flood of obscenities and warmth. He was more interested in the question that was now troubling me: Why had we been arrested?

"It was the fucking *takyia*," he told me excitedly down the phone. "They arrested dozens of Sufis. That was where the trouble started."

Saddam was always paranoid about those around him and never more so than in the days before April 9. Wherever he met his sons and his top aides, the Americans seemed to bomb the place soon after. He suspected a captain, who was part of his entourage, of being the traitor, according to Abu Tiba, Uday's bodyguard.

So, on April 7, Saddam gave the man warning that the top brass would be meeting at a house in Mansour.

"We went inside and then out the back door," Abu Tiba told me.

"Ten minutes later it was bombed. So they [Special Security] killed the captain. One of Saddam's bodyguards did it." It would be days before the Americans realized that they had not killed any of Saddam's inner circle in this much-touted attack.

Still moving about Baghdad freely, in civilian vehicles, Saddam stopped in the Adhamiya neighborhood at one point to greet some of his rather startled citizens. He had a cameraman with him, Abu Tiba said, as he nearly always did. The resulting footage of Saddam surrounded by a small group of Iraqis was broadcast on Iraqi TV and then around the world. It was a body double or outdated footage, most people assumed. No, Abu Tiba told me, it was real.

These were dark days for Saddam and his two sons. The American army was now toying with Baghdad. Armored columns were passing through the city. The airport was in American hands. What had happened to the three defensive rings? Saddam and his sons were furious at what they believed was the treachery of their commanders.

The four buses drove west, past the towering mosques of Fallujah and on to Ramadi, where the regime was strong and still popular among the Sunni Arabs who lived there. The prisoners waited for at least an hour outside a police station, and then the buses turned around and headed back along the way they had come. Saad sat next to an Egyptian prisoner, and they talked about how they wanted nothing more than to go back to Abu Ghraib, to the Americans and the freedom they would provide.

Instead, the buses stopped outside another police detention center in Fallujah; within minutes the station was full of the prisoners who had populated the Arabs and Foreigners Department, both the old-timers like Saad and the pajama-wearing, stinking, unshaven Hakmiya detainees. The efforts to separate them quickly broke down, and they were soon mingling in the courtyard. Saad, trained after seven years to avoid danger, kept away from the Sufis from the Takyia Kasnazan, with their long hair and their quiet ways.

Saad and the other professional prisoners complained to their guards. These Hakmiya guys have fleas, they said. They walk all over our blankets and they're always asking for food and cigarettes. This place is filthy, still covered in the red dust from the huge storm.

For three days they griped to their increasingly accommodating captors, who Saad believed sensed that the end was coming and therefore it might be wise to be nice for once. The Americans were closing in on Fallujah, and the guards were once again nervous about their own fates.

A bus came and the permanent prisoners were ushered out of the station, leaving the Hakmiya prisoners behind. They drove around the besieged city and eventually arrived at dusk at a large prison in Diala, about thirty miles east of Baghdad. The forty-five Arabs and foreigners joined the three hundred prisoners who were already being held there. Saad's Mukhabarat jailers signed them over to the prison authorities, said their quick goodbyes, and fled in three cars. That was the last Saad saw of them. It was April 8.

"We took showers and cleaned up. We woke up in the morning. They did the count. We start talking to the other prisoners, finding out what the hell's going on. The prison was cooking—everybody tense, listening to the news. Everyone was excited, ready to do anything to get out of there. The guards locked the doors and maintained a big distance between us and them." At one o'clock in the afternoon of the next day, Saad was watching TV with some other prisoners when the first footage came of the tanks in the center of Baghdad. The prisoners erupted, screaming through the bars at the disconcerted guards, addressing their captors with language they would never have dreamed of using before.

"Why don't you open the door? The fucking Americans are in the middle of Baghdad. What are you guys doing? We want to see what happened to our families."

"We've sent a message to the minister and we're waiting for an answer," one of the guards shouted back.

"What minister? The Americans are in the *middle of Baghdad*. There is no fucking minister. Fuck the minister, fuck the whole ministry. We know what's going on outside. Why are you keeping us here? Don't you have families too?"

The guards would not listen to reason. There was only one thing to do—riot. Saad, the scent of freedom in his nostrils, found himself leading. He and other prisoners rushed into the cells and smashed up the beds, pulling off their legs and supports. They swung and crashed the metal bars against the locks. At last they broke through the door that kept them all inside.

Suddenly there were 350 prisoners swarming through the inner perimeter of the prison, smashing windows and flicking their cigarette lighters to set fires. There were three walls—three gates to break through before they could make it to the streets. The guards had retreated from the interior, making it easy for the prisoners to break through the first gate, but as Saad and the others reached the main gate they were faced with a score of guards carrying automatic rifles. The guards stood with one foot inside the prison, one foot on the street outside, frightened for their lives but still defiant. To let the prisoners go would be to defy Saddam for the first time in their lives. What if the regime was not really gone?

"They were negotiating and shooting," Saad said. "One shot the wall just next to me. We were six or seven meters away. They were trying to scare us."

The guards began to aim at the prisoners who were running all over the compound. Seven were wounded, one killed, on the very day that the regime fell.

"The prisoners went even crazier. We gathered these mattresses and documents, threw it all by the main gate and set it on fire. That was real stupid because the smoke and the fire actually came back toward us. We had to back up, the fire increasing in size. We were surrounded by the fire and had to back up to the center of the prison. What the guards did was to come forward and jump onto the roof of the prison, surrounding us with Kalashnikovs. We had nowhere to go. By this time all the prisoners were sitting in lines, ready to do the head count. Finally the guards came down, surrounded us and started hitting prisoners with aluminum bars."

Only one part of the prison was left undamaged by the riot and the fires: the isolation section. So all 350 prisoners found themselves crammed into tiny cells. There were about sixteen in Saad's cell. They could barely breathe.

At about nine o'clock that night, the guards decided to turn on the charm again, letting all the prisoners out to wash. Saad could not work out what was going on. He was sure it was a trap, that one of the other prisoners would tell the guards that he had been one of the riot's leaders. Ever since that prisoner had written his soapy message on the wall of Saad's cell in the Hakmiya, he had been convinced that he would not die in prison. Now he lost that certainty. Would he die as the regime breathed its last? He washed quickly and rushed back to the cell.

In the morning, he went out to wash again. He dunked his head under the tap and scrubbed his scalp and hair with his fingers, trying to wash it without any soap. When he looked up again, there was hardly anyone in the block.

"I looked in my room for all the foreigners and there was no one there. So I walk to the main gate, and this prisoner says, 'Come on, this way, this way. God bless you, God take care of you.'"

Saad walked toward the main gate. It was open. He saw local kids standing just inside the prison, gazing at the men who were staggering out toward the street. Saad counted about fifteen steps between the second gate and the main gate and then he took one final step, out of the prison and into freedom.

Outside on the street, local people were staring silently at the prisoners as they burst into tears and hugged each other. Saad found Mohammed Fakhri, and the two men, who had often been at loggerheads in Abu Ghraib, threw their arms around each other and kissed. They couldn't let go. "We were crying from the bottom of our hearts," Saad said.

Then he found other friends. An Iraqi-born Swede, an Indian named Mohammed Sabouleh, and a Palestinian named Khaled Walid. Mohammed had been in Abu Ghraib for ten years, Khaled for more than nineteen. Again Saad squeezed them and felt his tears running between his cheek and their necks.

"Come on guys, let's go, before they change their minds," said Saad. "Guys, step on it."

Uday Hussein, 39 years old and three months away from a violent death with his brother Qusay at the hands of American soldiers, sat in a house in Baghdad on April 9 watching television. Like millions all over the world, he was transfixed by the pictures of the Americans pulling down a statue of his father just across town.

"After he saw the fall of the statue on TV he was so tense," Abu Tiba said. "His nature changed. It became very hard to talk to him. . . . He used to get angry at us, shouting at us endlessly."

There were American soldiers all over the city, but they were by no means on every street corner, and the family continued moving about. "Once, in Mansour, we drove past a convoy in a normal vehicle, not with blackened windows," Abu Tiba said, laughing. "Maybe they would not recognize Uday's face. He used to laugh at them. He saw one soldier with a red face and said, 'This guy doesn't have a face for fighting.' "

On the morning of Friday, April 11, Saddam, Uday, and Qusay publicly attended Friday prayers at Abu Hanifa Mosque in the Adhamiya neighborhood. As the world was asking where the most wanted men in Iraq could have gone, they were still in Baghdad, lingering among their people, parading themselves within a few hundred yards of the oblivious Americans. When prayers were over, the three men and their entourage left the mosque. Word had spread quickly among the congregants that Saddam was there and a small crowd gathered around him, Abu Tiba told me. An old woman in a black *abaya* approached Saddam and spoke to him with the kind of honesty that at any other point over the past thirty-five years would have led to her disappearance. Many in the crowd began crying, Abu Tiba said. "He had told them one thing, and another thing had happened," he said. "She was an old woman and she was not afraid."

"What have you done to us?" she berated her president.

Saddam hit himself on the forehead with his open palm.

"What could I do? I trusted my commanders. . . . They have broken the oath they took upon themselves to protect Iraq. We hope we will be back in power and everything will be fixed."

Saddam's protestations and surprise were genuine, Abu Tiba said. "They never planned to leave because they had a very good plan to prevent the Americans reaching Baghdad," he said, referring to the defensive rings that had collapsed so quickly. It was clearly not such a good plan. And now the deposed ruling family had to come up with a new one.

Meeting in a house in Adhamiya, the Iraqi president and his two sons joined with a handful of other senior regime officials to discuss the future. "There was a closed-door meeting five or six days after the fall of Baghdad so that no one would know the details of the resistance," Abu Tiba said.

He did not know the specifics of what was discussed inside the room, he told me. But he was sure that the former president and his sons were planning to orchestrate a campaign of guerrilla resistance against the occupiers. Not that they could possibly be responsible for all the attacks on the American soldiers that were taking place in the months after the war—Islamic and nationalist sentiments were fueling the resistance, Abu Tiba told us. It would go on, with or without Saddam and his sons.

Soon after the closed-door meeting, Uday spoke to Abu Tiba and told him that it was time to separate. "We'll send for you when we need you," were the last words of the subdued Uday to his trusted bodyguard. Uday gave him $1,000 as a farewell gift. Abu Tiba never got the call.

Saad, Mohammed Sabouleh, and Khaled Walid teamed up. The Indian and the Palestinian had some money. Saad had a family and a home they could head for.

The three men walked around Diala, asking residents where the bus station was, where they might find a taxi. It was April 10 and the town was packed full of Baghdadis who had fled the bombing. They were desperate to get home now and there was not a single mode of transportation available for the three former prisoners. "No taxis, no buses, no trucks, no lorries, no horses, no donkeys. Nothing."

At last they found a taxi. The driver insisted on being paid the extortionate rate of 50,000 dinars to take them only the first twelve kilometers. Mohammed and Walid didn't want to pay. Saad wanted to tear his hair out. Pay the man, he told them. Who cares how much it costs? They drove for five minutes and then the argument between the two paying passengers and the driver became so heated that the car stopped and the three of them had to get out and start walking.

Over the next hours, they would get other rides, only to be turfed off in similar circumstances after another five minutes. Saad was going crazy. He urged the others again and again to simply keep walking. Finally, past midnight, they arrived at an American checkpoint on the outskirts of the capital. The headlights shone in the night. Saad was about to meet his fellow Americans.

He introduced himself as a U.S. citizen to the American soldiers, who couldn't have been more surprised if Saddam himself had walked up to them. They gave him and his friends water and told Saad that they would immediately take him to the airport and fly him home to the United States if he wanted.

"No, I want to see my family, my wife, my kid, my mother," Saad told them.

There was a huge line of vehicles and pedestrians at the checkpoint, all desperate to pass into the city, to go home and find loved ones. Saad acted as translator and explained the situation to the soldiers, who then opened the road and let the flood of families sweep into the city.

Saad and his two friends walked with the crowd. Eventually a passing pickup truck stopped and offered them a ride into town for 500 dinars. When they arrived in the chaotic city center Saad offered the driver another 2,000 to take them to his sister's house in the Zayouna neighborhood. After seven years in prison, however, Saad had a problem. He couldn't remember where the house was, exactly. He told the driver to just drop them off and he would find the place on foot. The three men looked suspicious, walking around late at night, looking lost. An armed group guarding the neighborhood approached them and asked them what they were doing. Saad told them whose house he was looking for and they gave him directions.

At about three in the morning, Saad found the house. His seven-year journey was over. Exhausted but elated, he knocked on the door.

13

This Is My Friend
and This Is My Brother

APRIL 2003

One of the volunteer gravediggers cradled the prisoner's rotting head on his lap, raising it slightly with his left hand. He couldn't get the cotton blindfold untied, so someone had given him a penknife. As tenderly as if he were holding the head of a living child, he sawed through the bind. It didn't seem respectful, all of the men clearly thought, to leave the cotton strips over the murdered men's eyes. He peeled it gently from the sticky flesh until the unseeing eyes were exposed to the sun that sat high over Abu Ghraib. And then he cut the tie that bound the prisoner's hands behind his back.

The men dug into the earth with shovels, sweeping away clumps with their hands when they found the outline of another body. They pulled out thirteen of them and lay them on the earth just next to the bulrushes. The wind that swept across the huge prison grounds left a coating of dust over the bodies.

The dead prisoners all wore the same clothes, the same ones I had worn in prison—blue-and-white striped pajamas, white undershirts, and plastic flip-flops. The blindfolds were strips from the same pajama material. They had been buried in a shallow ditch about fifteen yards outside the walls of the Arabs and Foreigners Department.

Bodies that are two weeks dead, as these were, give off a powerful smell, almost sweet and sour. It was an invasive scent that seemed to linger in my lungs for hours. To inhale it was to have an undesirable intimacy with the dead men who lay in the dirt. They were getting inside me. Most of the people standing around the grave pressed handkerchiefs, scarves, or T-shirts to their noses and mouths, and they looked at the bodies from a distance. Clutching a handkerchief to my face, I walked over to where some of the bodies lay. I had to get close to see if I recognized any of the faces, but even after only two weeks they were already very decomposed, the faces all blurring into a bloated flatness of yellow, black, orange, and pink. There was nothing left to match with my memories of the men who occupied the cells opposite me. But it was those men, ten of the thirteen, that we were looking at.

I knew that because of Saeed Ihsan Hussein. He was a prisoner in the Arabs and Foreigners Department until the end, and even though we never saw each other, he was one of my neighbors in Section Five. He was housed in the other wing of the section, in what Saad calls "second class"—the larger cells that slept as many as six. Now he had come back to help disinter the bodies. We stood several yards from the grave as he told us that "they killed them two days before I left the prison. Shooting, by Kalashnikov. They had Thurayas. And some of them, four I think, were Sufis."

I had often thought of tracking down my fellow prisoners across the corridor and asking them who they were, how they ended up in Abu Ghraib, and how they became free. I was not expecting the reunion to be at their shallow grave.

This was not my first time back at Abu Ghraib since returning to Baghdad after the war, but it was the first time I had been with my girlfriend, Catherine. Also a reporter, she had been on deadline when Moises and I had rushed out to Abu Ghraib as soon as we arrived in Baghdad a few days earlier. A unit of military police from the National Guard was temporarily guarding the prison. They let us in as a favor. We used our sob story. And then, in Section One, where we had checked in and put on our pajamas, I sobbed. I had to turn my back to the soldier accompanying us, but he could probably tell. He just waited. We walked to our cells and inside the six-by-ten room where I had not been able to spark tears, I now couldn't hold them back. I stared through my window and across the now withering, yellowing patch of bean stalks to the wall of the department. The glass was still in the window and I considered smashing it, but again I felt the impulse I had had when first placed in that cell: I just didn't want to contribute to the destruction, not of this room, this prison.

So by the time I stood with Catherine watching the bodies being unearthed a few days later, I had overcome the initial shock. The horror of seeing the fate that very nearly had been mine didn't move me as much as I kept expecting it to. I think that I had faced death for eight days, awaiting it at every moment, and even the awfulness of the deaths of my block mates could not match that fear. Besides, I had survived. To look into that grave was to feel, in a confusingly shameful way, relief.

For Catherine, who had been in the north of Iraq during my disappearance, the scene was a little more disconcerting. I saw her crouching on the ground, pressing her headscarf to her mouth and nose, gazing at the grave. I let her be.

She came with me and Saeed Hussein, the former prisoner, when I asked him to show me where he had been held and where exactly the executed prisoners had come from. We padded through the garden area, headed straight for Section Five, and once inside, turned left to our wing. "The people in these cells, they were killed," he said. "This area was for spies. There was contact between them and us. When they were interrogated we saw them walking past. In the same day they took ten from this block and three from our block."

Catherine counted the cells. There were fifteen. The five of us had been released on April 1. A week later—April 8, Saeed Hussein thought—the Mukhabarat investigators had tied the hands of the men, wrapped the same pajama blindfolds around their eyes that I had once worn, and marched them through the corridors, along the paths, out of the front door of the department and over to where they had been digging short trenches that they had planned to fight from. There they gunned down the men we had spent the week with, sharing food and the bathroom and occasionally nodding to each other across the corridor.

"I heard the gunshots and then the sound of a digger," Hussein told us. "It was at about five in the afternoon."

We walked out to the graveside and interviewed more family members. Their loved ones, they said, were arrested just before or during the war. They had had Thurayas, they acknowledged. And to have a sat phone meant only one thing to the Mukhabarat if you were an Iraqi: you were a spy.

Yousef stood with us, smoking one Pleasure cigarette after another, distracted from his translating duties by the sight of the digging and the bodies. It was his first time at Abu Ghraib also. A cloud of "what if?" hung over us both. He had not been the only person we had known before the war to be interviewed by the Mukhabarat because of their connection with us: Alan Enwia was at his record store one day when a car pulled up and a middle-aged Mukhabarat man stepped out of it. The man had asked the terrified Alan about the band's involvement with Moises and me. Alan had stayed cool and persuaded the man of the boys' innocent desire to make music and become well-known and, fortunately, the Mukhabarat had left matters at that.

Catherine had been gentle with me until now. She took me by the shoulders and turned me toward the grave.

"Look at that and tell me that you still believe you made all the right decisions?"

"Yes," I told her. "Under the circumstances, I believe that I did."

Now, I don't. Although I have no regrets about any of the decisions I made that ended up jeopardizing my own safety, I made one, perhaps unforgivable, error. Moises and I asked Yousef to hide our Thuraya.

"You know," Yousef said to me, without the rancor that might have been warranted, "if they caught that phone in my home, I would be with them." He nodded toward the grave. He had been smart enough to give the Mukhabarat the phone in a bag, telling them he had never looked inside to see what it held. They believed him.

"I'm sorry, Yousef," I told him, not for the first or last time.

In the early afternoon of May 29, I begged a favor from the bureau chief of the Qatari satellite news channel Al-Jazeera. I had heard that they had a tape of an Iraqi state TV news item that ran during the war.

In a hotel room that the Qataris had turned into an editing suite, an employee named Ali ran the tape for me.

An Iraqi official with graying hair, wearing a khaki uniform without rank or unit markings, held a microphone and gazed with casual seriousness directly into the camera. He sat on an ornate armchair with a black-and-white curtain behind him. Two pens poked their heads neatly out of a pocket on his left sleeve. After reciting a passage from the Koran, he got to the matter at hand.

"I present to you a sample of the agents of the American intelligence because the security services of the Iraqi people were able to catch them," he said. "They have succeeded in tracking international phone calls and specifying the positions of the people doing it."

The footage cut to two Thurayas. And then to a man whose face I knew. He told the interviewer that his name was Qader Ibrahim Qader and that he was from Erbil in northern Iraq. He had a Kurdish accent, my translator Mukhaled told me. I had seen the man in Abu Ghraib, on our block, walking past my cell to the toilet and back. I think he was once given cleanup duty, flushing all of our cells and the corridor with water and then pushing the dirty water toward a drain.

On camera, he sat on a couch of the same design as his interviewer and could barely force his confessional words out through his tightened throat. I had seen him in pajamas. On TV, he wore a green suit jacket and a white open-necked shirt. He described how he had gone to Suleymaniyeh in Kurdistan and had been recruited by a Major Kassem, whom he said was working for the Americans there. They had given him a Thuraya and some explosives—which the footage showed—and asked him to call Major Kassem during the war with information about whether American bombs had hit their targets or not.

"I did it for money," Qader said. "For one thousand dollars."

"You are very bad," the interviewer scolded him. Qader's eyes darted at the floor and at whoever was standing next to or behind the camera, and he agreed that he was very bad.

A recorded intercept of two men talking played while the camera panned over Thurayas, a global positioning system unit, and a charger that works in the outlet of a car cigarette lighter. The taped conversation was scratchy and proved nothing.

A second man took Qader's place to tell the interviewer that he had used his Thuraya's GPS unit to send similar targeting information to his American handlers in the north.

"I regret this," said the man, Ali Jasseb, whom I think I recognized but am still not sure about. "We didn't understand what we were doing."

The third and final man told the interviewer that a CIA agent named Mike had recruited him in the north in 2001. "He tempted us with money—four or five hundred dollars a month," said the strangely relaxed man, wearing a yellow-and-blue polo shirt. "He put us up in the best hotels and gave us drink and women. . . . He trained me on some instruments to point out important military installations around Iraq."

The tape was carelessly edited, with jumps that suggested retakes of the suspects' answers. Not self-flagellating enough, perhaps. Try again, Qader.

"It is a great thing for the Mukhabarat to have uncovered such a network," said the interviewer, addressing the camera at the end of the segment.

Ali couldn't remember exactly when the Iraqis had run the piece, but he was pretty sure that it had run on March 27. I had been in prison with Qader and the others for three days by then, so it was probably taped a few days beforehand, unless they took Qader from the prison for the interview.

As we drove away from the Al-Jazeera bureau I talked about the tape and the prisoners with Mukhaled. I felt a little shaken by having recognized Qader. I recognized in his face and in the words he forced out of himself the same fear that I had found in Abu Ghraib when faced with the questions of my interrogators. I didn't care whether it was true that Qader had used a Thuraya to contact opposition or American forces in the north, and I didn't care whether he had done it for money or because he wanted to help get rid of the government that had turned Iraq into a corner of hell over three decades. Although I had not been able to identify his corpse among those pulled out of the ground outside the department, I assumed that he was among them, that he had been executed. For one reason or another, Qader had contributed to getting rid of the regime that had imprisoned all Iraqis, including Mukhaled, for most of their lives.

A Sunni Muslim who had kept his head down, served as an engineer in the Air Force and joined the Baath Party because to have declined would have marked him as an enemy of the state, Mukhaled was delighted to see the end of Saddam. But Mukhaled had no thanks for Qader, whom some might consider a martyr.

"He and the second guy were particularly scared and ashamed," he explained, "because they had wives and children."

"Absolutely," I said, thinking of kids growing up without their father and his financial support. That was not what was on Mukhaled's mind.

"It is terrible for the children," he said. "They will forever have to live knowing their father was a traitor to his country."

If the suspected spies who shared my block and now shared a grave in the dun earth were killed on April 8, they were as unlucky as we were lucky. They missed the collapse of the regime by a day. American tanks had already made violent excursions through Baghdad, and it was on April 9 that the statues of Saddam were pulled down and the city erupted in looting.

It is possible that these men were the last people executed by Saddam's regime, the final names on a never-compiled list that could be hundreds of thousands long. We drove a few miles further west from the prison to the Kharq cemetery where the employees of Abu Ghraib used to bury the men they had hanged.

Kharq was, for the most part, a regular cemetery. But if you drove straight down the central track you would get to a section that was surrounded by a cinder-block wall. Someone had lately smashed a large hole in the wall, and for the first time in its history the relatives of the dead could visit. Once inside, though, they had another obstacle to overcome: There were no names on the simple, sheet-metal grave markers—only numbers. And there were hundreds of graves, packed tightly together, just raised columns of earth stretching in every direction.

The other challenge facing the families trying to locate the dead was that once your son or brother was arrested by Saddam's people, that's usually where the trail ended. Do not keep asking about him or you will be in trouble, families were told. Sometimes, with luck or bribes, you could get more information, but that rarely amounted to more than the simple revelation that the person in question had been executed. As long as Saddam remained in power, people had largely given up on ever finding the bodies of their loved ones.

But there was one thing now working in the favor of the thousands of searching families: the regime's meticulous record keeping. As obsessed as the Nazis to record their own acts, the Baathists noted down everything, no matter how incriminating. As the city had fallen, various groups and individuals rushed in to seize as many files from the Mukhabarat, General Security, and the other agencies as possible. The American-backed resistance group, the Iraqi National Congress, had millions of files. The Americans had many more. And a volunteer group of former prisoners, nearly all of whom had spent time in Abu Ghraib, had taken over a house belonging to a former Saddam acolyte on the western bank of the Tigris and had turned it into the headquarters of the Committee of Free Iraqi Prisoners. Trucks pulled up outside and men would leap down onto the street and begin carrying file cabinets and boxes into the building.

There was probably nowhere else in Iraq at that time that was such a focus of grief. The crowd spilled out of the front courtyard of the rococo house onto the street. Old women in black *abayas* sobbed on the sidewalk, able for the first time in their lives to express their fury and sorrow in public and to share it with others who had suffered similar losses. Everyone seemed to be carrying aged photographs and identification documents of the missing, hoping—and perhaps fearing—to match up their papers with one of the files being carted into the house. Some had photocopied the last pictures of their loved ones and were pasting them to the walls of the house, hoping that someone would recognize a face and reveal the story behind it.

The volunteer workers carried the files through the crowd and into the rooms of the house. Inside were small mountains of secret documents; one pile for General Security files, another for Mukhabarat files and so on.

For the hundreds of people outside, pressing against the doorway with their long-suppressed hunger for knowledge, there was only one question they wanted answered: What happened to the missing?

The prisoner volunteers, nearly all Shia, had rather amazingly managed to forge a little bit of efficient order out of the scene of pushing and yelling and crying. At one doorway, volunteers would take the details of one of the lost and would then retire to the mountains inside to find the answer to the only question.

Assembled at Kharq were a few people who now had the answers. Their sons and brothers had been executed and were now buried here. And, thanks to the government's meticulousness, they even knew which number on which metal grave marker corresponded to their loved ones.

Taleb Saddoun and his brothers had brought along a couple of chipboard and plywood coffins that they had borrowed from their local mosque. They were old, some of the wood splintering and crumbling, and had been used many times before. When the two men the family had come to find had been taken away and buried properly, Taleb and his brothers would return the coffins. They were poor and they didn't care much how they carried away their brother and friend, as long as they found them and gave them a decent Muslim burial in the holy Shia city of Najaf that they deserved.

"This is my friend," said Taleb, pointing to one open grave and then the one next to it, "and this is my brother."

The two men were arrested in 1997, Saddoun said. Now that the regime was gone, he could say with pride what the two men had done to end up in a numbered grave in the walled section reserved for the executed in this dusty cemetery.

"They bombed the Interior Ministry," said Saddoun, unable to hold back tears. "They did this because they felt the government was very bad. They tried to do something."

For two years, Taleb and his brothers did not know where his brother Hassan and his friend Hairi were. Eventually they found a bribable prison guard who told them that the men had been hanged.

While we spoke, Taleb rarely taking his eyes off the grave, another relative stood in the hole and used a shovel and his hands to pull out the bones and clothes of the two men. It took a long time. The man would dump a shovelful of earth next to the grave and others would rake the earth with their fingers, occasionally plucking out a vertebra or another small bone, perhaps from a foot or a hand. Two blankets, one for each dead man, received the bones and scraps of clothing. Taleb and his brother Jabar stood at the foot of the grave in silence. And then Jabar let out a primal wail and the two men hugged and shook in their grief.

"Thank God we found them," said Jabar, when he had turned silently to the grave again. "He has become a hero now that Saddam has fallen."

As family members lifted the worn coffins onto their shoulders and carried them through the smashed-in hole in the wall to their waiting cars, they called out two chants.

"There is no God but God," they cried. "Saddam is the enemy of God."

★   ★   ★

The waves of death during those first few days in Baghdad came with waves of euphoria. Yousef and I had rushed into each other's arms like long-lost brothers, kissing each other on the cheeks and lifting each other off the ground in bear hugs, our words tumbling out in an unstoppable rush. I lost sufficient words to properly thank my journalist friends and colleagues still hanging on in Baghdad after the war, and those who had come in later who had also helped in so many ways during our disappearance. And on the concourse of the Palestine, now guarded by American tanks, I saw the porters who had taken our bags and gear away from room 1122. The man to whom I had given the $20 bill rushed up and we hugged and laughed and kissed. And even though we shared only a little language between us, he told me that that night he had gone home after work and sat down with his wife and cried. It was all the joy of survival.

That was not a ubiquitous feeling in the city. One evening I went to the house of Phil and Julian's driver, Bassem, an old friend of Yousef's. We drank tea with two of his British-educated brothers, a doctor and an engineer on Saddam's missile program. In Bassem's kitchen, I noticed one of the brand-new microwaves that Julian and Phil had off-loaded before they had to leave Baghdad.

Before the war, Bassem had been unenthusiastic but realistic about the inevitability of the American victory. Now he had mixed feelings about the new occupiers. His brothers Saad and Hazem had entirely unmixed feelings: the Americans were to blame for everything going wrong in Baghdad—the looting, the lack of electric power, the lack of phone service. They were here to rob Iraq of its oil and then they would leave. They had decapitated a legitimate government and were humiliating and subjugating the population. It was only a matter of time before the Iraqi people would fight back and drive them out of the country.

Hazem, the missile engineer—now unemployed, like every former military man in Iraq—was a very large man with a very loud voice, and I found him particularly good at making sure that I got the points he was making.

"Saddam Hussein gave me this," he said, pulling up the left sleeve of his *dishdasha* and showing me something that was very distinctly no longer fashionable—a Saddam watch.

A little girl brought me white flowers with their stems wrapped in tissue paper from the garden, and this was my cue to leave. Yousef told me the next day that Hazem, whom I had wanted to ask about Saddam's missile program but then thought better of doing so, was convinced that I was indeed a spy. The Mukhabarat had arrested me and taken me to Abu Ghraib. Therefore I was a spy; therefore my release had been a mistake.

All over Baghdad I found an endless variety of feelings about the Americans. One Friday morning, a patrol of Humvees and fighting vehicles rumbled down a quiet main road in the west of the city. A group of kids ran toward the convoy, waving, smiling, giving the thumbs up, and shouting out in Arabic to the soldiers, who might have not waved back so cheerily if they had realized that the 10-year-old boys were informing them that they planned to have sex with the soldiers' sisters.

One afternoon, three members of Unknown To No One and Alan, their manager, came round to the Al-Hamra to chat. With the phones and the Internet down, I had become their link to Peter Whitehead, the British music entrepreneur who was now trying to organize a trip to Baghdad to re-record their best song, "Hey Girl," and to shoot a video. The boys were beside themselves with excitement at the prospect and wisely suspicious that it would never really happen. They were not sure about this new world they were now living in. Trust came hard.

"For thirty years we lived under his hands, so we lived his life," said Shant, not needing to name "him." "It's a big change. First new step. We don't know how to cross it."

"I bought a satellite and I have it for my first time," said Art, who seemed the most unhesitating enthusiast of the new Iraq. "For the first time I see the world. MTV, CNN."

"Even the air we breathe, we think it's different. I can be me. I can be myself now," said Alan.

Art saw the anti-American rallies then going on as simple expressions from a people that had never been allowed to demonstrate before. Their target was the Americans purely because the Americans were the ones in power.

In a rambling conversation about the U.S. performance so far, about its interest in Iraqi oil, Alan used the metaphor I had begun to hear over and over.

"We were in a big prison—Iraq," said Alan, pulling on a cigarette. Everyone from prisoners to ordinary civilians to the jailers themselves would say the same. "Now we are more than free, more than the word means. We have gone to prison and now we are free. For us, we know the rules and we behave straight, but other people, they rob banks."

"Thirty years of Saddam's rule—they destroyed morality," Art said.

Nadeem didn't like this moralistic tone about the looters who had been stripping government buildings, palaces, and the homes of members of the regime, and were now moving on to innocent citizens.

"Imagine yourself not being able to provide food for your families. How far would you go? Most people have spent thirty years in this prison. What do you expect them to do?"

"If you enter Saddam's house, you would rob it?" Alan asked Nadeem.

"Of course I would," Nadeem said. It was getting a little heated.

"No, I would not. No way. No, thanks."

Art, the diplomat, moved things back to their lives before April 9. And they spoke about how Nadeem's brother was arrested by General Security and imprisoned for nothing, and how six of his cousins were executed for suspicion of being members of the Dawa Party, the largest opposition Shia party. About the perpetual fear. About how Shant had one day taken a wrong turn in Baghdad and ended up having to bribe his way out of being arrested for driving past a forbidden ministry. About having to join the Baath Party to get the simplest things, like permission to stay in college. And about how these stories can be found behind every front door in Iraq and how they never, ever thought it would end, that Saddam would just be replaced by Uday.

"Is there some such a novel called *1984*?" Art asked me. "It's the same as what happened here. As if Saddam Hussein had read it and then made the republic. Maybe worse than what [Orwell] wrote."

There was one other reunion I had in my first weeks back in Baghdad, a reunion with a man I had never met but had once written about.

During my time in Scotland I had read a story in the *Times* of London by my friend Steve Farrell. He had met an American citizen wandering around the halls of an interrogation center. His name was Saad Jassim, or Sam Jason. He had spent seven years in the Arabs and Foreigners Department of Abu Ghraib, Steve wrote. He had been accused of being a spy for the United States.

I couldn't believe it. This was one of the two men I had written about in October. And by the description, it sounded like the Arabs and Foreigners Department of Abu Ghraib was the same place that I had been held. Steve wrote that the prisoners had been allowed televisions. I was sure that the shelf in my cell had once had a TV sitting on it and there had been no TVs in the massive part of the prison where we had spent our final night. I had to talk to Saad. I dashed off an email to Steve and asked him if there was any chance that he had kept Saad's address or any way of contacting him.

"Sam is waiting downstairs in the lobby," Steve wrote back from the Sheraton in Baghdad. He had hired him as his translator.

When we were introduced several days later, we shook hands and smiled. Saad had heard already that I was coming and wanted to meet him. He was tall and his black hair was tidily cut. I would never have thought he had just spent seven years in Abu Ghraib if it hadn't been for his slightly forced air of cheeriness. There was sadness in his eyes.

"I've got a lot of questions for you," I said.

"No problem, guy," he said. "Anytime."

"I was in Abu Ghraib for eight days," I said, knowing that he already knew.

"Seven years," he said, pointing to his chest.

"You got me there."

14

The Jailer

MAY 2003

We did not have an appointment with Abu Firaz, the Mukhabarat jailer, but he welcomed us into his home anyway. He came to his front gate in the lower-middle-class neighborhood of Hai Jihad in his *dishdasha* and politely waited while my translator and I explained who we were and why we were there. "I found your name on a list of employees at the Arabs and Foreigners Department on the floor at Abu Ghraib," I said. "I spent some time there recently." He burst into a huge smile, all cheekbones and eye glints, and invited us in.

The first thing I saw in his living room was a large model of a Napoleonic-era ship, its hull shining with a careful varnish job, its rigging meticulously crafted, Iraqi flags stuck horizontally and motionlessly atop the three masts.

"Was that, by any chance, made by the Iranian prisoners in the big workshop?" I asked, and Abu Firaz laughed again, amused.

"Yes, and you can have it if you want. It's a gift from me to you."

"No, really, I couldn't. But thank you."

I was a little surprised and much encouraged by his warmth. It was late May, only weeks after the war, and I had been knocking on the doors of several former Mukhabarat employees at the Arabs and Foreigners Department. Along rural back roads around Fallujah and Ramadi, the heartland of Saddam's support and ongoing resistance to the American occupying forces, we visited surprised and suspicious men who were keen to cut short the conversations I imposed on them. At one farm to the south of Baghdad, one former agent and his brothers and father had given us tea and water and chatted for a while before informing me that, most unfortunately, they had to leave to attend family business, a common Iraqi way of asking you to leave. "Are you working for the CIA?" one of the brothers had asked as the interview came to an abrupt close.

"If I were, there would be a tank outside," I replied.

Saad had told me that he wouldn't be accompanying me on any of these house calls to the men on the list I had found. He looked through the names, each with its own history for him, and said: "You're on your own for this one, guy."

Abu Firaz, one of Saad's former jailers, was poor, fierce-looking, and unfailingly hospitable. He turned on the air conditioner and called through to the kitchen for tea; we offered each other cigarettes as his budgerigars chirped through the hum of the AC from their cage in his front yard. In his barren living room he had only a couch and two armchairs that barely held together. I lowered myself into one of the armchairs. Some of the coils in its seat cushion had erupted. Others had collapsed. I perched as comfortably as possible on the more even side of the cushion. The first thing he talked about was his salary: $450 per month in 1980, it had devalued to $150 by the time of his forcible retirement from the Mukhabarat when the Americans showed up in Baghdad. Now it was gone altogether.

Saad later told me that Abu Firaz "was the guy you don't hate but you don't like. You don't know how to feel about him. One day he's in a good mood and you can get whatever you want, any help from him. Another day he's in a shitty mood and he just punishes people for nothing."

I had come to see Abu Firaz in search of answers to the questions that had been haunting me since my release. Why was I arrested and released by the Mukhabarat? How did this machine, Saddam's most infamous security apparatus, live and breathe? My nightmares were over and I had stopped bursting into tears for no apparent reason, but I did not want to go through the rest of my life wondering why Moises and I were picked out of all the journalists in Baghdad during the war. Yousef's theory about the Sufis was still only a theory. Because I had felt its bite, I did not want to live in ignorance of how Saddam's intelligence agency worked, not just in our case but in the cases of hundreds of thousands of Iraqis who had disappeared over thirty-five years. Nor how his bricks-and-mortar symbol of terror, Abu Ghraib, functioned on the inside. And I did not want to keep wondering what it was, exactly, that had delivered us from Abu Ghraib when our ten block mates had been executed a week later.

"You are so lucky. I don't know how you got out," he said, and we laughed because it was the only response. Every officer I have met from the Mukhabarat and other security services has said the same thing, and we always laugh in the same uneasy way that required me to move the conversation along for everyone's sake.

I already felt that I had some traces of answers to the question of why Moises and I were arrested. With Julian and Phil gone from Baghdad, we were, I believe, the only journalists left who had come in with the human shields. We had managed to become legitimate, but only at the last minute. There was also the visit to the *takyia* and Yousef's conviction that we had inadvertently stumbled across a Mukhabarat surveillance operation and aroused their suspicions. But that did not begin to explain everything. How had we come to be associated with Molly, Johan, and Philip, people we hardly knew, if at all, and who had come into the country much later on tourist visas? Why had they been arrested but others in their group left alone?

Almost more puzzling was why we had been released. *Newsday* had mounted an astonishing campaign to get us out, including using crucial contacts in the Palestinian Authority and the Vatican, which both still had missions in Baghdad. Ramsey Clark, the former attorney general, had helped also. I knew of at least three senior regime officials—the head of military intelligence, the head of the Mukhabarat, and Tariq Aziz, the deputy prime minister—whom *Newsday*'s intermediaries had managed to contact indirectly or directly. But I was not convinced that it was *Newsday*'s superhuman efforts that did the trick. Most of them came to fruition in the last two days of our detention and it was on the third day that we began to be told that we were going to be sent home. Furthermore, I simply didn't understand why, under any degree of international pressure, a collapsing regime would care enough about its image in the world to bother releasing us. A long and highly public campaign had not helped Farzad Bazoft, who was also innocent.

Abu Firaz, I knew before I went to see him, was not from the section in the Mukhabarat that had arrested me, held me, and released me. But as both a Mukhabarat officer and an employee of the Arabs and Foreigners Department, I thought, he could provide more insight into the prison and the nature of the Mukhabarat.

In conversations with Saad and others, I had learned that a month before the war began, the Hakmiya had abandoned its quarters in downtown Baghdad because it thought that it would be bombed in the coming war.

The Hakmiya had chosen the Arabs and Foreigners Department as their new, temporary home, planning to wait there until the army had repelled the Americans. At first the Hakmiya officers took over Section One, the block where they had processed us. Then they spread out to Section Two, and as the war approached they took over every part of the department except Section Four, where Saad and the remaining twenty-eight prisoners were now housed. To make room, on the day before the war all of the Iranian prisoners were released and bused to Iran.

The Arabs and Foreigners Department was known in the prison as the Sheraton of Abu Ghraib. In spite of the beatings and the constant spying and mistrust, the prisoners there lived with liberties that were not to be found in any other prison section in Iraq. It may all have been for the benefit of the visiting diplomats and Red Cross officials, who had the right to see citizens of their own countries, but it certainly made life easier for the foreign prisoners. That all changed when the Hakmiya men arrived. Suddenly, the department, for all its flower beds and Ping-Pong tables, became the new Mukhabarat detention and interrogation center. The brightest part of Abu Ghraib became the darkest corner of the Mukhabarat.

With the keys long lost because of the open-door policy within sections, the Hakmiya men had rings welded on the cell doors so that they could padlock their prisoners in. There was no talking allowed; there were no rights to anything. Everyone had to wear standard-issue Hakmiya pajamas. The department's prisoners, like Saad, were warned not to talk to us or look at us from their new home in Section Four. But Saad did see. He saw us walking across the garden past the disused fountain. He saw us sitting in the sunshine signing our statements. And through the walls, he heard the torture of our fellow prisoners in the interrogation rooms of Section Three, just as we heard the screams more faintly, carrying across the garden to our cells in Section Five.

But between 1996 and late February 2003, the Arabs and Foreigners Department was run by men like Abu Firaz. As the ranking Baath Party official in the department, he was the third most powerful man, after the director and the security officer.

He joined the Mukhabarat six months before the war with Iran began in 1980 and was given a classic Mukhabarat job—hunting down foreigners who were inside Iraq illegally. He was a spy catcher. After years on the job, he grew tired and was happy to be assigned to a quieter life at Abu Ghraib. There he enforced the strict discipline of the prison.

"Drugs, gay sex, we stopped everything like that," he said, sitting in a *dishdasha* and worn flip-flops. "Pills, gays, illegal letters, fighting."

How would you punish them? I asked.

"Oh, we'd raise their legs and place their feet into this sort of wooden frame and we would beat them on the soles of their feet and shave their heads, and put them in a one-meter-by-one-meter room for twelve days," he said.

There were no hard feelings, he said, as if he thought that the prisoners would forgive and forget. The guards would play soccer with the prisoners, sometimes in mixed teams, on the packed earth field in the northern half of the department's compound. There were volleyball games, basketball matches. The prisoners could cook their own food and sell it, keeping the money. The Syrians were especially good at falafel and *shwarma*. The medical care was good, and a Syrian prisoner with medical training tended to guards and prisoners alike when the doctors weren't available. When the Mukhabarat took over the section there were fifty tuberculosis cases. The new director ordered the wealthier prisoners to pay for meat for the TB patients and made sure they had medical care; three months later, there were only three active cases left. One of the fifty prisoners died.

Prisoners were allowed televisions and refrigerators in their cells if their families brought them to the prison. They could play Ping-Pong and pool. They planted all the flower beds and grew vegetables in neat plots around the compound. They could wander around and talk to each other at any time. The only times they were locked in was at night, and then only the doors to each of the five sections were locked.

Their families could visit them and bring them cigarettes, money, and other things they needed. Diplomats and Red Cross officials also had access.

When the department needed repairs, the prison authorities sent over some inmates from other departments. "They described the place as just like heaven," Abu Firaz said.

Other officers I spoke to all described this similarly beneficent regime in the department. But that was the official line from people who made their living from the prison. Saad always had a different story; the beatings, the infighting, the suspicion. "Everyone is your enemy in prison," Saad told me. And then there was the gnawing knowledge that he was spending twenty-eight years in prison for nothing. Like thousands of Iraqis, his life was slipping away because of the regime's paranoia and assumption that anyone who looked vaguely guilty was guilty.

Other guards from different parts of the prison I spoke to later told me that everyone in Abu Ghraib was guilty. "We had no innocent prisoners," said a man who would give his name only as Jassim. He lives nearby the prison in the Sina quarters, a rundown government compound that houses the families of 175 prison employees. "They were all criminals." A conviction in Jassim's eyes equaled guilt.

So I asked Abu Firaz about how fair the Hakmiya's investigative methods were.

"Anyone who is innocent would be set free, but anyone who is guilty would be punished," he began, simply.

"But how would they know if they were really guilty when people would confess under torture?"

"The investigative methods prohibited hitting and harming prisoners," he said. "No prisoner would be held at the Hakmiya without a judge's approval, and he would have a Ph.D. in law. The judge must be sure."

"But again, there was torture, so how could the judge know?"

"Before, yes," he said. "But lately, any officer who built up a case and was wrong would be punished. All officers must make sure of their cases before writing to the Hakmiya. But being beaten and hit is normal. Even in a police station it's normal."

I wasn't following his logic, and I was not convinced that he was either. He continued.

"If they confess, they won't be beaten," he said. "If they don't confess, they would be beaten. On the soles of their feet. With an electric stick. It's so important for the investigators to get the prisoner to confess."

"But surely they could just beat a confession out of an innocent man," I said.

"That's normal. This happened to everyone. They would start hitting someone and they would get a false confession. When it came to human rights, there weren't any, to be honest."

"So the system wasn't fair, then? It didn't work."

"Yes," he said. "You're right."

This was like the rest of my conversations with former security officers: no matter how cooperative or hospitable they were, there was an unsettling lack of insight. They insisted on their loyalty to their country and their own fairness and humanity even as they acknowledged beating confessions out of their terrified countrymen. I saw the tendency in other Iraqis too, especially as crime gripped their neighborhoods. That yearning for the sense of order and unquestionable simplicity that Saddam had supplied echoed the post-totalitarian nostalgia that had seduced many Russians and Serbs after the collapse of their own regimes. With the rapid rise of organized crime and the spread of unemployment and poverty, many people in those countries yearned for a return to iron-fisted rule. Only time and a new stability, and perhaps a few reasoned discussions like the one I was trying to have with Abu Firaz, can move Iraqis toward accepting that future freedoms are worth more than gone-forever rigidity.

But just when I thought that this oddly endearing tool of the regime had gained some insight into the absurd brutality of Saddam's world, he stripped his former president of any responsibility and, by implication, excused the entire system. The torture was an aberration.

"Saddam Hussein gave an order," Abu Firaz told me, "not to use hitting or beating during an investigation, but they still didn't follow his orders."

In a corner of Abu Ghraib is a building distinguished from the other cell-block structures in the prison by the unusual elevation of one side of the roof. If you walk through the gray metal front door and turn right, the reason for the unusual height becomes clear. On the left is a concrete ramp with a white metal handrail running along its open side. It leads onto a platform, which has in its center a cream-painted metal box with a lever sticking out. You can push the lever down without much effort and watch as two metal catches pull back from the center of the two square holes in the platform. When the building was in use, trapdoors that have now been ripped off would drop to either side and the two men who had been standing on the doors a moment earlier would be hanging with ropes around their necks above the floor below.

Dr. Fadhil Franghoul always refused to attend the executions—it was a privilege he held as the prison's ranking doctor. He would send the visiting doctors, the physicians who counted the days they would have to work in Abu Ghraib as keenly as did the prisoners. Someone had to be there to verify that the hanged prisoners were indeed dead. Now and then a body would show signs of life.

But usually, the fall would sever the vertebrae and the prisoner would only struggle and convulse for about ten seconds before he died, dangling there in the red pajamas that Abu Firaz said condemned men would change into before their hanging.

Wednesdays were the most common execution days. There were no executions on Fridays, Muslim holidays, or public holidays.

The visiting doctors would do anything to avoid working on Wednesdays. If they were on duty, they would pick lots. Their other duty, besides checking that the prisoners were really dead, was to extract their corneas. Specialists from Baghdad's eye hospital would come on Thursdays to collect the dead men's corneas.

"Maybe in America a patient needs years to get a cornea, but in Iraq it took one week," Dr. Fadhil told me as we sat in his office in the Saint Raphael Hospital in Baghdad, where he works three days a week. "The receptionist here has an executed man's corneas. It was not ethical. But my colleague is very happy, of course, because he can see again."

Reaching the noose required a prisoner to be dragged through at least ten hoops of Iraqi bureaucracy, according to the former governor of the prison, Dr. Tamim. Again, the Baathist system required meticulous order: The execution order would go from the first court to another court and on up to the president's office; it would then take another several journeys to various ministries and courts and committees before finally landing at Abu Ghraib. Then time was up for the man on death row.

Officials would inform the family on the day before the execution that they could visit their relative at 10:00 A.M. the following morning for the last time. At 8:00 A.M. guards would take the condemned man out of his cell to a larger room, where he could shower, read the Koran, pray on a prayer mat, and eat his last meal. That's where he would also see his family for the last time. They had to leave at noon.

In the late afternoon, guards would come to take the prisoner on his final walk. If the man was considered violent, the number of guards would be greater. They handcuffed him and put a hood over his head. They weighed him; if the man was particularly heavy, the hangmen would use a thicker rope.

Tamim said, not altogether credibly, that he never witnessed an execution in all the years he was the prison's governor, but Abu Firaz didn't hesitate to acknowledge that he saw the room in action. An Egyptian prisoner, already convicted of murder, one day seized a guard's pistol and killed another Egyptian he had a dispute with.

"I signed his hanging order," Abu Firaz told me, deadpan as ever.

In the twilight, he took the prisoner from the department, across the prison compound to the execution section, which sits on the south side of the prison. The Egyptian ambassador was present, along with a judge, the prosecutor, and an official from the Ministry of the Interior. The prisoner was called before the judge, who had the Egyptian's file. A General Security officer tied the prisoner's hands behind his back and slipped a black hood over his head.

"Say you believe in God," the judge said.

"I do," the Egyptian said.

There were six prisoners to be executed that day. One by one they were led up the ramp. The lever and trapdoor system had, in fact, stopped working years earlier. So the hangmen had placed a metal rod across the gaping hole and guided the men onto it. Then they pushed them off, one by one.

Abu Firaz was friendly with the Egyptian. As the man stood on the iron bar, he called out to his friend and executioner, "Don't be angry with me."

The Egyptian died instantly. But an Iraqi prisoner was still alive when the doctor shook his body to see if he had any signs of life. "They hanged him another time," Abu Firaz said.

When it was all over, guards removed the body and took it to the prison's morgue. The family came the next day to collect the body.

The executions in the hanging room were all for criminals, Tamim told me. The regime's security services didn't bother with the charade of legitimacy with political prisoners. "They executed them in their own places, but we'd issue the certificates of execution. They didn't have to follow all these procedures. They acted very fast."

Then Tamim laughed bitterly. "For the mass graves, if they'd followed all these procedures no one would have been executed by now."

As the prison's head doctor for six years, Dr. Fadhil walked and worked among its tens of thousands of tubercular, mentally ill, and drug-addicted inmates. He had prisoners lining up at his office in the long-term prisoners department to show him their hemorrhoids and their bloody sputum and to beg for morphine or Valium to feed addictions that took them away from their desolation and reality for a few hours.

There was often little he could do for them. He had enough medication and equipment for three to four thousand prisoners and there were usually at least twenty thousand inmates in the prison. He was the only permanent doctor, with others being forced to come in for two, three, or four weeks from hospitals in Baghdad to bring the number of doctors up to four. There were four dentists and three or four pharmacists. Dr. Fadhil had a small lab and one x-ray machine. A small operating theater took care of things like appendectomies and fractures; for more serious conditions prisoners would have to be taken to Noor Hospital in Baghdad. But getting permission from the prison authorities to transfer a prisoner there was infuriatingly hard, and permission was often denied.

It was the same for people with malignant tumors. Countless signatures were necessary for the patient to be sent to a hospital with treatment facilities for cancer. Bribes would have to be paid, even to the ambulance drivers. Most patients didn't get all the signatures in time. "So they died," Dr. Fadhil said.

Scabies was a big problem; tuberculosis even bigger. The overcrowding made Abu Ghraib a petri dish for TB, its bacteria floating easily between inmates in the air of the crammed cells. Two prisoners every week died from the highly treatable disease.

"When Saddam Hussein released the prisoners [in the amnesty of October 2002], Abu Ghraib discharged a thousand persons with TB into the community," Dr. Fadhil told me.

The prison had a separate room for TB patients, with twenty-four beds. It was always full. And it was luxury compared to the cells—there were air coolers for the brutal summer months and heaters in the winter.

A psychiatrist came once a month for two hours. "I had ten thousand psychiatric patients," Dr. Fadhil said. "The psychiatrist would tell me that he would need at the very least a quarter of an hour for each patient. When the prisoners would hear that the psychiatrist was there, he would see two to three hundred patients show up at his door. He tried not to come. Said he was busy."

Patients with the most serious mental health problems would find a razor and cut away at themselves, begging for Valium. Dr. Fadhil, if he was around, would give them an injection to calm them down, knowing that he was feeding their habit but seeing no option. The drug problem seemed insurmountable to him. Particularly popular was a psychiatric drug imported from Iran called Tophranil. It would make a prisoner euphoric, hallucinatory, and then finally sleepy. People often take drugs to escape. Abu Ghraib's addicts had more of a reason than most to yearn for a temporary reprieve from their lives. Dr. Fadhil would see beatings two or three times a week.

"They were tortured by holding their legs up and beating their feet, or they would be put in a small room for three months with one glass of water a day," he said. "Everyone who was engaging in homosexual practices or drugs would have to give the guards money or get hit and go upstairs to the small room. But anyone who had money or behaved would be okay."

Dr. Fadhil, a man of independent means who was paid $15 per month for a job that he did not have to do for as long as he did it and who had to drive twenty-five miles in his Volkswagen Passat from his house in the Zayouna neighborhood of Baghdad out to the prison, could barely tear himself away from Abu Ghraib. He stayed for six years, right up to late 2002. The prison was empty but for the few inmates still left in the Arabs and Foreigners Department. He had nothing to do then.

"I loved it," he said.

It wasn't just the feeling that he was helping patients who were suffering so much. For him, going into prison was a way of tasting a little freedom that he did not have outside the walls of Abu Ghraib. Dr. Fadhil had to go in to the very center of Saddam Hussein's world of killing and imprisonment to sample the liberty to talk about the horrors of the dictator that neither he nor anyone else outside the walls of Abu Ghraib could enjoy. Because in the safety of his office, he could talk with jailed ex-ministers and other educated men— doctors and engineers—about the regime they all hated. Their treasonous words bound them together in a vow of silence. They would sit in the air-conditioned room on the six chairs Dr. Fadhil had in front of his desk and drink tea and talk inside about things they could never talk about outside.

"It made me happy to hear these stories and I would just keep them in my mind," he said. "Of course I couldn't tell other people."

Toward the end of my second long talk with Abu Firaz in his tatty living room, I asked him to theorize as to why I had been arrested and released. We talked about our visas and moving around Baghdad without minders, and he said, yes, these could have been factors. But when I mentioned that we had visited the *takyia* he grinned and began to explain the regime's attitude toward the Sufis.

"They were suspected of not being loyal," he began. "They were caught in conspiracies at times. Lately an increasing number of *takyias* were closed. That had been going on for seven years. . . . They wanted to overthrow the regime. They had officers from the army who were helping them."

The lines on his face crinkled in disgust as he began to describe the Sufi ceremonies, especially the acts of self-mutilation.

"These things in Islam we call food for genies. Some people who are not Muslim, in India, do the same. They eat pieces of glass. The drumming brings out the genies and then they come into their bodies."

According to his orthodox Sunni belief system, he explained, genies are real beings made of fire. And because they are from fire, and not the mud from which God created humans, they believed they should not obey humans, as all other creatures were supposed to.

"It's a tribe, like a human tribe," he said. "They live beneath the ground in dirty places. They can see us but we can't see them. To see them you have to read the Koran in an inverted way—or wear the Koran on your shoes when you go to the toilet. Then you will see the genie and he will obey you."

He explained it all at length, but because I am not a scholar of Islam I became lost in the doctrine and suspicion. But it was now clear that the humanistic, peace-loving Sufis that I thought I had met at the *takyia* had been, in the eyes of the Sunni-dominated regime's enforcers, both a political and a religious threat. My translator, Mukhaled, is also a Sunni, and he considers Sufism almost a form of devil worship. So does Saad, a Shia.

By showing up without a minder at one of the most important *takyias* in Iraq, as the war seemed imminent, Moises and I had walked into a building that the regime considered the source of one of its greatest internal challenges, a magnet for spies and plotters and Mukhabarat agents trying to catch them.

15

Tea with Abu Ibrahim

Gandhi Kasnazani did not look much like his spindly, bald, humbly dressed namesake. His stomach was only just losing the battle to pop the buttons of the blue shirt that Gandhi wore under his well-pressed gray suit. He had a full head of hair, and armed guards kept watch on the *takyia,* where his new black Mercedes was parked in the driveway. I looked at him and doubted whether his older brother Nehru wore the eponymous jackets. And yet the names seemed somehow appropriate for the sons of a Sufi leader who, unlike many of Iraq's Muslim clerics, preached that all humans are equal in the eyes of God and welcomed all at the Takyia Kasnazan. Less appropriate was Gandhi's account of the decidedly nonpacifist approach of his brother and many members of the *takyia* toward the regime before and during the war. It was probably true, he laughed, that Moises and I had become primary targets of the Mukhabarat's attention the moment we had stepped into the *takyia*'s grounds in early

March. The place had for years been a site of opposition activity and meetings, and the congregation was well penetrated by agents of the security services.

I was keen to know the extent of this opposition movement within Iraq. In a country where even criticizing the president's family was a capital crime, exactly how possible was it for any group to organize an opposition to Saddam? Various generals and ranking members of the regime had plotted and failed over the years to assassinate Saddam or topple the regime, and they had all suffered the same terminal fate. The most successful effort had been the attempted assassination of Saddam's oldest son, Uday, as he waited in his car at a traffic light next to a popular ice cream parlor in the wealthy Mansour district of Baghdad. That attack left Uday close to death and in need of medical attention for the rest of his life. The assailants, amazingly, were never caught. All other attempts to overthrow the regime had been disastrous. These were generally well-publicized events, and anyone considering any attempt to undermine the regime would know the price of failure. I had seen that price when I had watched the thirteen bodies clothed in blue-and-white striped pajamas being unearthed outside the Arabs and Foreigners Department.

Three of those men were from the *takyia*, Gandhi explained: a farmer with three children named Abdul Majid Khalifa al-Samarai; another farmer called Abbas, who also had three children but whose family name escaped Gandhi; and a laborer called Abdul Karim Mohammed Jawad, who had one child. They were all in their forties or fifties, and yes, Gandhi said, they all owned Thurayas. But the terrible irony, he said, was that they did not happen to be part of the underground movement that was centered at the *takyia*. Like Gandhi and many other traders, they were merchants who used Thurayas to organize clandestine business deals with people in Kurdistan without the regime listening in on a land line. The government—mainly Uday—took a dim view of merchants who did not give them a cut. Uday was Iraq's chief smuggler, and he wanted it to stay that way. These three lesser smugglers had been among the nearly 100 Sufis arrested after the third day of the war from various *takyias* around Iraq, and because they had confessed under interrogation to owning Thurayas, they had been executed, Gandhi said.

Not among the 100 were three or four other Sufis who also had Thurayas, Gandhi told me. These men were indeed using them to contact opposition forces in the Kurdish town of Suleymaniyeh.

"When we felt that the war was inevitable," Gandhi said, in his slow, measured voice, "we started militias in the north and inside Iraq, and we prepared for any uprising that might take place."

This was a bold claim, and I questioned Gandhi carefully about the extent of the armed Sufi militia. In 1991, Gandhi said, members of Takyia Kasnazan had begun to use the building as a meeting place for those who opposed the regime. He said their chief aim was to educate people about the brutality of the regime, a modest if dangerous goal. It wasn't until after the events of September 11, 2001, that the group decided that war was likely and that they should do their best to join in an uprising if one happened. There were now about 1,500 rebels in the north, based around Suleymaniyeh, he said. They coordinated their activities with the dominant Kurdish party in that part of the country, the Patriotic Union of Kurdistan, taking care not to step on the toes of the party's leader, Jalal Talabani. Around the rest of Iraq there were small cells of twenty to thirty members. Gandhi said that while the Iraq-based militias did not really take part in an uprising—no real uprisings took place during the war—the militia in the north had helped liberate Kirkuk and Diala. They operated under Nehru, who lived with his father, Mohammed Kasnazani, in Suleymaniyeh.

The militia now forms the basis of the Coalition of Iraqi National Unity, one of the hundreds of new Iraqi political parties.

I had earlier visited the party's headquarters and had met officials who made such wild claims of antiregime activity that I had dismissed it all as opportunistic fiction. Gandhi's claims were relatively modest, but nevertheless some details made no sense to me. He said that the group's supporters at Uday's Youth TV station would intentionally query government ministers with unexpectedly hard questions. According to conventional wisdom among Iraq watchers, this was Uday's way of undermining ministers he did not like. Gandhi also said that members of the organization would send false letters from one minister to another, causing disputes between them. Not a tactic that would bolster unity, perhaps, but not one that would topple a dictator, either. What I found particularly damaging to Gandhi's credibility was his own status as a quasi-minister in the government, in charge of religious affairs in the north. His family is Kurdish. He was jailed, as is commonly known, but then released and reinstated in his post. And his obvious wealth—the Mercedes, the nice suit, the deferential guards—made me wonder how he could have obtained it without some degree of cooperation with the regime.

But it had nevertheless become clear to me that Nehru and other members of the *takyia* were involved in stirring up some kind of opposition before and during the war. Mukhaled and I spoke to two PUK officials, including one of its military commanders in Suleymaniyeh, Sheikh Jafer Nabou. Yes, he told Mukhaled on the telephone, the Sufis under Nehru did have a force of between 1,000 and 1,500 in and around the town before and during the war. There was neither cooperation nor disagreement between the Sufis and the PUK, he said.

The very ownership of Thurayas and the location of their father, the movement's leader, in Kurdistan was enough to constitute guilt in the eyes of the regime's intelligence agencies. The arrests did happen. The executions happened. And, as Mukhabarat men like Abu Firaz and Abu Thar had so vividly explained, the Sufis were constantly under surveillance. Yes, Gandhi said, the security services had closed many *takyias* over the past several years.

"These religious places were full of people from the north," Abu Thar had told me at our first meeting, in his home. "They were all being monitored. The regime was cautious about some people at the *takyia* working against the government. There were many high-up people in the government who attended the *takyia*. So we would go there to watch. There were strangers going there to interfere with the thoughts of those high-ranking officials."

My guess was that the Sufis were a target for two reasons: First, they were genuinely stirring up opposition to the government, albeit in a way that caused no real threat. Second, their unorthodox religious practices and beliefs were such an affront to the Sunni-dominated regime that the *takyias* could only be seen as a source of trouble. I could think of only one way to find a reliable answer to this question and to so many other questions I still had about the workings of the Mukhabarat and how Moises and I had come to be snared up in it. I had to find Abu Ibrahim.

In front of his sons and neighbors, who had come round for lunch, Abu Thar scornfully laughed off my request that he help me track down Abu Ibrahim. I had explained why I wanted to meet him, and I had described him carefully: tall, thin, graying hair, a slightly high voice, speaks a little English, very calm with his body movements. I mentioned what I believed to be his real name. "You're ticking off the boxes," Abu Thar couldn't help saying, his mouth curling into a smile, and I knew then that I had a solid lead. Earlier hints as to his identity and address had left me, after nearly three months of looking, with nothing but a name. But Abu Thar wasn't interested. "You want me to lead you to a fellow intelligence officer?" he asked, not expecting an answer. "You want me to do this in front of my sons?"

After lunch, Abu Thar led Mukhaled and me to our car in the narrow street outside. It was the audience, not the request, that had been the problem. "I'll get the details of his case," he told Mukhaled quietly. "And I'll do my best to fix up the meeting."

A few days later Abu Thar came to my hotel room, and we had a long talk and then some lunch. He spotted the bottles of scotch on my shelf and insisted that I drink with him even though it was only one o'clock. He preferred to eat in the room and not be seen dining with me in public.

I took it gently, not pressing too early or too much for details about my interrogator, a man who I believed had the power of life and death over me for eight days, who I believe had been involved in the execution of my block mates. I had radically conflicting feelings about him. In my cell, I had decided that I would never wish any harm to come to him or any of my captors. And indeed, he had not hurt me physically. At times, he had shown me kindness and courtesy, even if they were only part of his good-cop routine. Ultimately, he had let me go, let me live. I refused to let myself feel any anger toward him. And yet there were occasional times when I wanted to hurt him very badly. Shortly after returning to Baghdad I had been walking toward the copper bazaar, scanning the dozens of faces that passed me, hoping to chance upon a familiar one from Abu Ghraib. And there in front of me was Abu Ibrahim. I was about to hurl myself at him and wrestle him to the sidewalk—for some reason I had a particular urge to twist his left arm behind his back—before I realized that it was not him after all. More recently, I had been lashing out at people I loved, venting emotions naturally intended for Abu Ibrahim and the other men who had held us in prison. The elation that I had felt immediately after being released had begun to curdle into a confused and multilayered resentment.

Further complicating the prospect of seeing Abu Ibrahim, or for that matter men like Abu Thar and Abu Firaz, was the gnawing knowledge that I had to protect them. Torturers, jailers, men who had sent other men to their deaths and, for all I know, had personally killed innocent Iraqis. I believe passionately in prosecuting war criminals and people who use the cover of an authoritarian regime's laws as a rationale for violence against its own people. But I assured Abu Thar, when trying to persuade him to arrange the meeting, that I would rather go to jail myself than to give the occupying forces or a court information about the true identities or addresses of my sources. It's a matter of some debate within journalistic circles whether it is acceptable for reporters to testify at war crimes trials. Some journalists have, indeed, testified against suspects from the former Yugoslavia. That is a grave mistake. To maintain the integrity of not just one's own reputation but that of the whole profession, we must all make sure that when sources talk to a reporter, they are not talking to a proxy for a prosecutor or a government. Agonizing as it may be—and I have interviewed some Serbs, for example, who deserve to spend the rest of their lives in prison for their crimes—in the long term journalists must remain completely independent of governments and courts if they are to retain their ability to uncover the truth in their own way.

There was no avenue open to me but to suppress all of these mixed emotions of revenge and conflicted interests. Abu Ibrahim was the sharpest corner of the regime that I had encountered, and to understand it better, I had to meet him. I wanted to understand why educated and seemingly reasonable men like Abu Thar and Abu Ibrahim could so easily find themselves devoting their lives to a murderous tyrant. Why didn't all the doctors and lawyers and engineers who joined the Mukhabarat in the early 1970s work at making sick people better, defending the innocent, and building bridges? Why, at least, couldn't they use their intellect to realize what they were becoming and what they were supporting as Al-Bakr's proud and affluent Iraq turned into Saddam's world of suspicion and death?

As we talked, sometimes Abu Thar would bring Abu Ibrahim into conversation. I tried not to look especially interested or to follow up with overenthusiastic questions. I did not want him to think that I was luring Abu Ibrahim and him into a trap, an arrest.

I told Abu Thar that the greatest weapon that Abu Ibrahim had used against me had been fear.

"Yes, it's a human instinct of any person considered guilty to fear interrogation," he said. "It's also to do with the raising and the family of the investigator. Some, like Abu Ibrahim, most people he interrogated would feel he's a friend to them and are quite open with him. Some people would die of high pressure during investigation—they would see the investigator and simply die from his looks. It would be a blood pressure thing. That's why in most investigations we'd blindfold the guilty person. For Abu Ibrahim, most people wanted the blindfold off. He's very good at making friends."

How good was Abu Ibrahim? I asked.

"Very, very good. He's a very educated guy. That's the reason for his successful career—he's a just and educated guy."

Abu Thar explained that Abu Ibrahim was a Shia, like himself, and that he had little time for the regime loyalists from Tikrit and other towns in the Sunni heartland.

"The main reason for his success was his education and his success in interrogations. He's calm and educated and a law graduate.

His main job was to investigate cases such as yours. Some cases, very important ones, they would assign him to them for his brilliance."

Abu Thar promised to do his very best to arrange a meeting. I prayed that I had found my final degree of separation between Abu Ibrahim and myself, that my lunch guest was not just leading me on. So I asked him one more question about Abu Ibrahim.

Are you friends with him?

"We are like brothers," he said.

Saddam may have lost his seat of power, but he has not lost his power to breed suspicion. I saw it everywhere in the faces of Iraqis I would approach. And I felt it inside myself. Mukhaled and I set out one day to find Intesar, the guide at the Amariya shelter whose name had so startlingly come up during my interrogation. She was not at the shelter, which had been taken over by an Islamic political party. But we found her at home and knocked on the door.

She looked surprised to have visitors and showed no sign of recognizing me. I wished her no ill, even if she had been a Mukhabarat informant, but I wanted to know. She and her husband invited us in and served us Pepsis. I told her my story and her already big eyes widened. She was as kindly then as when I had first met her. I realized quickly that my suspicions stained only myself, that she had nothing to do with what had happened to Moises and me. I apologized to her children for interrupting the movie they had been watching on television, and we left.

On the morning of Sunday, July 13, I paced around my room with the nerves of a teenage boy waiting on the appointed street corner for his date, full of excitement and dread that I might somehow blow it. I was waiting for Mukhaled to show up. He was due to come with Abu Thar and perhaps even Abu Ibrahim.

The hotel phone rang and Mukhaled said, "We're coming up."

When I opened the door it was just Mukhaled and Abu Thar, dressed in navy slacks and a neatly pressed blue shirt. I was disappointed. While I made coffee Mukhaled came into the kitchenette and

I gave him the thumbs up, thumbs down sign, my eyebrows raised. "He's met with Abu Ibrahim and has the story," he whispered.

Abu Thar had given Abu Ibrahim some line about meeting a guy who was working with foreign journalists who wanted to know the true story about the five Westerners who had been arrested during the war. Abu Ibrahim's story confirmed my suspicions: The combination of our irregular visas, our possession of Thurayas, and our visit to the *takyia* had convinced the Mukhabarat that we were spies. They were so sure of it that they had arrested us, even though usually the Mukhabarat, on the orders of Saddam, preferred to escort foreigners suspected of spying out of the country or to ban them from obtaining visas again.

What had begun to intrigue me more was why we had been released. Nothing had counted in our favor. Everyone connected with the case had expressed their amazement that we had made it out alive; with the regime on the brink of collapse, surely the Iraqi authorities had nothing to lose by killing us. And we were in the custody of an organization that tended to see suspicion as guilt—Saad being a tragic but typical example. Saad Majid Ali, the former governor of Abu Ghraib, had told me that 75 percent of the people released from the prison in the October amnesty were innocent—perhaps a slight exaggeration borne from his insistence on his own innocence, but even a significantly lower figure of guiltless inmates would be a horrifying statistic. Not to forget the roughly 300,000 Iraqis believed executed by the regime over the years.

Abu Ibrahim had explained to Abu Thar that there were two main factors that had prevented our becoming part of that number.

First, our stories had held together. By the end of our interrogations he had decided that, after all, we were not spies. They had no tape recordings, no documents, no confessions. The evidence was circumstantial. To execute us would simply not have been proper, not consistent with the old-school Mukhabarat's pride in its investigatorial integrity. Bizarre as this sounds, given the way that parts of the organization tortured and executed the innocent, I believe it. A spy agency does not think with one brain. The Mukhabarat had its mindless and brutal elements, especially those from Saddam's tribe and their allies. If the wrong interrogator had been appointed to our case, we might have ended up in the shallow grave outside the Arabs and Foreigners Department. We were lucky, Abu Thar told me several times, to have the fair-minded and well-educated Abu Ibrahim as our investigator.

The five-day wait after we had signed our statements was an inevitable by-product of regime bureaucracy. We didn't know it but we were already safe by the afternoon of day three. Abu Ibrahim and his colleagues had not been trying to torture us psychologically by leaving us alone with our brains for all that time, even though that was the effect. They had, in fact, been trying to get rid of us. The paperwork had to go to the right senior officers in the Mukhabarat before we could be released. Under war conditions, Abu Thar said, we had again been lucky that it had taken only five days—four, if you consider that our last night in prison was necessary only because the man from the residence directorate could not get our exit visas in time—to get all the right signatures.

And then there was the second reason that we had been released, one that might shed light on other matters far more important than our fate. I don't for a second want to suggest that Moises, Philip, Johan, Molly, and I were a deliberate part of Saddam's grand plan for his legacy. I'm sure he never even heard of our case. But his legacy-building system was already institutionalized and, perhaps a little ironically, it contributed to saving us. Saddam's need to appear righteous on some level helped pluck us from the depths of the murderous, paranoid machine he had so carefully and tirelessly constructed.

In spite of knowing Farzad Bazoft's story, I had whispered to Molly while we were checking in to Abu Ghraib that "they wouldn't be that stupid" as to harm us. I didn't believe it then, but I believe it now, in light of what Abu Thar told me. Saddam's earlier decision to avoid the inevitable bad publicity and controversy over other suspected foreign agents had become institutionalized within the security services. "The government policy was to avoid any international incident with foreigners," Abu Thar told me. "For the Iraqis, we could deal with them in the right way. But for foreigners it was very difficult to take hard decisions against them." Ever the player of world public opinion, the self-deluding Saddam did not want to bolster his reputation as a brutal and unreasonable man. For years he had been using the sanctions, the UN weapons inspectors, and his opposition to Israel and support for the Palestinians as tools to garner support in the world at large and the Arab and Muslim worlds in particular.

To a great extent, he succeeded in tricking much of the world into seeing him and his country as victims of an American-led conspiracy. Nothing was more powerful than the images of children dying because of the sanctions. But much of it was a hoax, Iraqi doctors explained to me after the war. In May 2001 I first visited Ibn al-Baladi Hospital in the huge Shia slum of Baghdad that was then known as Saddam City. Doctors, speaking in the presence of my Ministry of Information minder, told Sandro Contenta of the *Toronto Star* and me that Iraq's appallingly high mortality rate among children was due to the sanctions. The hospital did not have enough medicine, and families did not have clean water and sufficient food. "It is one of the results of the embargo," Dr. Ghassam Rashid al-Baya told me. A dehydrated baby named Ali Hussein had just died on Al-Baya's treatment table, the second to die in the wards within seven minutes. "This is a crime on Iraq. What is wrong with these poor children? Are they soldiers that they have to be treated like this? They are not soldiers."

I returned to the hospital after the war and now the doctors could speak freely. "We had the ability to get all the drugs we needed," said the hospital's chief resident, Dr. Hussein Shihab. "Instead of that, Saddam Hussein spent all the money on his military force and put all the fault on the United States. Yes, of course the sanctions hurt but not too much because we are a rich country, and we have the ability to get everything we can by money. But instead, he spent it on his palaces." Shihab and his counterparts at another hospital told me that they were also forced to refrigerate dead babies until the Ministry of Information and the Mukhabarat were ready to gather the corpses together in a monthly convoy of small coffins on the roofs of taxis for the benefit of Iraqi state television and visiting journalists. The parents were ordered to wail with grief—no matter how many weeks had passed since their babies had died—and to tell the cameras that the sanctions had killed their children, the doctors said. Afterward, the parents would be rewarded with food or money. People all over the world denounced the sanctions as responsible for the deaths of hundreds of thousands of Iraqi children. In many ways the sanctions did directly harm the Iraqi population, especially the sometimes absurd vetoes often exercised by the British and Americans on the UN committee that approved Iraqi requests for imported goods. Items considered of potential dual use—in other words, those that had civilian uses but could also be used for military purposes—were often blocked by the committee. One legendary example was the block put on the export of pencils for fear that the carbon could be used for military purposes. But whatever happened in the meeting rooms of the UN, Saddam continued to exploit the sanctions for his own benefit. It was all an enormous coup for Saddam and his public image.

His ultimate, and ultimately fruitless, achievement had been the massive worldwide condemnation of the coming war and the failure of the United States and Britain to gain approval for their war at the UN Security Council. And it appears now, as of this writing, that he had indeed ordered his chemical and biological weapons programs destroyed, that there was nothing for the inspectors to find. And that the stated American and British rationale for the war—that Saddam had weapons of mass destruction ready to use at a moment's notice—was mistaken. I imagine that wherever he is, Saddam is enormously enjoying the failure of the Americans and British to find those weapons.

It all served one of the things that mattered and probably still matters most to Saddam—his legacy. He has always wanted to be seen as a great pan-Arab hero. The busts of him dressed as the Muslim conqueror Saladin (who was, ironically, a Kurd) that still stand on two of his most spectacular palaces in Baghdad are constant reminders to Baghdadis and American troops of that ambition. I don't think he considered the slaughtering of countless Shia and Kurdish citizens after the 1991 uprisings a blot on his legacy. In his mind, I imagine, it was just punishment for disloyalty. And, depressingly, the stories about mass graves in Iraq have already dropped out of the pages of our newspapers. Saddam was right that the world powers did not sufficiently care about these mass murders to unseat him from power. It was bad press, but not bad enough ever to spark a war—or to stain his image.

What would have forever made him a worldwide outcast, however, especially with the German and French governments who had so strongly opposed the war, would have been killing Westerners. And I do not mean just the five of us. Early in the war, Saddam had a group of American prisoners of war in his hands. Although he paraded them on Iraqi state television, which passed on the footage to Al-Jazeera, the Americans were all found alive and well after the war. As were we. And so whatever his crimes, Saddam will not go down in history as the killer of Western journalists, American peace activists, or American POWs.

But why, then, I asked Abu Thar, did Saddam order Bazoft executed? Few actions could have more alienated Saddam and Iraq from the world community than that.

Those were different times, Abu Thar said. The war with Iran was over and Saddam was claiming victory. He felt emboldened, powerful, perhaps even invincible. So much so that later that year he invaded Kuwait, convinced that he would get away with it. Killing Bazoft was just another way of pulling up his shirt sleeves and showing off his biceps.

"Saddam wanted to show how strong he was," Abu Thar told me. "He didn't care for any other country at that time. One of the tough speeches of [then British Prime Minister Margaret] Thatcher was about wanting [Bazoft] alive, to come back to Britain. But on his coffin he wrote, 'You wanted Bazoft alive, now you take him dead.' It was a political stand more than an intelligence stand. He just wanted to show how strong he was."

Saddam may find it easier now that he is out of power—now that he is the underdog—to cement his legacy than if he had remained president of Iraq. He has become a focal point for a resistance movement to an occupation, a role far more noble and romantic than the ultimate power he once held. Even if he is killed or captured, he will have gone out resisting, hiding, claiming responsibility for a growing wave of anti-American violence that could greatly appeal to an Arab and Muslim world ever more hostile to the United States. As with the Saudi government's disavowal of Osama bin Laden, the nascent Iraqi government and most Iraqis may see Saddam as an enemy. But for some other Arabs and Muslims he has turned into a symbol of anti-American resistance that he could never quite be while at the head of a regime whose brutality was unsurpassed perhaps anywhere in the contemporary world.

The knock came on the door of my hotel room and, as on March 24, the Mukhabarat was outside coming to see me. Only this time they were out of a job, and I wanted them there. Mukhaled burst in without waiting for me to answer. He was sweating. "Abu Ibrahim is here. You've never met Abu Thar before, okay?"

My hands began to shake slightly. I was not prepared for this, even though I had been preparing for it ever since we were released. Dirty teacups lay all over the coffee table. Abu Ibrahim, I was sure, was an obsessively clean man and he would disapprove of my mess. It was as if he were a strict father who was dropping in on me unexpectedly at my junior-year college dorm room. I didn't want his disapproval. I also didn't have a notebook handy, and my mind was suddenly scrambled.

There was nothing in the world I wanted more than this meeting, and still I dreaded it. Shortly after the war I had asked a group of former prisoners how I might find my interrogator. They had laughed at me. "Only if you see his face in the street," one of them had said. "It's a one-in-a-million chance."

I cleared away the cups. Moments later Abu Ibrahim walked into the room. "Matthew," he said in that gentle, high-pitched voice. He came toward me, smiling broadly.

"Abu Ibrahim," I said. And he embraced me. Not the usual handshake or the more affectionate three or four kisses on the cheek. I hugged him back and we squeezed tightly. I found myself kissing him quite passionately on the cheek once.

"How are you?" I asked.

"Fine," he said, and we were all nervous laughter.

Abu Thar sat on an armchair and Abu Ibrahim sat on the beige, two-person sofa. "Matthew, come," he said, patting the space next to him.

"I'll get you some tea first," I said, not knowing what to do with myself. I lit a cigarette, my hands trembling, and made for the kitchenette. I mulled over making a joke about putting truth serum in his tea and then thought better of it. I ordered some Arabic salads from room service and sat down next to my interrogator.

I had not been expecting him. Mukhaled had been working for days, trying to persuade Abu Thar finally to arrange the meeting. At last they had gone to Abu Ibrahim's house and Mukhaled had spent a long time persuading him to come. Their story was that Mukhaled was a cousin of Abu Thar, and that was how he had found my interrogator. Abu Ibrahim worried that it was a trap, that I would have American or British soldiers waiting for him. "But if you come right now he won't even know we're coming and couldn't possibly have anyone ready," Mukhaled argued. "And listen, I'm telling you, all he wants to do is thank you for saving his life." Eventually Abu Ibrahim went to his bedroom, took off his white *dishdasha* and kaffiyeh and came out in navy slacks, black shoes, and a well-pressed shirt of thin blue-and-white stripes. He was ready to go.

I gazed at the face that was now two feet from mine: the slightly hooked nose, the black moustache with only a few strands of white, the short salt-and-pepper hair receding from a high round forehead. His legs looked so thin in his pants. I could break this man in two, I thought, and pushed the impulse away. He wore a big silver ring, embedded with a swirling brown stone, on the wedding-ring finger of his left hand. He played with a string of black prayer beads. When he looked at me, his dark brown eyes fixed on mine and barely blinked.

He took the cigarette I offered him and smoked it in a way I had never before seen. He held it tenderly in his fingers, pointing it slightly upward, and kept his lips apart so that when he sucked a quiet hiss of air mixed in with the smoke he was inhaling.

I asked him how his family was, how he was, and we continued with uneasy pleasantries, picking up our teacups from the white Formica coffee table. At last, I thought, I have what I've been looking for. And I saw how privileged I was. I remembered Dr. Ahmed, the former political prisoner I had met only once, the man who had cried when I asked him what he wanted to ask his interrogator if he ever met the man. Dr. Ahmed was among the vast majority of Iraqis who would never have the time and the resources to track down their tormentors. They would never have the extraordinary luxury that I enjoyed of spending months finding one man. They had to get on with their lives, make a living, feed their kids, and go on without answers to their questions. Nor would they have the balm of storytelling, making sense of it all so that they could move on with ease. Saad told me one day, three months after the end of the war, that he had not had a single hour alone with his wife and his son to talk about what had happened to him. He was too busy with work and family obligations and was sleeping on the couch at his sister's house.

"This time I get to ask the questions," I said to Abu Ibrahim. And I realized that this was the revenge I wanted, to sit where he had sat and make him talk, make him give me answers. I wanted to interrogate him.

"This is only a private conversation," he said. He insisted that I not publish his real name, and so we agreed on Abu Ibrahim. I didn't tell him that the name he had used in Abu Ghraib had already appeared in *Newsday* and that anyone who wanted to see it could find it on the newspaper's website. But a deal is a deal. I pulled out my notebook and he began to talk in a slightly defensive, philosophical manner about truth, fairness, Islam, and the generally honorable nature of the Iraqi people. He didn't want me to see the looters and criminals who had scarred the country in recent weeks as representative of Iraqis. And, in hints, he acknowledged the misdeeds of the organization he had spent his life working for.

"I was raised in a village," he said. "I love nature. I've never been polluted by the city. I've traveled to most countries in the world. I have learned one thing from my family and my work—to always tell the truth. Only God knows how many mistakes were done by some people, and we did make great efforts at reform. Now that things have been revealed, some uncultured people need to be raised up severely."

Which I took to mean that since the end of the regime, the reporting about its crimes had been a good thing and that those who were guilty needed punishment or reeducation. Or maybe he was talking about those Iraqis now damaging the country. Maybe he wished he still had the power to deal with them in the ways he considered appropriate.

"That's why we used to be severe," he said, "to elevate people. When the regime collapsed, Baghdad was looted. How could a man destroy a school or hospital that had no connection to Saddam Hussein? We were raised with ethics. We wanted our people to be elevated. This isn't propaganda for the Mukhabarat. Maybe there were a few mistakes here and there."

He continued exculpating himself from crimes that I had not even asked about. He was an honest and ordinary man, he seemed to be saying.

"It's in my nature that when I would finish work I would go to the country. I have fifty sheep. I have birds and a wolfhound. I love it. I like to wear my *dishdasha* and walk around. And I respected my job. I fast a lot, I pray a lot, I believe a man without faith has no values. It's a spiritual power and it protects you from falling into bad ways. Human beings must live with a clean conscience."

I was impatient with his philosophizing.

"So," I said, "why were we arrested and why were we released?"

He evaded the question, told me it was time to move on from things in the past. There were certain matters he could not speak about, he said.

"Okay," I said, "but how about if I run past you what I believe led to our arrest." And I told him about our visas, our Thurayas, and our crucial visit to the *takyia*. He listened and sucked on his cigarette, and when I had finished he paused.

"I worked for more than three years as a press consultant in the Mukhabarat," he said. "I know the interests of journalists. When your file came to me I found that these journalistic missions were at the heart of your job. There was nothing to convict you. That's why you were released. I really understand your mission as a journalist."

Abu Thar put down his glass of scotch. "Abu Ibrahim's role was unique in these cases," he said. "If you had had a man without his experience, you would have been in trouble."

"But if you knew so much about journalists and what we do, why were we arrested in the first place?" I asked.

"You were followed by observation officers," Abu Ibrahim said. "Maybe they were confused, so the judge issued the order for your arrest. Then the file went to me for investigation. When I saw the file I was convinced you were journalists."

"But you didn't release us immediately," I said.

"As a professional investigator I would not predecide a case. I would go through all the steps and then weigh things up to see if you were innocent or guilty. Your testimony and the evidence led to the point that you were innocent. It was the same as in any case. Anyway, I had made up my mind that even if you had been intelligence people I would have set you free."

"Why would you have released us if you thought we were spies?" I asked.

"You could have executed him," interrupted Abu Thar, who liked to make jokes like this. Abu Ibrahim didn't laugh.

"Yes, I had the authority to decide whatever I wanted about your case. We were in extraordinary circumstances because of the war, so I had all the authority."

My questioning was making Abu Ibrahim uneasy and Abu Thar tried to wrap it up early. "When is your birthday, Matthew?" he asked.

"November 2," I told him.

"Well, from now on you should have a second birthday. April 1, the day Abu Ibrahim released you. You should have a romantic evening with your girlfriend and a bottle of whisky."

I tried to laugh, telling him that I would be like Queen Elizabeth then, with her real birthday and her official birthday. But I steered conversation back to our case. I wanted to know why Abu Ibrahim would have released us even if he had thought we were spies. I found it hard to believe.

"Let me rephrase it," he said. "When God created man, he honored him and asked the angels to kneel in front of man. Man is God's creation. No man can decide to kill another man whom God has honored."

He went on in this vein, talking about how all religions forbid killing. I thought about the thirteen bodies I had watched being disinterred from outside the Arabs and Foreigners Department, about the collections of transparent plastic bags full of bones in Muhawil, about the sobbing brothers at the Khark cemetery, about the hanging room in the prison, about Saad Jassim's torture and wasted years. But I had to save that for the end.

"Religion is like a fence to protect men," he concluded.

"When exactly did you decide that we were innocent? After the second interrogation at night or the following morning before we signed our statements?" I asked.

"I decided at night."

"I'm sorry, but I have to ask a difficult question. Why were we not beaten? If you had beaten me I would have confessed to anything you wanted."

"As a professional investigator I have no belief in beating and torture. I think investigation is like mind wrestling and legal wrestling between the investigator and the accused. Any investigator who uses force will be a failed investigator. Any confession taken by force would be weak. A true confession the investigator would get by dialogue. That's the main principle. I believe in dialogue and persuasion."

I sensed that I was running out of time. Abu Ibrahim asked if it was time to go. I had a few more questions I had to get in.

"You say you don't believe in force or killing people. But prisoners were beaten outside my cell and I heard screams at night. And thirteen other prisoners were executed and left outside the Arabs and Foreigners Department. What happened to them?"

"I don't know," Abu Ibrahim said with the same quickness he

had used when he had declined my prison request to call my friends in the Palestine Hotel to let them know I was all right. He was lying. I don't blame him for not admitting to knowledge of or participation in the men's executions. But it was impossible that he knew nothing about it.

"I have to tell you one thing before you go," I said. "On my first day in prison I made a decision that no matter what you or anyone did to me, torture or execution, I would bear you no ill will. And I still feel that. But after we were released I had nightmares and I would cry often, and I have to say that sometimes I felt great anger toward you."

He stared straight ahead for a moment.

"You are forgiven," he said. "We apologize for what happened. What happened, happened. The event took place because of the circumstances at the time. I respect your speech, and if I didn't respect you I wouldn't have come here. I know the Americans are looking for the Mukhabarat, but I respect you and know that you do an honest job."

I was forgiven? For what? I let it pass, putting it down to his abstruse ways.

"Do you think it's better that Saddam Hussein is gone, or would you still want him to be president?" I asked.

"I love Saddam Hussein," he quickly replied. "There may have been some madness, but he was a patriot and he loved his country."

"But he killed hundreds of thousands of his own people, your fellow countrymen."

"Let me tell you something. The Americans have killed three times as many Iraqis as Saddam Hussein did. In 1991, during the sanctions, in this war. Children were killed in the streets, women and children in cars. The Americans diverted the media's attention away from civilian casualties to the mass graves."

"No matter how many Iraqis the Americans have killed, does that excuse Saddam from killing people?" I argued. "You just told me that it is forbidden by God to kill another man."

"It's his philosophy, his way of ruling Iraq. It was not our choice.

I'm not defending Saddam Hussein. That stage has passed. It's gone and will never be back."

Lunch and the interview were clearly over. They were itching to go. I thanked him for coming and told him that he had helped me gain some peace of mind. He leaned forward and rested his elbows on his knees. "I am no longer Abu Ibrahim your investigator, I am Abu Ibrahim your friend."

"And I am no longer Matthew the prisoner. I am Matthew your friend. Come back here anytime. I'll be here for a while. And the food is better here than in Abu Ghraib."

"I wanted to invite you to my farm, but under the circumstances people might think the wrong thing."

"Maybe in a year," I said.

"God willing," he said.

We all stood up, and as we walked to the door he stopped. Again we embraced and I felt like I was hugging a man who was not evil, who lived what he believed to be a moral life, but who was a killer nonetheless. He had not saved my life, as Mukhaled had said. He had spared my life. There's a big difference. I am not his friend.

16

Working on It

Mahmoud Abdullah leaned against his roasting-hot car and gazed at the American troops standing behind the barbed wire at the entrance of the long-term prisoners' compound at Abu Ghraib. It was July 2, less than three months after the demise of Saddam's regime. Abu Ghraib was up and running again. Contracted by the American interim authority, Iraqi laborers were patching the walls and fixing up the cell blocks. Mahmoud, a 22-year-old college student majoring in management, had come to the prison looking for his brother, Hamid, who had disappeared forty-one days earlier. Behind the wire and walls of the compound were an unknown number of Iraqi men rounded up by the Americans. The soldiers at the gate had told Mahmoud that they were sorry, but they could not even answer the most basic question: Was his brother inside? As for visits from family members or lawyers, forget it. The American Constitution did not apply in Abu Ghraib.

"In Saddam's time we never came here," Mahmoud told me. "This is my first time here. I never imagined coming here. The American occupation forced us to come here to look for our brother. He has his exams tomorrow."

When I returned to Iraq, I had begun asking people what they thought should happen to Abu Ghraib, thinking their answers might indicate how they now felt about both their past and their future. Should the symbol of Saddam's terror be torn down, easing the memory of a population that already has enough living nightmares to deal with? That option might suggest that people did not want to dwell on the painful past and were choosing to look to the future. Perhaps, I suggested to people, it should be made into a museum, like Robben Island in South Africa or Tuol Sleng in Cambodia, a living reminder for Iraqis and visitors alike of the evil they are now rid of. That answer might suggest people's inclination to preserve the symbols of their oppression as they worked more slowly through their pain. Or perhaps the country and its American rulers should accept the banal reality that Iraq, like any other country, has its criminals and needs prisons and here is a huge one that happens to be available. With some work, it could be fully operational in a few months, and the criminals who have so terrorized the people of Iraq, and especially Baghdad, in the months after the war and the thirty-five years before it would have somewhere to be kept.

This was a debate I had with many Iraqis. I could find no consensus, and often the answers were unexpected, exposing scars in surprising places. Abu Firaz, who had for so long made his living from the prison as a Mukhabarat guard, wanted it turned into "a rubbish yard. It was a destructive place, a very bad place to be. It holds bad memories, so no one should keep it as a museum." But some former prisoners I spoke to wanted at least parts of the prison—the execution room and Khasa, the political prisoners' wing—preserved as cautionary evidence of their suffering. And other guards yearned to have their jobs back. "We have no other job," said one of them, a man who would give me only his first name, Alwan. "It's our way of living. It's an ordinary prison for criminals, a reformatory prison."

The debate was now academic. The American administration had already made its decision: Abu Ghraib was a working prison again. Some of the American soldiers at the gate of the long-term prisoners' section, which was the only part of the prison they were using again, showed some small awareness of the history of the place.

"It's kind of frightening for them coming back," acknowledged Lieutenant Sheri Brunette, the National Guard military police officer who came to speak to me at the gate. "Some say their brothers were here or family members were here. . . . We get a lot of family members coming here and we let them know that there's nothing going on here. . . . They assume something is happening to them, but of course we reassure them that that's not the case."

When Mahmoud and another of his brothers and an English-speaking neighbor showed up to inquire about Hamid, Brunette was polite and apologetic but firm. Visiting was impossible. "We're working on it," she told them.

And so it is with many things in postwar Iraq. Self-appointed fixers of a broken country, the Americans decide hugely sensitive issues, bypass the sort of fundamental rights that Americans are constitutionally ensured, and stomp all over the complicated feelings of a people bursting with the right to speak out for the first time in thirty-five years. Iraqis feel, dangerously often it seems to me, that their newfound voices are not being heard by their new masters.

On August 1, I took an army tour with some other journalists of the renovated part of the prison. It was coming along. Two blocks were newly painted in beige and cream, and many of the cells were furnished with bunk beds, mattresses, pillows, wastepaper bins, and red plastic wash basins. Ceiling fans waited motionlessly for the electricity that would come in about two weeks, the soldiers said. The power and the water would allow the Americans to move indoors the roughly 400 prisoners who were then being held nearby in the prison behind coils of barbed wire in tents under the Iraqi sun.

"Why are we staying here?" shouted the prisoners to the pack of journalists, who were forbidden by the soldiers from talking to the detainees. "What's the story? They just picked us up from our houses.

Come on, rescue us. We've been here for two months. Shit on Saddam Hussein. Shit on the Baath Party. We're going to burn down this camp."

This wasn't part of the scheduled tour and two soldiers strode over to warn the prisoners to shut up, while another pulled out his handcuffs and threatened to arrest one reporter who had taken photographs of the detainees. He told us that it was a violation of the Geneva conventions to take pictures of the prisoners. But just a few minutes later another soldier was telling us that these were not prisoners of war, just ordinary criminals. Therefore, I was tempted to point out, they weren't subject to the Geneva conventions. Besides, it was not a violation of the conventions for the prisoners to talk to journalists if the prisoners themselves chose to do so, I told the soldier who bore the handcuffs. "I'm not going to talk law with you," he barked, when I tried to discuss the matter with him.

They were generally nice, the soldiers at Abu Ghraib, but largely clueless. They had no idea what kind of prisoners the specific compound they were renovating formerly housed. One sergeant thought the prison was built in the 1930s or 1940s. As he showed us the execution room, he rather irresponsibly told journalists rumors he had heard about how prisoners were electrocuted and burned as they were hanged, rumors I knew to be false. I asked a lieutenant colonel in the Engineers what he thought of the original structure of the prison. "It's not up to Western standards," he told me, and I didn't bother mentioning to him that it was an American company that had designed it.

What the soldiers did have going for them, however, was a degree of sensitivity about Abu Ghraib's history. The execution section, they said, would remain untouched. It would remain as a memorial for the Iraqi people, and when an Iraqi government was in place, they could decide what to do with it. What to do with the whole prison, for that matter.

It's perhaps unfair to pick on the American soldiers; they joined the military to fight enemies of the United States and are now spending their time building a country that is not their own and won't even necessarily remain an ally when the work is finally done. They are tired and scared, and every one I've ever spoken to wants desperately to go home. They don't want to be policemen or cultural ambassadors. They try to be friendly with the Iraqis who come up to them in the street, but their officers tell them, understandably, not to accept cans of soda from kids in case they are packed with explosives. But the reality is that they are the face of the United States in Iraq, and they are, for the most part, simply not trained for the job. They are trained for war, not peace. Ordinary soldiers tend not to have language skills or a wide understanding of the cultures of the countries they are ordered to invade. And sometimes they make very stupid, easily avoidable mistakes.

In slow-moving traffic in downtown Baghdad one afternoon, I found myself stuck behind a Humvee. Poking out from either side of the rear of the vehicle were coils of barbed wire, and parked cars soon had scratches all the way down their sides. One after another, pedestrians failed to notice the wire and found their shirts snagged. I was just waiting for a kid to run past and have his eye pierced.

I got out of my car and walked up to the soldiers inside the truck.

"Excuse me, do you realize you have barbed wire sticking out the sides of your vehicle?" I asked, as politely as possible.

"Yes," said the soldier in the passenger seat, glaring at me. I instantly lost my temper, a common though unwelcome event for me during those initial postprison weeks.

"It's catching on people's clothes and scratching cars. You think that's a way to make friends with the Iraqi people?"

They said nothing and drove on, scraping a white line along the side of a light blue sedan.

It was a small matter, but my frustration felt justified. I had wanted this war, and now I wanted the Americans and British to succeed in creating a prosperous and democratic Iraq and then get out. I wanted the war so that more than 23 million people would not have to live in the fear that I first scented in 2001 and tasted more strongly inside Abu Ghraib. Weapons of mass destruction seemed to me the least pressing reason for war, and the dubiousness of the American and British arguments over these weapons is now evident.

The American soldiers charged with rebuilding Iraq would have a much easier time of things if their presence in the country were not built, in the eyes of Iraqis, on a lie. I have never met a single Iraqi, even those who supported the American-led invasion, who believed that the United States, sitting thousands of miles away from Iraq, attacked their country because it was afraid of Saddam's military capabilities or his alleged links to terrorism. While the defeat of Saddam Hussein was welcome to the vast majority of Iraqis, they felt that the invasion was based on an untruth. That's not the way to get off on the right footing, particularly with a population so isolated from the world and weaned on distrust and paranoia.

If the war had been fought on the grounds of human rights and moral obligation, Iraq and the United States would be less likely to be facing the potential catastrophe of suspicion and violence that threatened post-Saddam Iraq. First of all, the message to the Iraqi people would have been clear and consistent: We are coming to save you. Second, the invading powers might have made an effort not only to plan a highly flexible war strategy but to plan a highly flexible peace strategy. They had months to do so and simply messed it up. It was not a priority. The Bush administration planned a brilliant war and neglected to prepare properly for what came next.

The American occupation of Iraq was, and still could be, an unprecedented opportunity to demonstrate to the Arab and Muslim worlds that the United States is a beneficent power intent on bringing them freedom and prosperity. At no time or place have Americans and Arabs, other than in the United States itself, lived among each other in such numbers. The Americans are squandering this chance.

Even though the reuse of Abu Ghraib and one Humvee team's mindless coils of barbed wire may be comparatively small mistakes compared to the poor policing, massive unemployment, and power outages that really enrage so many Iraqis, they are horribly damaging nonetheless. Every young man who has his new shirt torn by the barbed wire or finds himself in what he will remember as Saddam's worst prison without being able to contact his family will find it hard to see himself as rescued by an act of military generosity.

Perception is everything in Iraq and the occupying forces are failing to see through Iraqi eyes. It is intellectually lazy to dismiss the growing resistance movement as a Sunni aberration that can be wiped out with force. The Sunni minority and other loyalists thrived under the regime and are afraid of the ascendant religious Shia leaders. They must be quickly made to feel that their lives have improved since April 9 and that their voices will be heard in the new Iraq. "If I don't get paid in two months, I'll go out with my Kalashnikov," Abu Thar, a secular Shia, told me the first time I met him. Over lunch another time he seemed less defiant but no less desperate. I asked him what he would do for work now. "There's nothing, only being a taxi driver. If you have a job for me, that would be very good. After being a successful intelligence officer for twenty-seven years I will turn into a taxi driver. How can I raise my children? How can I keep my house? The big mistake of the coalition is to dissolve the security systems. I know there are some bad people in there, but they could have them retired. If they had intelligence people on the streets, not a single bullet would be shot and they would keep the country secure. They could make use of their experience and deal with criminals. Now they are paying retired cleaners in dollars. I did my service for twenty-seven years out of patriotism, no matter what the regime's thoughts. I did it because it was the best thing for my country. And now I'm like a housewife. Now I know how to make salads."

The very idea that Abu Thar, a top officer in the Mukhabarat, who may well be on a list of those the Americans want to arrest, believed that the occupiers should pay him his salary or give him his job back seemed delusional to me—until the *Washington Post* reported in late August that the American-led administration was rehiring and retraining some members of the Mukhabarat to help them gather intelligence on anticoalition forces in Iraq. Protected by his layers of self-righteousness and patriotism, Abu Thar was incapable of seeing himself for what he was: an agent of appalling evil. I took a flash-lit walk through the abandoned Hakmiya building one morning in late July. The second and third floors were draped in darkness. The lightless cells where Saad and countless others had been held had been repainted a calm, creamy white after the October amnesty. But scratch the surface and a violent red bled through. It was impossible to get to the basement, to the torture room, because it was flooded. Anyone who could have woken up, had his breakfast, said goodbye to his wife and kids, and then driven to work in this building, I thought, deserved to spend a long time in prison thinking about his chosen profession.

But dismissing Abu Thar's fretting about how he will pay his rent and feed his children is horribly dangerous. In July, my *Newsday* colleague Mohamad Bazzi interviewed the leader of some resistance cells in the town of Fallujah, where Iraqi guerrillas have been attacking American soldiers since the end of the war. The fighter gave Mohamad some flyers aimed at recruiting Iraqis to the cause. One in particular appealed directly to men just like Abu Thar.

> To all members of the Baath Arab Socialist Party, the Republican Guards, Special Republican Guards, Military Intelligence and intelligence apparatus, security services, Fedayeen and Emergency Brigades: Now is the time to prove to your people that you are men, and that you will sacrifice your blood in order to wipe the shame that has tainted the forehead of the great Iraq. Be aware that whoever runs away from the American dogs or hides, fearing them, will receive death in his shelter, because they will not leave you alone and they will do to you what they did to the Germans two months after occupying Germany. Read history carefully. Prepare yourselves. Contact each other because you know one another very well. Organize your ranks and be a model and a support to the mujaheddin in order for the people to forgive what some of you did to them.

That last sentence, a startling acknowledgement of past misdeeds, was perhaps the most threatening for the Americans. The people's oppressors were consciously working to turn themselves into the people's champions. And the more justification the Americans gave them, the more their warped logic might attract adherents. Just weeks later, three huge bombs ripped into the fragile détente of postwar Iraq—at the Jordanian embassy, at the UN's headquarters, and at the shrine of Ali in Najaf. They are unsolved crimes, but even if they are partly the work of foreign Islamist terrorists, they could hardly have been carried out without the aid of disaffected Iraqis.

There are only two ways to deal with a man like Abu Thar: you either give him a job or you lock him up. And if you lock him up, give him a lawyer, a fair trial, and, if the evidence supports a conviction, a short prison term. While he's away, make sure that his family is well taken care of so that his brainwashed sons don't grow up with a life-long hatred of the United States. Understand his sense of pride and integrity, no matter whom he tortured and sent to the gallows. After one lunch I insisted on giving Abu Thar a bottle of scotch as a sign of respect. He is fond of a glass or two. But for many minutes he refused to accept, interpreting it as a payoff or a bribe for the information he had given me. If he is left sitting on his torn couch in his run-down rented house, he will feel that his integrity demands him to fight against the occupiers who are doing him wrong. There are thousands like him.

By definition, disillusioned men like Abu Thar are no longer fighting for Saddam; they are simply fighting the invaders of their country. And with the deposed leader in custody, the Americans have one fewer explanation for why the Iraqi insurgents still refuse to accept that they have been liberated by the United States.

Under interrogation, an unhelpful Saddam told his CIA inquisitors that he had not been directing the ever-more-sophisticated insurgency, and the continuing attacks suggested that the chronic liar might be telling the truth. During the mid-December days after Hussein was captured by American soldiers, his supporters stormed municipal buildings in the Sunni towns of Fallujah and Ramadi. They bombed police stations, the ultimate symbols of collaboration with the American occupiers. They shot at American soldiers. The

Americans had scored a substantial propaganda victory and a morale boost, but it looked as though the head they had cut off was barely, if at all, attached to the snake that was biting them.

There's a more long-sighted strategy worth pursuing: Smother Iraq's Sunnis with sympathy and jobs and reliable electricity, and their paranoia will ebb far more quickly than it will in the face of further American search-and-destroy missions. If you keep giving people reasons to hate you, they will keep hating you, Saddam or no Saddam.

"Whenever I see the Americans I want to kiss them," Yousef told me one afternoon as we drove around town. "I want us to be state 51."

Ever consistent in his hatred of the regime and faith in the long-term benefits of the American occupation, Yousef remained a voice of reason to me. I don't know how he escaped untainted by Saddam's country-sized prison but he did. He mistrusted the intentions of the Shia leaders who claimed not to want an Islamic state, but his dislike of them did not come from the paranoid ethnic or religious enmity so many Iraqis feel for one another. His teenage daughter, Doa, brainwashed at school like all Iraqi children, still revered Saddam. (Her parents, conscious that the security services would often trick children into informing on their parents, had been too afraid to criticize the leader in her presence.) But Yousef just wanted to be able to earn money, drink whisky, and enjoy life with the freedoms that he never dreamed would come to Iraq.

Iraq has its fundamental problems, not least the complicated religious and ethnic makeup of its population. It is an artificial country, a collection of competing tribes and ethnic groups shoehorned into statehood by the British and French after World War I. But even as the Kurds in the north yearn for autonomy and the Shia in the south push for the political dominance that their majority status implies is their right, most Iraqis I have met are passionately proud of their patchwork nation. Even the independence-minded Kurds may have come to understand that the world and regional powers will never let them have their own country, because such a venture would mean taking chunks out of Iraq, Iran and Turkey; they know they must make the best of being partners in the new Iraq. It is a country of phenomenal natural resources, and as it was affluent once so it can be again. Everyone stands to gain. But that will happen only if the Iraqis can break through their own individual and collective layers of paranoia, victimization, and mistrust and learn to take responsibility for their own destinies in ways they have never even been allowed to before.

"Let me tell you a little story," Saad told me one day. "I walked past this journalist from some Arab network. People are surrounding him, complaining. 'When will we get good water? When will we get electricity? When will things be back to normal?' He said, 'Guys, I tell you one thing, but please don't get mad. Please, when you go to a gas station, stop your cars in line. When you get propane, stand in a queue. When you drive in the street, drive like normal people. You guys are not helping yourselves and you want everything. Start with yourselves.' They told him, 'You're absolutely right.' "

And that is what inclines me, on the whole, toward optimism. The Americans are slowly learning to think like Iraqis. In the proregime Sunni town of Fallujah, for example, where attacks on Americans have been frequent, the Americans have stopped shooting and started listening and learning deference for local customs. One of their first acts was to pay blood money to Iraqis they have injured or to the families of those they have killed, as tribal customs dictated. It may not have stopped the hard-liners but it was one way of neutralizing the breeding ground for the Sunni guerrillas who are attacking the Americans. And the Iraqis are slowly learning to think like free citizens, setting up Internet cafés, gazing at the world beyond their borders through satellite TV, and waiting hungrily for the reissuing of passports so that they can travel abroad once again. And both the Americans and Iraqis are now sitting on a desert land that boasts centuries of learning and culture and a huge ocean of oil that can fast-track Iraq into the world of capitalist democracies.

The Americans have made mistake after mistake and continue to do so, but they are learning. They could barely do any worse than they did in the first three months of the new Iraq. The anger of moderate

Iraqis will simmer down once the electricity works again and the summer heat recedes, once the streets are safe, once their embryonic government has greater power, once their oil leads them to employment, once they can vote for the first time in Iraqi history, and once Saddam Hussein is dead or in custody. I find their public anger refreshing and unsurprising. They have spent thirty-five years unable to voice that anger that bubbled inside their heads. Now they can sit in tea shops and be furious with the authority that runs their country without worrying that their words will lead them to execution.

It worries me, however, that most Iraqis do not have a way of channeling their anger and grief. Very few Iraqis have the time and resources to seek psychiatric help, even though there are probably millions who could do with it. It is a nation of traumatized people, a country whose psychological infrastructure is as in need of major overhaul as its physical infrastructure.

In spite of the damage, stubborn hope oozes from the words and deeds of people like Jaber Husseini, the guardian of the Muhawil mass grave, and Mohammed Msayer, the painter of the killings. "There are some great factors that will help," Mohammed said. "Their faith in God will help them to overcome the problems of anger. Secondly, they need time to overcome these feelings. The people who were killed are symbols to us, like candles that have lit the way for Iraqis so that we will never tumble into such a catastrophe again."

Jaber and Mohammed had solid, tangible projects that could help them with their trauma in the most positive of ways, but most Iraqis do not. But even the eruption of looting and burning that followed the collapse of the regime, depressing as it was, seemed to me to be more of a long stifled roar of antiregime fury than an indication of rampant criminality. To me, it seemed like a huge prison riot, a magnified version of the destruction that Abu Ghraib's prisoners inflicted on the prison when Saddam released them in October 2000. (Having said that, it's worth remembering that Saddam did release all of Iraq's criminals in that amnesty, and I'm sure there were a lot of criminally minded opportunists at work during those first days of freedom.)

Saad feels differently from me. He thinks Iraq is "doomed." He sees drivers who won't let other cars through in traffic jams for no good reason. At the military bases where Saad now works construction, he comes across Iraqi translators whispering in the ear of the contracting officer that Saad is charging the army too much for the walls he is building. But I believe he is wrong. There are financial jealousies and bad drivers in every city in the world, not just Baghdad.

Kevork Toroyan, one of the unwitting builders of what would become Saddam's worst prison, remembers Iraq with genuine fondness. The people were educated and showed an unparalleled hospitality, he told me. But they could also be brutal and cruel to each other. I think of the boys slapping the puppies and the men gazing lovingly at the angelfish in the pet market, and I think that Toroyan would find today's Iraq largely unchanged. It is easy to scratch at Iraqi society and to see a violent red underneath, as on the creamy walls of the Hakmiya cells, but the redness is just another layer of paint. Behind the different coats of politics and pain, Iraq has a solidity and pride that will see it through these hard times.

I visited Abu Ghraib several times after the war, but it took a few weeks for Saad and me to coordinate a trip. When we did finally head out there, he couldn't find it. We drove around and around Baghdad for nearly three hours, and he could not work out how to get to the place where he had spent seven years. "My wife is the expert in finding this place," he said, a little embarrassed.

Along the way he told me how he had spent one of his seven years in prison. "I wrote a movie script—for Jim Carrey."

The script is a comedy about two brothers. And here we were, driving around Baghdad like Dumb and Dumber, trying and failing to find a place that had been so important to us both. Bob Simon, the CBS correspondent who was held in Iraqi prisons for forty days with three colleagues in 1991, has written about the brotherhood that former prisoners have with each other. I did not like talking with Saad just because he had a good story. And I suspect he was willing to spend so much time with me for reasons beyond his naturally accommodating nature, even if my own eight days of incarceration barely registered on his scale of suffering.

"I was never really free," Saad told me another time. "I never really enjoyed the moment." When he had knocked on his sister's front door that night in April to come home after seven years, he immediately had to play host to his two fellow ex-prisoners. He led them to the bathroom, found clean pajamas for them, got them drinks. The next morning he was up early, met Steve Farrell of the London *Times* and was immediately hired as Steve's translator. He stopped working with Steve after a while and ever since had been hustling for contracting work with the Americans. He had no home of his own and never had time to be alone with his wife and son. It wasn't easy being free, having choices but no time to yourself, being without a routine and the discipline of prison life.

"It's really hard to get used to. You know one of funny things I complain about? In my prison time I always had an ashtray beside me. Now, whenever I smoke I can't seem to find an ashtray. Everyone laughs at me. Kids surrounding me drives me crazy. It used to be that everything was quiet. I had a lot of time to think. Now it's completely different. Never alone, never alone."

It's not only you who's having trouble adjusting, is it? I asked him.

"You know the reaction now, what's going on. Everybody thinks of his own way of freedom. People are looting, robbing. People are trying to express themselves in a strange way. They don't know what freedom is. They don't know how to react to freedom. It's been thirty-five years now."

Like many Iraqis, even those with American citizenship, Saad was not keen on having the Americans stay for too long, but at the moment, he told me, they were a huge improvement on what came before.

"Saddam took the oil and took the freedom and took the right of speech and took our lives. Let the Americans take the oil. They can't take the freedom of speech. I'm sure the Americans will give us something in return, but not Saddam. Saddam never gave us anything in return. This is reality. Let's face it, most of the people are saying that they're here for the money. The oil is gone, with or without Saddam, with or without the Americans."

Saad wasn't always consistent in his analysis—Iraq was doomed, things would be better now that Iraq had the Americans and their commitment to free speech—but I thought his mixed perspectives largely typical of Iraqis as they struggled to make sense of their confusing new world.

We drove across an overpass, and I asked Saad who he wanted to play the other brother in his movie. "I don't know, but the main part is for Jim. I thought I'd leave it up to him to pick the other guy." He laughed. "But dude, I'm gonna do it."

"But do you still have the script?" I asked him.

"No, I had to leave it behind. I hope it's still there."

Unlike Saad, I had seen the state of the Arabs and Foreigners Department. I had sifted through the huge piles of paper scattered all over the floors of the cells. I had not seen anything that looked remotely like a movie script.

"What if it's not there?"

"I'll rewrite it."

At last we arrived at the front gate where Moises and I had come to find him after the amnesty. We drove through the modest gateway and into the compound, past the foundations of the unfinished blocks and over to the Arabs and Foreigners Department, where Moises and Yousef were waiting with understandable impatience. Saad gave us his own personal tour, explaining to us the place we had been held in and that had been his home for seven years.

"Iraq is everybody's country. We must protect Iraq and the President," read a sign over the door of the office.

Inside was the visiting room for diplomats and Red Cross officials. Our boots crunched on broken glass and burned sheets of paper. There was a hole where a sheet of pink-colored glass had once been, concealing an enclosed room from which the guards would secretly film the visits. This was where Saad had met with the Polish diplomats who represented the American government, his government. It's a matter of some bitterness for Saad that the American government did not work harder for his release. And I wondered why Saad's case had not been widely publicized in the United States. He was an American citizen, unjustly held by the Iraqi regime. That would have been a huge story in the 1990s. So why the silence?

An official with the State Department emailed me an answer in late July. Saad had refused to sign away his right to privacy, as is required under federal law before the government can go public with the details of such a case. The State Department knew all about him but could do nothing to help. Saad himself had told me often that he knew the Mukhabarat was listening in to the conversations in that room with the Poles. He was constantly calculating whether anything he said in there could get him hanged.

We passed through the director's office, which I recognized as the place where I had undergone my second interrogation. There was another room that had been full of closed-circuit TV monitors. And another where guards used to sleep. One in particular, Mohammed Ismail, used to take his afternoon nap there and sit out on a white plastic chair scanning the prisoners, deciding which one to beat next. The chair was still there, upturned in the grass.

We heard a noise behind us, and suddenly there were two American soldiers creeping round the corner of the building with their pistols drawn, their tense expressions announcing they were ready to shoot.

"What are you doing here?" one asked.

"Just taking a look round," one of us said.

"We were prisoners here," I said.

They demanded to see our passports and ID cards and led us out to meet their officer, who took down our details and let us go back inside.

"That would have been great—shot by Americans in Abu Ghraib," I said. It irritated the hell out of me to have the Americans bossing us around, giving us permission to be in the Arabs and Foreigners Department. It was Saad's place and, less so, Moises's and mine. For a moment I sensed how ordinary Iraqis must feel every day as they see Americans controlling the country where the Iraqis suffered, where they lived their stunted lives, where they have ownership rights, and, in spite of everything, where they retain pride in their nationhood.

We walked past a fence of blue wire attached to Section Five, where the five of us had been held as the war raged outside. It had also been Saad's home for three years. We found books among the debris along the way. Nietzsche, *The Winds of War.* Books from the department's small library, an enormous privilege in Abu Ghraib.

Inside Section Five we found the remains of Saad's pool table, the one that the guards played on all throughout our incarceration. It was a coup for Saad to have that brought into the prison. He used to charge 75 dinars for each game from the prisoners but the guards, of course, played for free. The Abu Ghraib Sheraton, indeed, I thought.

We turned left along the corridor in which I had been held. The first cell on our side had been Saad's, cell number 1. It still had the blue flowery wallpaper he had pasted up himself. Toothpaste, the prisoners discovered, was an excellent glue. He had shared the cell with an Iranian. Looters had taken everything of value: shelves, his television, the air cooler, the fan. The one new addition to Saad's cell, and the rest of them on our block, was the new metal loops on the doors. "These are for you guys," he chuckled. Then he pointed to the Arabic numbers scribbled on the wall just outside each cell. "And these numbers are for you guys. They didn't used to be there."

Cell number 3 had been Moises's. An Indian and another Iranian had been held there before the Hakmiya men took over. My cell was number 5, and it had been home to two Iranians, Haidar Ali and Mohaned Mossadeh, until all the Iranians were released one day before the war began. Saad had, over the years, visited my cell often. Yes, he said, the shelf had held a television. He translated some words on the torn poster on the wall above where I had slept. "Enjoy life and health with our product," the advertisement read. "We are not the only ones in the business but we are very special."

I stood in the cell and remembered the prayers I had offered to a God in whom I had not believed. Had it lasted, this newfound faith? I felt vaguely guilty that my atheist's reasoning was daily grinding down the existence of a God who may have saved me, who pulled off the miracle. Was I ungrateful and courting his wrath, or had I just conned myself into believing because when you're faced with death you play the odds, you try anything? I didn't know. I walked back into the corridor.

Beside the other Arabic numbers written on the wall outside my cell were three small Western numerals penciled in red onto the cinderblock. 276. My number.

Saad explained that when the Hakmiya officers took over the department, he and his fellow residents on our block had been moved out and forced to clear everything from the cells. They were stripped down to the bare shells that we had found when we arrived. The Hakmiya wanted to reconstruct the sparseness of their usual cells downtown. But before then, the prisoners had referred to these cells as "first class." The slightly bigger ones in the adjoining block of Section Five were "second class." The larger ones in other sections were "third class."

"This was my room before the amnesty," Saad said, gazing into cell number 6, where Molly had been held. It was on Saad's wall that Molly and I had tapped out proof of our survival to each other. "So we're neighbors."

We walked through the sunburned gardens, the grass and flower beds dried up into yellow straw, to the last place Saad called home in Abu Ghraib—Section Four.

"My Oxford dictionary, man," he said, leaning down to pick up a section of a book. He found more chunks of it as he walked around, collecting them together as if they were shards of a Ming vase. Among the mess I came across a rather appropriate bit of reading matter, a copy of Alexander Solzhenitsyn's *One Day in the Life of Ivan Denisovich*.

Just outside Section Four was a spot where the prisoners had sat in the sun. A wall separated them from Section Three, which the Hakmiya officers had turned into their main interrogation area and where I had experienced my first interrogation. "We used to sit here and listen to the interrogations," Saad said. "This is where you guys were." He pointed to the spot just beyond the wall, a few yards away, where he had watched us sit in the sunshine at the white plastic table and sign our statements. Saad and the other prisoners were told not to look at us, but they did anyway. They had also heard the beatings and screaming through the wall as the Hakmiya men gave the Iraqi detainees harsher treatment than they gave us.

We walked around the rest of the department. "They made us dig bunkers all day long during the war," Saad told me as we looked out at the trenches in the sun-baked soccer pitch.

I had thought that going back to Abu Ghraib with Saad would be good for both of us. He could explain it all to me, and we could both share a little in the unhappiness of the place, perhaps dulling that impulse that still makes me break down now and then for no good reason. It didn't work. We ran out of meaningful things to say and small talk seemed painful, so we settled into silence quite often. I felt a familiar surge of violence rising from my diaphragm, and I would have done anything for Saad, Moises, and Yousef to leave me alone. I wanted a sledgehammer and a lot of time to use it, and I wanted to bring as much of the place crashing down as I could. I didn't tell Saad that; instead, I asked him what he thought should happen to the prison.

"Level it down. It's too old. It's not fixable. Abu Ghraib has left very, very sad memories in the Iraqi people's mind. I think we have enough bad memories of what Saddam did. Young people have so many places to see what Saddam did. They don't need Abu Ghraib as a reminder."

Some weeks later, with the prison operating again, I sat in Saad's living room and asked him again how he felt. "It's okay to use Abu Ghraib again," he told me, rather to my surprise. "But only for temporary use because the Iraqis are going crazy now. We have real criminals in Iraq. They are really out of control. In April and May, they were shooting each other on the streets and they could get away with it. It's good to let them know they can't get away with what they are doing right now. Abu Ghraib is a total fear for the Iraqis. So for the Iraqis to know if they do something wrong they will go back to Abu Ghraib, not just a prison, is another way of straightening things out.

So I kind of support the idea of using Abu Ghraib. . . . With the things going on right now, they need a couple more Abu Ghraibs. The robbers are making checkpoints, they're stopping cars, killing the drivers, and driving the car away."

I reminded Saad of his words to me in the prison that day, about wanting to see the prison leveled.

"I didn't change my mind. Abu Ghraib is the worst place on Earth for the Iraqis. But it serves a purpose at the moment."

My own destructive urge had gone too by that stage. It might be temporarily satisfying to take a sledgehammer to the place, but I knew I would feel empty, and somehow dirty, afterward. Eight days didn't make it my prison to destroy. True, I had suffered in Abu Ghraib, in Saddam's Iraq, but only a little. Iraq had real scars to contend with. And now, its people had realized, was the time for building.